SPORTS ECONOMICS

SPORTS ECONOMICS

Current Research

Edited by
John Fizel, Elizabeth Gustafson,
and Lawrence Hadley

Westport, Connecticut
London

Library of Congress Cataloging-in-Publication Data

Sports economics : current research / edited by John Fizel,
   Elizabeth Gustafson, and Lawrence Hadley.
       p. cm.
   Includes bibliographical references (p.   ) and index.
   ISBN 0–275–96330–6 (alk. paper)
      1. Sports—Economic aspects—United States.   2. Professional
   sports—Economic aspects—United States.   3. Sports administration—
   United States.   4. Collective bargaining—Sports—United States.
   5. Athletes—Salaries, etc.—United States.   6. Sports—United
   States—Statistics.   I. Fizel, John.   II. Gustafson, Elizabeth.
   III. Hadley, Lawrence, 1945–
   GV716.S594   1999
   338.4'7796'0973—dc21   98–44670

British Library Cataloguing in Publication Data is available.

Library of Congress Catalog Card Number: 98–44670
ISBN: 0–275–96330–6

First published in 1999

Praeger Publishers, 88 Post Road West, Westport, CT 06881
An imprint of Greenwood Publishing Group, Inc.
www.praeger.com

Printed in the United States of America

The paper used in this book complies with the
Permanent Paper Standard issued by the National
Information Standards Organization (Z39.48–1984).

10 9 8 7 6 5 4 3 2 1

Contents

Tables and Figures   ix

Preface   xiii

Section I: Introduction

1. An Overview   3
   John Fizel, Elizabeth Gustafson, and Lawrence Hadley

Section II: Sports Leagues and Markets

2. The College Football Industry   11
   Rodney Fort and James Quirk

3. A Test of the Optimal Positive Production Network
   Externality in Major League Baseball   27
   Daniel Rascher

Section III: The Location of Teams and Stadiums

4. Emerging Markets in Baseball: An Econometric Model for
   Predicting the Expansion Teams' New Cities   49
   Thomas H. Bruggink and Justin M. Zamparelli

5. Mega-Sports Events as Municipal Investments:
   A Critique of Impact Analysis   61
   Philip K. Porter

6.   Baseball and Basketball Stadium Ownership and Franchise
     Incentives to Relocate   75
     Gerard C. S. Mildner and James G. Strathman

Section IV: Managerial Decisions: Inputs and Outputs

7.   Alternative Econometric Models of Production in
     Major League Baseball   95
     Elizabeth Gustafson, Lawrence Hadley, and John Ruggiero

8.   Technological Change and Transition in the Winning Function for
     Major League Baseball   109
     Thomas H. Bruggink

9.   Streak Management   119
     Rodney Fort and Robert Rosenman

10. Trading Players in the National Basketball Association:
     For Better or Worse?   135
     David J. Berri and Stacey L. Brook

11. The Benefit of the Designated Hitter in Professional Baseball   153
     Craig A. Depken II

12. Participation in Collegiate Athletics and Academic Performance 161
     John Fizel and Timothy Smaby

Section V: Labor Market Issues in Team Sports

13. Did Collusion Adversely Affect Outcomes in the Baseball
     Player's Labor Market?: A Panel Study of Salary
     Determination from 1986 to 1992   175
     Timothy R. Hylan, Maureen J. Lage, and Michael Treglia

14. Baseball's New Collective Bargaining Agreement: How Will It
     Affect the National Pastime?   191
     Daniel R. Marburger

15. "These People Aren't Very Big on Player Reps": Career Length,
     Mobility, and Union Activism in Major League Baseball   203
     Donald A. Coffin

16. The Impact of the Salary Cap and Free Agency on the

Contents vii

Structure and Distribution of Salaries in the NFL 213
Sandra Kowalewski and Michael A. Leeds

Bibliography 227

Index 239

About the Contributors 243

Tables and Figures

TABLES

3.1	Sample Statistics of the Game by Game Baseball Data	31
3.2	Regression Results of the Demand Specification Analysis	37
3.3	Fixed Effects Regression Results of the Demand Specification Analysis	40
4.1	Means and Standard Deviations of Variables	52
4.2	Predicted Values for MLB	54
4.3	Viability Index for Top Ten Cities	57
5.1	Super Bowl Impact Summaries	65
5.2	Regression Results in Selected Super Bowl Host Counties	67
5.3	Hotel Price and Occupancy Regression Results	70
5.4	Real Room Revenue Increases: Compatibility with Sales Regression Results	71
6.1	Franchise and Stadium Trends in Baseball and Basketball	79
6.2	Inter-Metropolitan Franchise Move	82
6.3	Sports Franchises by Metro Areas, 1997	85
6.4	Determinants of Inter-Metropolitan Franchise Movement	87
6.5	Determinants of a Public Stadium Ownership	88
6.6	Determinants of Attendance	90
7.1	Descriptive Statistics	101
7.2	Winning Percent Regression Results	103
7.3	Attendance Regression Results	104
7.4	Canonical Regression Results	106
9.1	Runs Tests for Streaks	121
9.2	Cumulative Periodogram Analysis for Streaks	122
9.3	Non-Random Streaks and Win Percentages	123

9.4	Attendance Regression Data	126
9.5	Attendance Estimation (American League)	129
9.6	Attendance Estimation (National League)	131
10.1	The List of Variables	137
10.2	Estimated Coefficients from Equation (3)	140
10.3	Estimated Coefficients from Equation (4)	140
10.4	The Reduced Form Coefficients	141
10.5	The Marginal Values	142
10.6	Estimated Coefficients from Equation (5)	144
10.7	The Trades to Be Examined	145
10.8	Net Benefits from Player Transactions	146
10.9	Expected Net Benefits from Player Transactions	148
11.1	Descriptive Statistics of the Data	156
11.2	Probit Analysis Results	157
12.1	SAT Averages by Group	164
12.2	College GPA and Enrollment	165
12.3	Academic Achievement Model (RevAthl and NoRevAthl)	168
12.4	Academic Achievement Model (All Varsity Sports)	169
13.1	Descriptive Statistics of Salaries for Pitchers and Hitters—By Year	179
13.2	Definitions of Variables	181
13.3	Descriptive Statistics—Hitters	183
13.4	Descriptive Statistics—Pitchers	184
13.5	Regression Results—Hitters, 1986–1992	185
13.6	Regression Results—Pitchers, 1986–1992	186
15.1	Descriptive Performance Statistics for Pitchers: Means with Standard Deviations in Parentheses	204
15.2	Descriptive Performance Statistics for Position Players: Means with Standard Deviations in Parentheses	206
15.3	Regression Results: Career Length in Years for Pitchers	207
15.4	Regression Results: Career Length in Years for Position Players	208
15.5	Regression Results: Likelihood of Moving between Teams for Pitchers	209
15.6	Regression Results: Likelihood of Moving between Teams for Position Players	209
16.1	Descriptives of the Variables	221
16.2	Results of the OLS Estimation	223

FIGURES

8.1	Year-to-Year Means for Batting Average and Power Percentage	113
8.2	Year-to-Year Means for ERA and Fielding Percentage	113
8.3	Year-to-Year Means for the Speed Variable	114
8.4	Regression Coefficients for the Batting Index in the Five-Year Moving Average Winning Function	115

8.5   Regression Coefficients for the Power Index in the
        Five-Year Moving Average Winning Function   116
8.6   Regression Coefficients for the Pitching Index in the
        Five-Year Moving Average Winning Function   116
8.7   Regression Coefficients for the Fielding Index in the
        Five-Year Moving Average Winning Function   117
8.8   Regression Coefficients for the Speed Index in the
        Five-Year Moving Average Winning Function   117
16.1   Lorenz Curves for NFL Salaries in 1992 and 1994   219

Preface

In November 1996, Praeger published *Baseball Economics: Current Research*. That volume is a collection of readings written by professional economists for professional economists. The genesis of the 1996 volume was the annual convention of the Western Economic Association International held in San Diego, California during the summer of 1995. Most of the chapters in the 1996 volume started as research presentations to professional colleagues during the San Diego convention. The best of the presented papers were reviewed by professional colleagues, revised by the authors, and edited for the *Baseball Economics* collection. We believe that the volume has been well received.

We have continued to use the Western Economic Association's annual summer convention as a forum for the presentation of research by sports economists. During the summers of 1996, 1997, and 1998 the Western conventions were held in San Francisco, Seattle, and Lake Tahoe, respectively. At these conventions, the emphasis of the research presentations was broadened to include all team sports—professional and collegiate. The presentations were made by approximately fifty different economists who label themselves as sports economists to one degree or another.

In 1998, Praeger agreed to publish a second volume of professional sports economics research. We have titled this second volume *Sports Economics: Current Research*, and it compiles the best of the work presented in San Francisco and Seattle. We have selected the parallel title because this volume has much in common with the earlier *Baseball Economics* volume. There is the common origin of the Western Economic Association International's convention. Many of this volume's contributors are the same, and their chapters have been reviewed by the same editors. We hope that the main similarity between the two volumes is high-quality professional research on sports economics topics.

Indeed, we believe that this book does contain high-quality research that will be
frequently cited by professional sports economists in the future. Thus, our primary
thanks is to the authors for these contributions. We also acknowledge the assistance
of Cynthia Harris of Greenwood Publishing Group. We thank Jacquee Bayles for her
editorial and typing assistance. Finally, a special thanks to Sandy Murphy for her
expert computer skills and typing assistance.

John Fizel
Elizabeth Gustafson
Lawrence Hadley

Section I

INTRODUCTION

1

An Overview

John Fizel, Elizabeth Gustafson,
and Lawrence Hadley

The sports industry continues to be the focus of much research by professional economists. A few seminal contributions by Simon Rottenberg (1956), Walter Neale (1964), James Quirk (El-Hodiri and Quirk, 1971), Roger Noll (1974), Gerald Scully (1974 b), and George Daly (Daly and Moore, 1981) have been followed by an explosion of research in the past fifteen years. The reason for this, in our view, is that the sports industry provides unusual opportunities for both theoretical and empirical research.

A central issue addressed on the theoretical side of sports economics research is the duality of market cooperation and market competition that is unique to the sports industry. Walter Neale was the first to analyze the "peculiar economics of professional sports" in his seminal 1964 article. The industry is unique because the legitimate monopoly goals of the team owners must be balanced against their illegitimate monopoly objectives. That legitimate goal is the preservation of competitive balance on the playing field. Without this balance, fans lose interest in the game and the league is an economic failure. The illegitimate monopoly objectives of the owners are the exploitation of the fans and the players. Owners appear to use their monopoly power in the product market to restrict output by limiting the number of teams. In the past (and perhaps even to some extent in the present), they appear to have used their artificial monopsony power to capture monopoly rents from the players. The theoretical problem for sports economists is to develop a model with policy prescriptions for achieving balance with neither monopoly nor monopsony exploitation.

The empirical side of this body of research exhibits almost limitless opportunities to test various economic hypotheses related to market structures. These seemingly endless opportunities are largely due to the nature of the available data. These data are both extensive and unique. They are extensive because fans thrive on the measurement of every aspect of a sport. They are unique because the inputs and output of firms (teams) can be directly and accurately observed. A team's output is simply team wins. The inputs are observed as the performance statistics of the athletes. The availability of these data is especially unusual because it provides direct detailed measurements of the workers' (players') productivity. The upshot is that the sports industry provides some of the best opportunities for testing various economic theories that address the unique institutional characteristics of that industry.

Sports Economics: Current Research contains both theoretical and empirical research. Our book opens with two chapters that address the central theoretical problem of a sports league: competitive balance. In the first of these two, Rodney Fort and James Quirk create a model of the top-level college football industry that yields expectations in keeping with observations of that industry. The model assumes that college football programs are profit maximizers, although the "profit" is generally in the form of athletic program budget or subsidies for the college's operating budget. Within a cartel organization, colleges compete for players and coaches. The impact of play-for-pay on competitive balance among teams is examined, and motivations for cheating are discussed.

The other chapter in Section II of *Sports Economics* is by Daniel Rascher. Sports leagues have the peculiar problem of positive production network externalities, which means that too much domination by one team is bad for all teams. Professor Rascher examines the assumptions of sports league models of demand, which assume that fans prefer contests between two high–quality teams that are closely matched and that fans are more sensitive to the quality of the home team. He uses a game-by-game demand analysis for Major League Baseball's 1996 season to determine whether these assumptions are credible. Results support these assumptions and show that fans prefer the home team to have twice as good a chance of winning as the visiting team.

Section III includes three chapters that examine the location of teams and their impacts on local economies. In the first chapter, Thomas H. Bruggink and Justin M. Zamparelli develop an empirical model that predicts the ability of a metropolitan area to support a major league baseball franchise. The main application of their model is the prediction of the cities that baseball will select for expansion franchises during the next inevitable round of expansion. Assuming that there will be two more franchises added in the next few years, Bruggink and Zamparelli predict that Washington, DC and Charlotte, NC will be the next two metropolitan areas to win expansion teams, while Salt Lake City, UT is identified as a close runner-up. Their model is also useful in identifying cities that currently have a baseball franchise, but can expect problems supporting that franchise in the future.

In chapter 5, Philip K. Porter examines the economic impacts of mega-sporting events on local economies. Specifically, he attempts to identify the economic impacts of several Super Bowls on local economies by analyzing sales data around the time of the event. He concludes that the economic impacts of these events are negligible in terms of increased local sales revenue. This is explained by short-run capacity constraints in the hotel industry that restrict the normal tourist traffic. These constraints cause suppliers to raise prices for hotel rooms, and this crowds out other potential tourists at the time of the event. In other words, the spending of Super Bowl visitors is simply a replacement for the spending of regular everyday tourists that would normally occur in the absence of the mega-sporting event. The primary beneficiaries are the owners of the scarce hotel space.

In chapter 6, Gerard C. S. Mildner and James G. Strathman develop a model to explain the relocation of franchises in Major League Baseball and the National Basketball Association. The primary focus of their chapter is the relationship between team ownership of the sports arena/stadium and the likelihood of franchise relocation. They hypothesize that the public ownership of sports facilities creates greater mobility for team owners and opportunities to threaten local public officials. In turn, this increases the probability that an owner will relocate the franchise. Their empirical analysis supports this hypothesis for Major League Baseball but not for the National Basketball Association.

Section I Vincludes six chapters that analyze managerial decisions related to the production of outputs. In the first, Elizabeth Gustafson, Lawrence Hadley, and John Ruggiero consider different ways of modeling the production function for Major League Baseball. In sports economics paper presentation sessions at the Western Economics Association meetings and elsewhere, it is not uncommon for questions to arise about the appropriateness of using ordinary least squares to estimate a single equation production function for sports teams. There is concern that the dual objectives of sports teams, success on the field and economic success, imply that joint or simultaneously produced products should be modeled. In addition, the requirement that the mean winning percent for teams in a league must be 0.5 is known to imply that there is correlation among the disturbances of a model for winning percent. This suggests that a generalized least squares estimation technique will enhance efficiency (Chapman and Southwick, 1991). Chapter 7 models baseball production using a simultaneous equations model, a canonical correlation model of joint production, and generalized least squares estimation of the single equation model in addition to ordinary least squares. All methods lead to extremely similar results with the exception of the canonical correlation estimation. The chapter shows that the rigidities of canonical correlation results indicate that this method of modeling is inappropriate for baseball production.

The second chapter in this section, by Thomas H. Bruggink, examines long–run changes in Major League Baseball's technology for the production of team wins. The author analyzes the shift from the "deadball era" of Ty Cobb to the lively ball era of Babe Ruth between 1901 and 1940. Over these four decades, the shift in technology was away from hitters with speed and high batting averages (like Ty Cobb) and toward hitters with power (like Babe Ruth). The coefficients of Bruggink's long-run production function support this change in technology. Team speed, measured by a team's stolen bases plus triples, became less important and power hitting, measured by team slugging average minus the batting average, became more important in the production of team wins over these forty years.

In chapter 9, Rodney Fort and Robert Rosenman search for non-random streaks in wins and losses for baseball teams, and they find that non-random streaks do occur for a few managers. Streak management involves reallocating team resources to extend a winning streak or to end a losing streak rather than sticking with a plan aimed at optimizing overall season performance. For successful streak managers, there is a payoff in terms of gate revenues and enhanced season performance. However, inappropriate or unsuccessful streak management attempts can have negative results for team performance. The authors also speculate abut the chances for inefficient resource allocation when owners find it difficult to determine which are streak managers.

The fourth chapter in this section, by David J. Berri and Stacey L. Brook, examines the behavior of general managers in the National Basketball Association regarding the trading of players. The authors adopt a model from the work of Gerald Scully to estimate the marginal value of a player to his team's owner. The model analytically combines an estimate of the wins produced via a player's performance with an estimate of the value of those wins to the team owner. If general managers behave rationally, then they would trade away players whose marginal value to the team is less than the players acquired in the trade. Surprisingly, Berri and Brook find that general managers often trade for players whose marginal value to the team is lower than the players traded away. More surprisingly, they find that general managers could correctly forecast the poor nature of these trades with readily available performance data on the players.

Chapter 11 by Craig A. Depken II, compares the quality of play in the American League and National League. This comparison is complicated by the designated-hitter (DH) rule in the American League. This difference in rules will likely impact the personnel strategies of teams. Professor Depken's regression analysis of interleague play controls for various factors including the DH rule. He concludes that the average National League team is stronger than the average American League team. However, American League teams are expected to win more interleague games because of their advantage from the DH rule.

The last chapterer of this section, written by John Fizel and Timothy Smaby, examines the academic performance of college athletes. The authors' model explains the academic achievement of students as measured by their grade point average. The model is estimated with data for all baccalaureate students at Pennsylvania State University (University Park) in Spring 1995. Their analysis is disaggregated by individual sports, and for most sports, participation in intercollegiate athletics has no significant impact on the athletes' grade point averages. However, they find that men's football is an important exception. After controlling for human capital, home environment, university support, and student activities, Professors Fizel and Smaby find that the football players' academic performance is significantly lower than their cohorts.

Section V contains four chapters that examine various labor markets in professional sports. Chapter 13, by Timothy Hylan, Maureen Lage, and Michael Treglia, uses a rich panel of salary and performance data for Major League Baseball players to identify the impacts of the owners' collusion from 1986 to 1988. Because of the rich database, their regression analysis can control for many variables including individual fixed effects. The estimates generated by their equations suggest that the owners' collusion reduced the salaries of hitters by 24 percent and reduced the salaries of pitchers by 29 percent.

The second chapter in this final section, by Daniel R. Marburger, provides a comprehensive overview of the new (1996) collective bargaining agreement negotiated between Major League Baseball owners and the Players' Association. He discusses the luxury tax provision and the new revenue-sharing provisions. Also, he analyzes the likely implications of these provisions for the small-market teams. Finally, Professor Marburger analyzes the possible implications of the new agreement for Major League Baseball's antitrust exemption. His overall assessment is that this agreement is not the final solution, and that more labor conflict in baseball is a distinct possibility.

The third chapter relating to labor market issues is written by Donald Coffin. Are the Major League Baseball players who represent the Players' Association targets of the owners? The Players' Association believes that owners do not like player representatives and they try to purge them from the team roster by trade or termination. Thus, the expectation is that player representatives will have shorter careers and will move between teams more frequently. Professor Coffin's empirical analysis finds no evidence to support this position. On the contrary, his regression equation suggests that player representatives have longer careers and are perhaps less likely to be traded than other players.

The last chapter in this volume is by Sandra Kowalewski and Michael A. Leeds. The authors analyze the 1993 collective bargaining agreement between the National Football League and the football players that introduced free agency and a team salary cap. The main focus of the analysis is the impact of free agency and the team cap on the distribution of income among the players. As expected, the central impact has been to create a less equal distribution of players' salaries. Comparing the distribution of salaries in 1994 to 1992, Kowalewski and Leeds demonstrate that star players have gained while journeymen and rookie players have lost. They also conclude from their salary regression equation that a player's position is less important under the new agreement. In contrast, starting players in all positions have gained under the 1993 agreement.

This introductory chapter is intended to give readers a preliminary insight into the relationships among the fifteen chapters in this book while stimulating interest. Readers should note that each chapter is a self-contained work that can stand by itself. Therefore, they can be read selectively and/or in any order. We have enjoyed the process of assembling this volume, and we hope that our readers find the research in *Sports Economics* useful, thought provoking, and even entertaining.

Section II

SPORTS LEAGUES AND MARKETS

2

The College Football Industry

Rodney Fort and James Quirk

INTRODUCTION

The analysis of college sports has proceeded without any comprehensive, rigorous theoretical foundation. Seeking a remedy, we derive many well-known, but heretofore casual, observations about the players' and coaches' markets, examine the effects of play-for-pay on profits and competitive balance, and profile cheating by coaches and athletic departments. The analysis sheds light on arguments that paying college players will only benefit large-revenue colleges. No new empirical investigation is undertaken, but our results are related to past findings by other researchers. The conclusion lists further testable implications of the model for future reference.

THE MODEL

Major college football production is comprised of three components. Players choose between different scholarship offers. The level of coaching talent chosen is based upon its contribution to winning programs. Player and coaching talent markets also are distinguished by their relative level of competitiveness, in the economic sense of that word.

We model college football programs as profit-maximizers. There are two reasons why this is justified. The first argument follows the same logic that Fleisher, Goff, and Tollison (1992, p. 21) offer concerning the NCAA:

The fact that the NCAA is a nonprofit organization simply changes the balance sheet item which is maximized. Instead of "profits" or returns to shareholders, it may be implicit subsidies to the university general operating expenses, coaches' salaries, office facilities, and so on which are maximized. The accounting practices of colleges and universities merely mask the recipients of cartel rents.

The same can be said for individual athletic departments. Even though athletic departments are nonprofit organizations, accounting practices simply show the flow of rents as administrative and coaches' salaries and operating budgets. But profit maximization by athletic departments is also supported by its appealing, stable equilibrium characteristic. As argued below, an equilibrium for a league in which all members forego profit opportunities is inherently unstable.

Finally, we assume that the college football industry is organized as a cartel. McKenzie and Sullivan (1987), echoing some earlier work on professional sports by Canes (1974) (see also, Barro, 1996, pp. 153–157, for nearly the same argument), argue that the NCAA is not a cartel. Instead, they argue that the NCAA is simply the enforcement mechanism used by college football teams that compete through joint ventures. Under this view, NCAA restrictions are remedies to pecuniary talent externalities associated with individual team talent choices (since winning percents are zero-sum, if one team chooses to increase its talent level and winning percent, it does not take full account of the impact on other teams). Also under this view, cheating could be interpreted as franchise cheating rather than cartel cheating. If so, then college football teams and leagues face the same enforcement problem that any franchise/joint venture faces. If the demand for college football is greater under the perception of amateur play, then the NCAA just enforces amateurism by monitoring colleges that want to cheat on that goal.

On the other hand, Koch (1971, 1973, 1978, 1983) offered the earliest, definitive, cartel interpretation. A compelling list of reasons why the NCAA is a cartel, rather than a franchise "joint venture," is given by Fleisher, Goff, and Tollison (1992) and we do not repeat it here. The idea seems so well-entrenched that economists in the popular press simply take it for granted (Becker, 1985, 1987; McCormick and Meiners, 1987; Barro, 1991) and Noll (1991) does not even pause to discuss it on his way to a full characterization of NCAA cartel behavior. Given all of this, plus the fact that a major argument against the monopsony power of colleges simply holds no water (detailed later), we go with the cartel view.

The model only treats the upper level of college football teams. We are well aware that most college players are playing for the joy of it without any unrealistic dreams of an NFL career. On the other hand, it is the small group of premiere players with NFL potential who are most important in determining the success or failure of a top-level college team. The decision making of those players, their coaches, and athletic departments is the focus of this chapter.

Players

Just like other students, players have their eye on income after college. They are assumed to be rational economic actors, choosing among different colleges to maximize their "permanent income." We also assume complete information as to their athletic abilities, coaching inputs at various colleges, and how these components translate into the probability of a professional football career and its associated income.

Player i with SAT score s_i chooses from among the j colleges in his attainable set,

$A_i = \{j \mid s_i > s_j^{min}\}$, where s_j^{min} is the lowest SAT score for admission to college j. The probability of an NFL career, given attendance at college j, p_{ij}, is determined by the entering player's talent level and coaching at college j. At the time of recruitment, the raw athletic talent of player i is $p_{ij}(0) = p_i(0)$ for all j. Coaching talent at college j, C_j, moves the player away from this initial point, that is, $p_{ij} = p_{ij}(C_j)$. [Leonard and Reyman (1988) offer an entertaining article about adjusted probabilities of attaining professional status; around 20/1,000,000 in football, 3/1,000,000 in baseball, and between 3/1,000,000 to 7/1,000,000 in basketball.]

If this player does indeed achieve an NFL career, then NFL (p_{ij}) denotes the discounted present value of NFL earnings for player i, given that he played at college j, with a football talent level that resulted in NFL participation with probability p_{ij}. The discounted present value of non-NFL earnings for player i at college j is $DPV_j(s_i)$. Let T denote the expected NFL career length and r the discount rate. Given this notation, the expected present value of income for player i at college j is:

$$V_{ij} = p_{ij}\left[NFL(p_{ij}) + DPV_j(s_i)(1 + r)^{-T}\right] + (1 - p_{ij})DPV_j(s_i). \tag{1}$$

Then, for two colleges j, $k \in A_i$, player i prefers college j to college k if and only if $V_{ij} > V_{ik}$. Our characterization takes to heart a critique of college sports analysis by McKenzie and Sullivan (1987), who argued that it is *expected* pay, not *actual* pay, that matters and that players get a chance at the pros as well as higher pay because of their exposure to the educational benefits offered in college. Below, we analyze their argument concerning expected pay and monopsony in the market for college athletes. In addition, Long and Caudill (1991), working on a sample from the 1970s, found that participation in major college football programs does indeed drive incomes up, including non-NFL incomes, and that athletes had higher graduation rates than other students.

We assume that higher academic standards are associated with higher expected present values of income, so that

$$s_j^{min} > s_k^{min} \Rightarrow DPV_j(s_i) > DPV_k(s_i), \quad \forall\, s_i > s_k^{min}. \tag{2}$$

Under NCAA rules, athletic scholarships to different colleges are treated as though they are equivalent in that restrictions are imposed on the number of scholarships that can be offered, rather than on their value. This means that there is a built-in recruiting advantage for schools with higher academic standards:

Proposition 1: Under NCAA rules, if coaching inputs are equal at all colleges in player i's attainable set, the player's preference ranking over colleges is the same as the academic ranking of the schools.
Proof: $V_{ij} > V_{ik}$ when $s_j^{min} > s_k^{min}$, since $p_{ij} = p_{ik}$ when $C_j = C_k$ (equal coaching inputs) and $DPV_j(s_i) > DPV_k(s_i)$.

Now, the expression in equation (1) could be interpreted as a discrete choice. But if there is a wide variety of colleges with continuous p_{ij} alternatives, then the following interpretation makes sense. Even if not, a flavor of the marginal consideration that players seek can be had. The first-order condition for maximization of equation (1) yields:

$$p_{ij}\left(\frac{\partial NFL(p_{ij})}{\partial p_{ij}}\right) = DPV_j(s_i) - \left[NFL(p_{ij}) + DPV_j(s_i)(1 + r)^{-T}\right]. \tag{3}$$

The student-athlete chooses the college where his expected increment to NFL earnings is just equal to the difference between earnings without an NFL career and earnings with such a career.

With V_{ij}^* as "indirect" expected present value of income (that is, equation (1) evaluated at the optimal p_{ij} that could be solved from equation (3)), the envelope theorem yields:

$$\frac{dV_{ij}^*}{ds_i} = \frac{dV_{ij}}{ds_i} = \frac{\partial DPV_j(s_i)}{\partial s_i}\left(p_{ij}^*\left[(1 + r)^{-T} - 1\right] + 1\right) > 0. \tag{4}$$

It is greater than zero since $(1 + r)^{-T} > 0$ and higher SAT scores generate higher lifetime income whether or not a player has an NFL career. Thus, at an optimum, expected present value of income increases with entering SAT score. Put another way, for two players with the same NFL probability at college j, the one with the higher entering SAT score has a higher expected present value of income.

Coaches

Turning to coaches, we look first at coaching as an input and then at the structure of the market for coaches. The coaching input raises individual skill levels and, as a result, the playing strength of teams. Let

$$L_j = \sum_{i \in I_j} p_{ij} \tag{5}$$

denote the playing strength of team j, where I_j is the index set of players at college j. C_j is the level of coaching skills at college j. Coaching works its way into the talent process through college-specific skill development. We characterize this with

$$p_{ij} = p_{ij}(C_j), \text{ where } \frac{\partial p_{ij}}{\partial C_j} > 0. \tag{6}$$

The idea here is that coaching is in large measure a training and teaching occupation. The raw talent of entering freshmen is transformed into the skills of a professional player. The larger the coaching input, the more skilled the final product, all else constant.

In stark contrast to the players' market, where NCAA rules are highly restrictive and market imperfections abound, the coaches' market is relatively free from economic restriction. There are rules limiting the number and earnings of some assistant coaches. However, head coaches operate in a market that is close to the competitive ideal since colleges are free to make whatever dollar and fringe benefit offers they wish to coaches. The existence of NFL assistant and head coaching jobs serves to intensify college-level competition over coaches.

In what follows, we assume that the market has cleared so that each coach is characterized by his contribution at his current college, C_j. The price of a unit of coaching talent is c. Because of indivisibilities, there is an admissible set of colleges that might hire any given coach. This set is characterized by its willingness to pay the going rate and the coach is indifferent about working for any of the colleges in the admissible set.

Athletic Department

The athletic department is constrained to obey the academic requirements of its college. Each college chooses its level of academic standards through its entering SAT score, s_j^{min}. It is assumed that tuition cost, t_j, increases with s_j^{min}. Further, we characterize DPV_j (s_i), the value of an education at college j, as increasing with s_j^{min} for all players with $s_i > s_j^{min}$.

Each college j belongs to its football conference J. Because of competitive balance considerations, football conferences tend to consist of colleges with roughly the same level of academic standards as well as roughly the same level of revenue potential, as discussed later.

There are some major differences between the athletic department of a college and the college's academic departments. Coaches, in general, and football coaches, in particular, are paid much more than professors but coaches typically are signed to relatively short-term contracts and are not covered by tenure and promotion rules. Moreover, as with many academic departments, athletic departments, on average, barely break even (the latest evidence is in Fulks, 1994, but earlier studies using the same data source found roughly the same results). However, football gate receipts, TV income, post-season earnings, and booster contributions typically are in excess of athletic department spending on football.

So, why do colleges typically support athletic departments with direct budget appropriations? If the typical athletic department generates any value to the typical college at large, it is through endowments and gifts from boosters that may be tied to football success, any sort of increase in the application pool derived from football success, plus any other spillovers to the rest of the college due to its affiliation with a "major conference." In many ways, the athletic department and its football program perform a development function for the college. The few extremely successful programs also provide direct revenues to their fortunate (but few) colleges.

It is well-established that winning enhances giving to the athletic department itself (Sigelman and Bookheimer, 1983; Coughlin and Erekson, 1984, 1985; Padilla and Baumer, 1994). But the value to the college, at large, is less well-settled. Brooker and

Klastorin (1981) and Grimes and Chressanthis (1994) find that winning boosts general giving to colleges. On the other hand, Sigelman and Bookheimer (1983), Gaski and Etzel (1984), and Sack and Watkins (1985) did not find such a relationship. Sigelman and Carter (1979) present sort of an intermediate finding; giving to the college, at large, only rises with dramatic program turnarounds. On other dimensions of interest to the college, athletic success has been found to increase the quality of the student body (McCormick and Tinsley, 1990) and enhance the size of the applicant pool (Murphy and Trandel, 1994).

It is commonly believed that college football programs are operated with little concern for net operating revenue generated for the college at large (for example, see Sperber, 1990). However, within the constraints imposed by a college's ethical framework and academic standards, we cast college football programs as profit maximizers. The rationalization for this modeling choice was discussed at the beginning of this chapter. The forces of stable equilibrium and competitive balance require the development to which we now turn.

Padilla and Baumer (1994) have established that revenues clearly go up with winning. Successful teams have larger direct revenues, as well as gifts and endowments to the athletic department, than less successful teams. To see how a stable equilibrium with competitive balance depends on profit maximization, suppose that all colleges in a given conference operate football programs that do not fully exploit profit opportunities. Such a situation cannot be stable since there are incentives for each college in the league to improve its team, hire a better coach, recruit better athletes, and gain a higher winning percent. Since, within a league, changes in winning percents are zero-sum, the improved team's revenues rise and all other teams' revenues fall. Unless they are willing to live with this reduced situation, other teams must respond by moving in the direction of profit maximization. Their only other alternative is to move to another league with lower revenue and profit potential. Thus, the only stable equilibrium is one where all athletic departments are pursuing something approximating profit maximization. That football programs often carry the other intercollegiate sports within the department only serves to reinforce this observation.

Ultimately, through the administrative branch of the college, athletic department budgets are subject to approval by external monitors of the college, usually some type of board of regents that serves at the state governor's discretion. Formally, then, individual coaches attempt to maximize winning percent subject to the athletic department allocation to the football program. While this does not necessarily imply a simple one-to-one relation to the profits generated in the department, in fact, athletic budgets and coaches' salaries are clearly directly related to the success of the team and the revenues that follow such success.

Let $w_j = w_j(L_J)$ denote the winning percent of team j, where L_J is the vector of playing strengths of teams in league J and

$$\frac{\partial w_j}{\partial L_j} > 0 \text{ and } \frac{\partial w_j}{\partial L_k} < 0 \text{ for k} \neq \text{j}. \tag{7}$$

Under NCAA rules, and assuming profit maximization, the college chooses its coaching level, C_j, and its number of scholarship offers, n_j, in order to maximize profits:

$$\Pi_j = R_j(w_j) - cC_j - n_j t_j, \qquad (8)$$

subject to $n_j < n_{max}$, where n_{max} is the NCAA scholarship limitation. Notice that all players who receive a scholarship receive the same amount, equal to tuition, t_j. The first-order conditions are:

$$\frac{\partial \Pi}{\partial C} = \frac{\partial R}{\partial w}\left(\frac{\partial w}{\partial C} + \frac{\partial w}{\partial L}\frac{\partial L}{\partial C}\right) - c = 0, \qquad (9)$$

$$\frac{\partial \Pi}{\partial n} = \left(\frac{\partial R}{\partial w}\frac{\partial w}{\partial L}\frac{\partial L}{\partial n} - t_j\right)\left(n_{max} - n_j\right) = 0, \qquad (10)$$

$$\frac{\partial R}{\partial w}\frac{\partial w}{\partial L}\frac{\partial L}{\partial n} - t_j \geq 0. \qquad (11)$$

In the usual Kuhn-Tucker way, note that $n_j = n_{max}$ yields

$$\frac{\partial R}{\partial w}\frac{\partial w}{\partial L}\frac{\partial L}{\partial n} - t_j \geq 0, \qquad (12)$$

and $n_j < n_{max}$ yields

$$\frac{\partial R}{\partial w}\frac{\partial w}{\partial L}\frac{\partial L}{\partial n} - t_j = 0. \qquad (13)$$

Equation (9) shows that additional coaching input increases winning percent directly (for any level of playing strength) and indirectly by increasing the playing strength of the team through both recruiting a better class of player and improving the skills of players that are recruited. Because coaching inputs are acquired in a competitive market, coaches capture their marginal revenue product, including increases in athletic department revenue resulting from both direct and indirect coaching impacts on winning percent.

The NCAA does not allow athletic departments to offer more than a full-ride scholarship (although athletes in some sports do receive partial scholarships) and recruiting rules restrict the number of full-ride scholarships that can be offered in any given sport. Thus, scholarship offers are not determined on the basis of their cost to the athletic department, or the value to players. Further, it is a meta-fact of college sports that athletic departments always allocate all of their full ride equivalent scholarships. As Noll (1991, p. 205) points out, "Hence, recruiting three or four additional first-rate athletes per year can move a school from being marginally profitable to being very successful, generating an additional million dollars a year or more in net revenues." These observations lead us to the following elementary propositions concerning economic exploitation of players by athletic departments.

Proposition 2: Under NCAA rules limiting the number of scholarships, every scholarship player at Division I-A colleges (except, perhaps, at the skill-level margin) is exploited in the sense that his marginal revenue product exceeds the tuition grant in Division I-A schools.

Proof: Under the usual Kuhn-Tucker interpretation of expression (9), if the scholarship constraint is binding ($n_j = n_{max}$), so that an increase in scholarships is expected to increase winning percent, then the marginal revenue product of the least-skilled player offered a scholarship exceeds or equals the tuition payment. All other higher-skilled players have marginal revenue products in excess of tuition.

Proposition 3: Under NCAA rules limiting the number of scholarships, the higher is a player's probability of an NFL career, the greater is the degree of exploitation of that player.

Proof: Also following expression (9), the greater the talent level, the higher the level of exploitation, that is, higher talent levels are farther from the skill-margin. But the greater the talent level, the higher the probability of an NFL career.

Earlier, we noted that McKenzie and Sullivan (1987) rejected the idea of monopsony because it is expected pay, not actual pay, that matters and athletes get a chance at the pros and higher pay because of the higher education exposure. But our characterization takes this criticism to heart, explicitly includes expected pay, and still implies monopsony behavior toward athletes. Thus, at the level of theory, the McKenzie and Sullivan critique is rejected. Instead, arguments like those by Goff, Shugart, and Tollison (1988) are supported. They argued that amateurism both redirects wealth from athletes to their organizations and lessens competition for the athletes' positions (by erecting low pay as an entry barrier).

However, we hasten to point out that there is some evidence that the returns to this exploitation may end up being spent in net socially wasteful ways. While tuition, room and board, books, and the chance at a higher expected future income represent the monopsony payment to athletes, recruiting costs are competitively determined. Unlike professional sports, there is no "draft" for new talent entering the college ranks. While the NCAA limits some types of recruiting spending, clearly large amounts are spent during the process. Rent-seeking ideas of the Tullock (1967) variety may mean that athletic departments already spend up to and including the added value of the recruit during the recruiting process. But, since only one school gets the recruit, and a cheaper way for talent to enter the Division I ranks is easy to envision, such expenditures by the other schools represent social waste.

Rushin (1993) cites an instructive example. George Raveling, USC basketball coach at the time, wrote around 100 letters per week to a potential recruit. As long as it was on two-color letterhead, this practice was within NCAA rules, but surely wasteful. Thus, exploitation in the presence of rent-seeking incentives may mean that coaches and athletic department administrators do not keep the difference between marginal revenue product and scholarships.

Equation (9) provides insight into competitive balance within college football leagues. Suppose that all colleges in a certain league have the same academic standard, so that the bias in favor of higher quality colleges noted in Proposition 1, above, does not apply. In this case, all colleges face the same competitive cost of coaching inputs, c, and the same tuition cost of player inputs, t_j. Let $MRP_j (C_j)$ denote the marginal revenue product of coaching at college j (shown in the right-hand-side of equation (9)). This leads us to the following proposition.

Proposition 4: Under NCAA rules limiting the number of scholarships, if colleges j and k in league J have the same academic standards, then $MRP_j (C_j) > MRP_k (C_k)$ → a higher level of coaching talent, a higher level of playing talent, and a higher winning percent at j than at k.

Proof: Suppose $C_j = C_k$ and $s_j^{min} = {}^{mi}_k$, but $MRP_j (C_j) > MRP_k (C_k)$. If college j is maximizing profit so that $MRP_k (C_k) = c$, the marginal cost of coaching talent, then college j cannot be maximizing profits. In order to do so, j must increase its coaching input. But doing so raises the level of talent and, in turn, the winning percent at college j relative to college k.

Proposition 4 asserts that the higher is the marginal revenue product of coaching for a college, the more coaching inputs are hired, the better are the players that are recruited and trained, and the better is the winning percentage of that college. Factors leading to a situation where $MRP_j (C_j) > MRP_k (C_k)$, even though $C_j = C_k$, include a larger and/or wealthier fan population, a larger capacity stadium, a stronger football tradition, fewer close substitutes (like professional football), and a better TV contract at j compared to k. Thus, just as in professional team sports, college football leagues face a problem of lack of competitive balance. Colleges in the strongest-drawing locations will field stronger teams, on average, than colleges in weaker-drawing locations.

One consequence of the imbalance is that if there is a great disparity in drawing potential between two conference colleges, either the weaker or the stronger, or both, will be under both internal and external pressure to leave the conference. Conferences thus tend to end up with members of similar drawing potential, just as they tend to end up with colleges of roughly similar academic standards. The University of Chicago, which dropped football and left the Big-10 in the late 1930s, is one historical example. A more recent example is Northwestern University; only the recent resurgence of its football fortunes have silenced rumors that the Wildcats would be leaving the Big-10 Conference.

THE IMPLICATIONS OF PLAY-FOR-PAY

One of the most controversial issues currently confronting college football is paying cash to college athletes, over and above the usual scholarship and expected higher income after graduation. Our model generates the following insights into the consequences of replacing the present set of NCAA amateur standing rules with a freely competitive market for player services.

Under a competitive market, players would receive money/tuition offers, as well as expected later income, that would reflect the skill levels of individual players. This is in stark contrast to the present system where, at any given college, all players receive the same scholarship regardless of skill levels. Because colleges differ from one another in the value of scholarships, schools with lower academic standards (and lower discounted present value of income for players who choose to enroll there) would have to offer higher cash payments to offset the differential in scholarship value. Also, since colleges differ in coaching inputs, which affect the probability of an NFL career, offers to players under play-for-pay would have to reflect this differential as well. Under a perfectly competitive market for players, with complete information, players would be completely indifferent between colleges, just as would be the case with coaches under the present system of NCAA rules.

Under NCAA rules, if colleges j and k in conference J have the same academic standards but different coaching inputs, say $C_j > C_k$, then for any player i with complete information, and for whom the two colleges are in his attainable set, college j is preferred to college k since $NFL\ (p_{ij}) > NFL\ (p_{ik})$. Thus, under NCAA rules, every recruit at college j would have more NFL potential than any recruit at college k. In contrast, under play-for-pay, players are indifferent between the two colleges. Under play-for-pay, the difference in playing strengths between the two colleges is determined by the number of units of playing skills signed by the two colleges.

Under play-for-pay, and given that colleges j and k in conference J have the same academic standards, Proposition 4 still holds. But because cash payments to players offset some of the drawing power of coaching inputs, we would expect the equilibrium level of the per-unit coaching input price, c, to fall under play-for-pay. On the one hand, NCAA rules do not permit colleges with low marginal revenue products for players and coaches to offset the coaching input advantage that colleges with higher marginal revenue products have under the rules. This generates part of the competitive imbalance result; better recruits are attracted to higher marginal revenue product colleges. On the other hand, high marginal revenue product colleges have a wider gap between player marginal revenue product and tuition cost and, hence, a larger unsatisfied demand for players. Just how these two forces balance out is problematic. We summarize their ideas along the lines of the following poroposition.

Proposition 5: Under play-for-pay,
(i) Players are indifferent between colleges in their attainable set.
(ii) The market price of coaching talent falls relative to its price under current NCAA amateur rules.
(iii) Proposition 4 holds, but whether competitive balance is harmed or enhanced is unknown.
(iv) Proposition 1 no longer holds; the talent advantage at colleges with high academic standards is eliminated under play-for-pay.
Proof: See the above discussion.

CHEATING ON NCAA RULES

We turn to the other important college football problem, cheating on the rules. While our focus is on athletic departments and coaches, there is evidence that players are willing to cheat as well (Sack, 1987, 1991). Let q denote the probability of being caught in a violation of NCAA rules. G denotes the gain achieved through cheating and H is the loss under NCAA sanction if caught. Then, the expected value of cheating to the athletic department at college j is:

$$EV = (1-q)G - qH. \qquad (14)$$

Cheating is more likely, the lower is q or H and the higher is G. Colleges most likely to gain substantially from cheating are colleges with high marginal revenues from winning. These would be colleges with low winning percents, large unused stadium capacity, and a large potential TV and gate audience.

Similarly, losses from NCAA penalties if a college is caught cheating are largest for the most successful football programs, that is, programs with lucrative TV earnings, wealthy donors, and perennial post-season play. Looking at things from a coach's point of view, older established coaches have made their reputation and figure to lose most if caught cheating while young unknowns have little in the way of reputation to lose and much to gain from establishing themselves as winning coaches. Thus, assuming that q is the same for all colleges, one would predict that a college with a currently weak football record, a high potential for financial gain if its team is a success, and headed by a young coach, is most likely to engage in cheating.

Further, coaches and boosters almost never bear the penalties imposed by the NCAA. Even if the coach is caught, the winning percent reward to cheating stays on his record and only seldom is a coach ever sanctioned for cheating. As Noll (1991, p. 198) states, "Cheating against the NCAA rules will continue—indeed, increase—because it is the profit-maximizing strategy for nearly all universities and the income-maximizing strategy for coaches."

There is evidence to this point. Padilla and Baumer (1994) analyze cheating at both the athletic program level and for individual sports. Programs with a history of NCAA violations tended to generate greater revenues and profits, while the short-run impacts of recent sanctions were negligible or zero. For football, sanctions did not effect revenues. They did for basketball, but only for a short time. Fleisher, Goff, and Tollison (1992) also found that "crime pays." Winning percents of violators were much different than others before they were caught even though there was a reduction in their winning percent after NCAA sanctions. It appears that Noll was correct.

But there are mitigating factors. The NCAA must surely be aware of these facts, which means that it should allocate its scrutiny heavily toward just such programs; the probability, q, of being caught would be higher for the teams most likely to cheat. Fleisher, Goff, and Tollison (1992) note the usual cheating incentives force cartel members to carefully monitor each other's output levels; the NCAA would be on the look-out for dramatic changes in winning percent, success in recruiting, and changes in conference affiliation.

There also appear to be incentives for schools to monitor cheating by their own athletic departments. Grimes and Chressanthis (1994) find evidence that NCAA sanctions reduce giving to the academic portion of the college. Such losses, if large enough, should bring the college's own watchdogs sniffing after the athletic department.

Also, there shouldn't be much cheating by colleges with high academic standards. By Proposition 3, they already have the advantage in recruiting the only type of players that they are willing to admit by virtue of the higher value of their scholarship. In a sense, these colleges are competing for different players than are other colleges.

Finally, Noll (1991, p. 207) points out that conference revenue sharing blunts the incentive to cheat. If each conference member only earns a portion of the reward to cheating and must share the rest with other conference members, cheating should be reduced. Further, teams in conferences with more extensive revenue sharing should cheat less. We summarize these ideas as follows:

Proposition 6: NCAA rules provide incentives for under-the-counter payments to highly skilled players, and for cheating on SAT and other entrance requirements, for players with low academic credentials at weak programs, with high potential payoffs, a young coach, low academic standards, and low revenue sharing imposed by its conference.

PAST EMPIRICAL WORK

In this section, we seek verification of the theory just developed by looking at the empirical work of others. The evidence is organized around the propositions in this chapter. Testable implications for those propositions without any related existing empirical work, and anything additional for those propositions with related empirical work, can be found in the conclusion.

Turning first to the evidence on monopsony exploitation of college athletes, Propositions 2 and 3 state that compensation to college football players will be less than their contribution to athletic department revenues and more so for star players. Past empirical work by others supports both of these propositions. Leonard and Prinzinger (1984) used an approach first applied by Scully (1974b) to Major League Baseball. They found monopsony exploitation in the 90% range. Brown (1993) put the level of exploitation at about $500,000 for college football stars, with the rate at 90%. In a related area, Brown, 1994, puts the estimate of marginal revenue product near $1 million for college basketball.

Noll (1991) provides an instructive example. Noting that quarterback John Paye was the only major roster difference in 1987 versus 1986, Noll finds about a $200,000 increase to Stanford's football program. The value of a scholarship that year was about $17,000. Without adjustment for Paye's future value as a pro (after the fact, it was not extensive), the exploitation rate in this example matches the 90% level found in other work.

There also are some interesting findings by others pertinent to Proposition 4, which dictates competitive imbalance based on different relative values of college football by fans at different colleges. Padilla and Baumer (1994) find no strong relationship between coaches' salaries and profits. But, by Proposition 4, higher marginal revenue products should drive higher salaries and higher returns to athletic departments. After noting that the data may have let them down, Padilla and Baumer add (p. 136), "Another interpretation is that there is also room here for cost-cutting, as spending for salaries is not strongly related to profitability in many cases." But Proposition 4 offers yet another explanation. They simply may have taken an empirical snap-shot of an equilibrium among similarly situated teams, from the marginal revenue product perspective.

Fleisher, Goff, and Tollison (1992) investigate some of the implications in Proposition 6. They find that variability in winning percent and conference switching both increase the chances for NCAA enforcement actions. In addition, the easier it is to monitor recruiting by other rivals, the less the chance of enforcement action by the NCAA. Further, they conclude that perennial winners and teams that never win are less likely to face such actions.

In summary, it appears that the empirical work of others offers some important verification of the theory in the last section. The three areas of significant past work concern Propositions 2 and 3 (college athlete monopsony exploitation), 4 (success and marginal revenue product), and 6 (cheating). This leaves substantial room for suggestions for future work, to which we now turn.

CONCLUSIONS: SUGGESTIONS FOR FUTURE WORK

Our goal was to add rigorous flesh to the informal bones of the analysis of the college football industry. Our set of propositions runs the gamut from player rankings of colleges based on the probability of an NFL career, to the monopsony exploitation of players, to competitive imbalance and its causes, to play-for-pay, to cheating. Significant support for the theory was found in past work, especially for monopsony exploitation and cheating. But much of the richness of the theory awaits empirical treatment.

There is no literature concerning Proposition 1; in a competitive market for coaches, there should be a one-to-one relationship between player preferences and academic ranking. This is reinforced by the findings in equations (3) and (4); even at the best school possible, athletes with higher entering SAT scores will have higher incomes and pro career chances, respectively. With modern record-keeping at major universities, as well as closer tabs on entering freshman athletes, there is potential to test this proposition. For example, tests of differences in means and variances of SAT scores at colleges of varying academic quality would help show that they draw from a different pool. Further, a retrospective look at the academic quality of schools producing pro players would lend further insight into the implications of the proposition.

The monopsony exploitation implications in Propositions 2 and 3 have been extensively treated in the empirical literature. But one issue remains. While we haven't followed through with the theory here, in our other work (Fort and Quirk, 1996) we have found that estimates of monopsony exploitation rates in professional sports are overstated by the amount of payment below marginal revenue product that can be attributed to revenue sharing incentives. Overstatements were estimated to be as large as 16%. Since the same techniques are being used by others to analyze exploitation in college sports, we expect that such rates have been similarly overstated for college athletes, calling for the type of correction we used in professional sports.

Even though it has received some empirical attention in past works, Proposition 4 dictates that sources of competitive imbalance are fan income, stadium capacity, tradition, few close substitutes, and better TV opportunities. The approach suggested is simple: look at the factors that should dictate higher marginal revenue products and see if better coaching, players, and winning percents line up. Given enough observations on athletic budgets, one could estimate the marginal contribution of winning to budget. Then, in a second stage, check whether or not the distribution of talent and winning lines up with the marginal contribution of winning.

Proposition 5 presents a real problem. Since the formation of the modern NCAA in the early 1900s, amateurism has been strictly enforced. There never has been play-for-pay, so its impacts cannot be evaluated directly. However, there may be a way of examining the competitive balance impacts of increased player mobility, such as would occur under play-for-pay. The idea is to find an episode where players in some college sport became more mobile after some exogenous change. For example, one might examine the variation in winning percent before and after the NBA allowed hardship cases, or before and after the NFL started drafting underclassmen. Another approach aimed at the same idea is to compare the variation in winning percents between baseball and football, given that college baseball players always have been the most mobile college athletes and football players the least mobile.

While Proposition 6 has received some treatment, more is clearly indicated. Cheating can be expected to occur where it is most profitable; under a currently weak football record, a high potential for financial gain if its team is a success, and a young coach. Mitigating factors include that the NCAA knows that these characteristics are most indicative of cheating, boosters and coaches tend to bear none of the costs of cheating, and that cheating should be lower at colleges with higher standards or in conferences with more extensive revenue sharing. Again, tests of different levels of cheating between high and low SAT score colleges should prove insightful. Also, revenue sharing formulas probably are available in order to check the variation in cheating along these lines.

There is plenty of room for theoretical extensions. In terms of the present effort, extensions should cover more fully the effects of revenue sharing and rent-seeking behavior on competitive balance. The effort here at covering cheating also is not very extensive. Game theoretical treatments would seem to hold promise, especially for further development on the player side of cheating.

In other areas, structure-conduct-performance has been analyzed empirically (Bennett and Fizel, 1995; Pacey, 1985; Pacey and Wickham, 1985; Fleisher, Goff, and Tollison, 1992), but absent rigorous theoretical underpinnings. And the analysis of government and the college sports industry could use a good dose of theory. Fleisher, Goff, and Tollison (1992) offer evidence that the NCAA is captured by powerful athletic schools and Hart-Nibbrig and Cottingham (1986) offer a more traditional political science view of the political economy of college sports. Surely the melding of solid institutional views with rational actor modeling can be as successful here as it has been elsewhere.

3

A Test of the Optimal Positive Production Network Externality in Major League Baseball

Daniel Rascher

Are the Bulls so good they're bad for the NBA?
—*The Cover of Sports Illustrated*, March 10, 1997

THE MODEL

Are both absolute and relative quality important in the demand for sports contests? Is the closeness of the contest a significant factor, and if so what is the optimal degree of closeness? Alternatively, what is the optimal distribution of talent across the league from the owners' perspective?

Unlike most businesses, firms in a sports league need viable competitors. While a certain amount of domination is optimal from an individual owner's perspective, too much will result in league dissolution, and thus a lower utility for every owner. Hence, there is a limited positive production network externality. Up to a point, many successful competitors are better than none, a major exception to classical economic theory. In fact, what Neale (1964) termed "the peculiar economics of sports" is just the positive production network externality.

Early in the history of professional sports, owners realized that contests with an uncertain outcome were important for attracting large crowds. In fact, the first professional baseball league failed largely because of the dominance of a few teams. Fans began to grow tired of the ``pre-determined" games and eventually stopped showing up (Scully, 1989).

In response, the owners began to insert rules to create more parity throughout the league. Most of these rules (the rookie draft, the waiver rule, salary caps, revenue sharing, luxury taxes, the Rozelle rule, player only trades with no cash involved) are either new or remain intact today. However, the reserve clause has been replaced by limited free agency. The efficacy of these rules in promoting league parity is questionable. Some of them have created a monopsonistic environment keeping player salaries down without necessarily affecting the distribution of player quality across teams.

The sports league model in Rascher (1997) posits a number of hypotheses regarding industrial organization and labor issues. Some of these depend directly on the assumption that both relative and absolute quality are determinants of demand. Most empirical analyses test the results of some theory directly. In this case, it is difficult if not impossible to test the effects of changes in revenue sharing or salary caps when neither have changed significantly more than once per league, and those that have changed have occurred concurrently with other structural changes. Thus, separating the individual effects is not possible. Instead, the analysis performed here tests the assumptions, not the results, to see whether they are reasonable. If the assumptions do not hold true, perhaps it is not worth checking the results; but if the assumptions prove to be acceptable, then we are one step closer to accepting the implications of the model.

The model assumes that the demand for a particular game has the form

$$Q_h = S_i(AT_i + BT_j + C(T_i - T_j)^2 + other) \tag{1}$$

and that $A>B>0>C$. Q_h is the demand for home games. T_i and T_j are the team talent levels of team i (the home team) and team j (the visiting team), respectively. A is the marginal propensity to attend home games with respect to the home team's quality. B is the marginal propensity to attend home games with respect to the visiting team's quality and is assumed to be less important to the home town fans. C is the marginal propensity to attend home games that is attributable to the closeness-of-contest portion of demand. S_i is a scalar which controls for the potential demand from market size, income, and other factors across cities. Q_h satisfies the consideration that the closeness of the contest as well as high-quality play are important aspects of the demand for sports contests. The restrictions on A, B, and C are consistent with the notion that demand is maximized when the probability that the home team wins a particular game is greater than 0.5, but less than 1. It is likely that the home team fans care more about changes in the home team's level of quality than changes in the visiting teams quality levels. This demand function prevents two equally rated low quality teams from enticing the same demand as two equally rated high quality teams.[1]

To test whether or not this demand function is credible, a game-by-game demand analysis will reveal if: (1) the absolute quality of the two teams is important (A and B are both positive and significant), (2) home town fans respond more to changes in the home team's player quality level than to changes in the visiting team's player quality level ($A > B$), and (3) fans want to see a close game where the winner is determined with uncertainty ($C < 0$ and significant). Additionally, a direct test of the optimal (from the league's perspective) *ex ante* probability that the home team wins a particular game will be performed.[2]

To accomplish this, the author created a large data set (2,267 observations for 58 variables) where each observation is a Major League Baseball game played in 1996. This data set is particularly suited to test demand because in the short run the supply of contests (and their quality) is fixed, and variation in the quantity sold should result from shifts in the demand function. A game-by-game or short-run demand analysis using attendance as a proxy for demand empirically verifies the above assumptions.

The next section contains a review of related literature. A description of the data comprises section three, followed by the analysis and results section. The last section summarizes the findings.

PREVIOUS LITERATURE

Most studies of the demand for sports contests have been long-run studies where the unit of observation was a team-season (i.e., each observation was a whole season for a particular team). Beginning with Demmert (1973) and Noll (1974), it has been typical to use attendance as a proxy for revenue. However, Siegfried and Eisenberg (1980) use average revenue in their study of minor league baseball demand, but find no significant differences in their results from the two prior articles.[3]

As expected, these studies have found that team quality (proxied by season winning percentage) has an important effect on demand.[4] However, they haven't tested whether relative, absolute, or both types of team quality are important.

Recently, there have been a number of short-run demand studies of professional sports. Hill, Madura, and Zuber (1982) examined baseball data from the 1977 season and found that the quality of the two teams was important (an absolute quality assessment). That study obtained other results that agree with the current study (higher population centers and weekend games attract more fans).[5] Borland and Lye (1992) show that the uncertainty of the contest is an important factor of demand, but only measure this uncertainty four times during their season of study of an Australian Rules football league. Thus, their results are interesting, but have low power.

Using a small data set, Welki and Zlatoper (1994) examine the National Football League and find that home team quality is important. Jennett (1984) and Peel and Thomas (1988) use soccer attendance data. Jennett shows that an *ex post* measure of uncertainty (the final score) is an important determinant of attendance. Peel and Thomas uncover evidence that the closeness of the contest matters using an *a priori* measure of closeness (pre-game odds data). Their study is similar in flavor to the current study because it directly analyzes the importance of closeness, but not the importance of absolute team quality.

Finally, an article by Knowles, Sherony, and Haupert (1992) uses 861 games and ten independent variables from the 1988 Major League Baseball season and concludes that the attendance maximizing *ex ante* probability that the home team wins (using gambling odds data) is about 0.6.

The current study has a larger number of observations and more independent variables than any previous study of this nature. It also specifically tests for the effect of absolute and relative quality concurrently as determinants of demand, so that their relative importance can be measured and an *ex ante* optimal probability of the home team winning can be estimated. In addition, it tests other factors such as race and pitcher quality in affecting demand.

THE DATA

The data set contains 2,267 observations for the 1996 Major League Baseball season, one for each game played. Each observation is a particular game and contains the dependent variable, game attendance, which is used as a proxy for game revenue or (without price) quantity sold. The sports league model being tested claims that teams choose player quality to maximize the owners' objectives. Owner objectives contain revenue (through a profit function) which is aggregated from individual game revenue. Thus, attendance is a natural outcome variable for testing the effects of owner decision making.

Dependent Variable

Table 3.1 shows sample statistics for a selection of the variables in the data set. Attendance ranges from about 6,000 fans (an Oakland A's game) to about 57,500 (the opening game of the Seattle Mariners) with a mean close to 27,000. Unlike the National Basketball Association where most games sell out, baseball games have a wide range of attendances allowing for the possibility of uncovering determinants of demand.[6] The source was from the internet web site www.sportsline.com.[7]

Time Varying Independent Variables

Included in each observation are variables that change from game to game for a particular team. Some of these relate to team quality while others relate to conditions of the game.

Two measures of game excitement are the average number of runs scored in the previous ten games for the home and visiting team, respectively. It is expected that the sign will be positive because pundits claim that today's fan enjoys a high scoring affair. However, it is possible for the sign to be negative if fans desire a pitching duel. This could be an interesting test of the pundits' claim.

To capture the effect of possible changes in player quality levels (from learning by doing or even trades) during the course of the season, the number of wins in the last ten games for both the home and visiting teams is used and is expected to exert a positive influence on attendance.[8]

Another measure of team quality is whether a team is in contention for a division title. A proxy, the number of games behind the division leader, is used, but is interacted with the percentage of games left in the season. This distinguishes between being ten games out in May (still in contention) or ten games out in September (out of the race). The current percentage of games played (e.g., thirty of 162 games is 18.5%) is used as a type of trend variable because many of the time-varying regressors (pitcher wins and losses) increase simply because the season wears on.

Unlike most other sports, the quality of a baseball team changes from game to game because a different starting pitcher is used each game (a rotation of four or five pitchers is used throughout the season). To capture this effect, the current wins, losses, and earned run average of both the home and visiting starting pitcher are used. It is expected that more wins, less losses, and a lower earned run average for both pitchers will increase attendance, but there should be a larger effect for the home team pitcher.[9]

It is possible that fans react more to the past career performances of a particular pitcher in making their purchasing decision at the beginning of a season than toward the end of the season. Career wins, losses, and earned run average for both the home and visiting starting pitchers are entered as covariates and are expected to have the same sign as the current versions of these variables.[10]

Table 3.1
Sample Statistics of the Game by Game Baseball Data

	Min.	Mean	Max.
Dependent Variable:			
Game Attendance	6021	26,868	57,476
Time Varying Variables:			
Prob. the Home Team Wins (Odds)	0.25	0.54	0.82
Prob. the Home Team Wins (Wpct.)	0.26	0.50	0.74
Current Home Team's Win Percent	0.28	0.50	0.64
Current Visiting Team's Win Percent	0.28	0.50	0.64
Home Team's # of Runs in Last 10 Games	0	5.02	12.5
Home Team's # of Wins in Last 10 Games	0	4.8	10
Home Team's Current # of Losses	0	40.03	108
Home Team's Current # of Wins	0	39.9	97
Home Pitcher's Career ERA	0	4.00	16.2
Home Pitcher's Career Losses	0	37.6	176
Home Pitcher's Career Wins	0	43.8	231
Home Pitcher's Season ERA	0	4.60	81.0
Home Pitcher's Season Losses	0	4.26	17.0
Home Pitcher's Season Wins	0	4.77	22
Visitor's Current # of Losses	0	39.90	103
Visitor's Current # of Wins	0	39.99	99
Visiting Pitcher's Career ERA	0	3.98	14.14
Visiting Pitcher's Career Losses	0	37.60	176
Visiting Pitcher's Career Wins	0	43.55	231
Visiting Pitcher's Current ERA	0	4.57	81
Visiting Pitcher's Current Losses	0	4.24	17
Visiting Pitcher's Current Wins	0	4.73	23
Visitor's Runs in Last 10 Games	0	5.02	15
Visitor's Wins in Last 10 Games	0	4.85	9
Night Game	0	0.66	1
Game is a Weekend Game	0	0.48	1
Cloudiness Index	0	2.06	9
Temperature at Game Time	33	72.5	100

Table 3.1 continued

Time Constant Variables:

Home Team's Previous Season's Wins	56	71.92	100
Visitor's Previous Season's Wins	56	71.99	100
Average Ticket Price	$7.95	$11.30	$15.43
Fan Cost Index	$81.31	$103.03	$121.76
Median Income of Local CMSA	$26,501	$35,046	$41,459
Percentage Black of Local CMSA	0.006	0.127	0.260
Percentage Latino of Local CMSA	0.005	0.099	0.331
Population of Local CMSA	1,640,831	5,997,132	18,107,235
Recreation Index of Local CMSA	81.32	93.72	99.02
Unemployment Rate of Local CMSA	0.034	0.061	0.113
Stadium Seating Capacity	33,871	50,655	64,593
Stadium Age	0	28.5	84

The independent variables above are the team quality factors that vary from game to game. There are a number of interesting game condition variables unrelated to team quality. A weekend dummy variable is expected to have a positive effect on attendance because the opportunity cost of attending a game on the weekend is lower than during the week for people that have a standard work week. Further, each team plays every Friday night, Saturday, and Sunday, but not each day during the week. Thus, the owners must feel that weekend games draw more fans than weekday games or else they wouldn't schedule so many of them. In fact, 48% of games are weekend games. An evening variable is also included for essentially the same reason. Additionally, an opening day variable is used to capture the well known positive effect that opening day has on attendance.

The temperature and degree of cloudiness at game time are probable factors in the decision to attend a baseball game. Warmer temperatures and clearer skies are likely to induce higher fan turnouts. The cloudiness index ranges from 0 to 9, with 9 being very cloudy. The average cloudiness of the 2,267 games is about 2. The temperature ranges from 33 to 100° Fahrenheit with a mean and median of about 72.5.

About 52% of the games were televised. Viewing a game on TV is likely to be a substitute for attending a game, thus having a negative effect on attendance. However, many pundits claim that these are not competing products because attending a game does not simply involve watching the contest, but also experiencing the atmosphere. Also, televised games are likely to increase product awareness and thus increase future game attendances. This argument has been used to advocate the removal of the blackout rule in professional football.[11]

One measure of the importance or excitement of a game is whether the two teams are rivals. Most rivalries are between two teams in the same division within the league. Additionally, divisions are usually geographically based. Thus, these official rivalries are also likely to be sociological rivalries, for example, the San Francisco Giants and the Los Angeles Dodgers. A dummy variable was created to denote a game between rivals.

Scully (1974a), using baseball data from 1967, shows that black pitchers were discriminated against at the gate with fewer fans showing up to watch them pitch. Indicator variables for Latino, black, and Asian starting pitchers for both the home and away team are created to assess whether customer discrimination against certain races is a factor of demand. About 6% of the starting pitchers are black, about 15% are Latino, and only two pitchers (Hideo Nomo and Chan Ho Park, both of the Los Angeles Dodgers) are Asian.[12]

There are two groups of variables that are of major interest for the empirical test of the sports league model. The first group contains the home team's measure of player quality (current home team's winning percentage, or T_i), the visiting team's measure of player quality (current visiting team's winning percentage, or T_j), and the difference of these two squared ($(T_i - T_j)^2$).[13] It is expected that the coefficients of these variables will be positive, smaller but positive, and negative, respectively. This corresponds to the test of the assumption that $A > B > 0 > C$. Because of the high variability of these variables at the beginning of the season, this test will be performed on the data corresponding to the last half of the season. Table 3.1 shows that both home team and visiting team winning percentages range from 28% to 64% with a predictable mean of 50%.

The second group of variables is simply the probability that the home team will win a particular game created by converting the pre-game odds data. On odds betting of this type, there is no vigorish or commission for the bookie.[14] Instead, the odds for betting on the favorite are not symmetrical to the odds for betting on the underdog. For example, if the home team's line is 175 and the visiting team's line is 165 with the home team favored, then a $175 bet placed on the home team will pay $100 if the home team wins, and a $100 bet placed on the visiting team will pay $165, if the visiting team wins, not $175. The bookie makes a profit because the odds are not symmetric and bettors place bets on both the underdog and the favorite.

To get a probability that the home team will win from the odds data, assume that the odds presented are for a fair bet. Then, if the probability that the home team will win is P_h,

$$100\ P_h - 175\ (1 - P_h) = 0, \tag{2}$$

implying that $P_h = 0.636$. For a bet placed on the visiting team the fair bet equation,

$$165\ (1 - P_h) - 100\ P_h = 0 \tag{3}$$

yields $P_h = 0.623$. These probabilities are not the same because the difference allows the bookie to make a profit. The average of the two will be used here for the home team's probability of winning. Thus,

$$P_h = \frac{1}{2} \left(\frac{H}{H+100} + \frac{V}{V+100} \right), \qquad (4)$$

where H is the home team's line (175) and V is the visiting team's line (165). Therefore, $P_h = 0.63$, or the home team has a 63% chance of winning the game. The resulting probabilities for the home team winning have an average of 54% with a minimum of 25% and a maximum of 82%.

For an interesting comparison, the home team winning percentage and the visiting team winning percentage can be translated into a probability that the home team wins by using the following formula (Fort and Quirk, 1995):

$$P_h = \frac{(1-w_j)w_i}{w_i(1-w_j) + w_j(1-w_i)}, \qquad (5)$$

where w_i and w_j are the winning percentages of the home and visiting teams, respectively.[15] This probability can be compared with the one generated from the odds data to see which is a better predictor of fan turnout. It can also be used in a forecasting model to see if it can beat the odds data in forecasting winners.

Time Constant Independent Variables

There are a number of potentially important independent variables that are constant throughout the season for a given team, but vary across teams. A straight average ticket price for each team is used as a proxy for the actual ticket prices paid by consumers. Obviously this may be an influential determinant of demand. However, as discussed in the review section, many previous studies have found ticket price to have the opposite sign or be insignificant. Average ticket prices range from $7.95 to $15.43 with a mean of $11.43.[16]

Perhaps a better measure of the real cost of attending a game is the Fan Cost Index from the Team Marketing Report.[17] This index assumes a family of four purchases a fixed number of products (four hot dogs, four sodas, two peanuts, two caps, four mid-level tickets, and parking).[18] The average Fan Cost Index is $103 with a minimum of $81 and a maximum of $122.

Median income, the local unemployment rate, and the local population are all candidates for inclusion in a demand model. The expected effects are positive, negative, and positive, respectively. The racial composition of the local geographic area, if baseball appeals to certain cultures more than others, may affect attendance levels. Rascher (1998) shows that National Basketball Association annual attendances are partially predicted by the percentage of the local population that is black. Here, the percentage black and the percentage Latino is used to capture cultural differences across baseball cities.[19] It will be interesting to see how the sports differ in this respect.

Owners believe that characteristics of the baseball park affect attendance since these are part of the product space. The data set contains two variables related to stadium age. One is an indicator variable which takes on one if a stadium is new (built since

1987, which is the new generation of stadia) and zero if it is old. Also, because of the allure of the two classic ballparks, Wrigley field in Chicago and Fenway Park in Boston, a dummy variable is created for them. Another constraining factor on attendance is the stadium capacity. Rascher (1998) shows that for every two additional seats that are added to a basketball arena, one of them gets sold each game. It is likely that the effect of an extra baseball seat won't be as large because games aren't as close to being sellouts in baseball as in basketball.[20]

Again, Rascher (1998) uses a measure of alternative recreation as a factor in determining annual attendances. This same measure is used here to capture the notion of substitute products for professional baseball. Pundits consistently claim that west coast fans are more fickle either because many more of them are transplants than fans in eastern cities, or because of the extra recreation available in west coast cities.[21]

Finally, the number of home team and visiting team wins from the previous season is used as a measure of expected quality. This may be more important at the beginning of the season, but is probably also a factor in season ticket sales, which in turn affect game by game attendances throughout the season.[22]

ANALYSIS AND RESULTS

Analysis

The primary analysis consists of three tests that are performed by running three multivariate regressions and interpreting the results. The first test examines whether $A > B > 0 > C$, using the demand function in the model. This determines if both absolute and relative quality are important factors of demand and their respective weights.

Using pre-game odds data, the second test solves for the *ex ante* optimal probability that the home team wins based on attendance. The regression uses a simple quadratic to allow for a maximum. Thus, the signs of the probability and the probability squared are expected to be positive and negative, respectively.

The current home and visiting team winning percentages can be converted into a probability that the home team wins and can be examined in exactly the same way as the second test. This third test can be compared to the second test to see whether fans use all of the data available to them in making their decision (pre-game odds data) or use winning percentages as a proxy for the quality of the contest. In predicting attendance, it is not obvious which piece of information is more likely to be used by the fans.

To predict which team will win a particular game, the odds data is expected to perform better than the modified winning percentage data. A test of which variable is a better forecaster of game outcomes will be undertaken.[23]

Because of the possibility of truncation of the dependent variable due to sellouts, a censored regression was run. It is similar to a tobit analysis except that it allows the dependent variable to have more than one truncation point, that is, a different one for each stadium capacity. The results are virtually identical to those from an OLS analysis. This is not surprising since there were only fifty-one sellouts out of a possible

2,267 games.

Another potential data problem is that the errors for an n-game series between two teams may not be independent. It is expected that independence of errors exists across different groups of games (a three game series for example), but not necessarily within groups. This type of clustered correlation leads to understating the standard errors. A robust estimator of the variance is used to correct the standard errors.

It is possible that the time-constant independent variables will be correlated with the error term (a causality issue). For example, larger population centers may exhibit higher variances in attendance that may or may not err or one side of the fitted equation. If so, the estimates will be biased. To correct for this, a team fixed effects model without any time-constant independent variables is used as an alternative to the full model. As with most fixed effects models, the fit is better because there are specific intercepts for each team which capture the omitted team-specific variables, like advertising and ballpark atmosphere.

Results

Table 3.2 shows the results of the three regressions using team specific variables.[24] The first column is the analysis of the demand specification directly. Home team current winning percentage has a positive coefficient ($A > 0$). Visiting team current winning percentage also has a positive, but smaller, effect on attendance ($A > B > 0$). Finally, the square of the difference between the two measures of team player quality has a negative coefficient ($0 > C$).[25] Thus, fans are more sensitive to changes in their own team's player quality level than to changes in the visiting team's player quality level. They also desire close contests. During the middle of the season, an average win increases an average team's winning percentage by 0.0125 leading to an increase in attendance by 690 fans for each game (695 more for a better home team and five less for a more certain outcome).

Table 3.3 contains the results for the team fixed effects regressions. The adjusted R-squared increased from about 0.62 to 0.73. Almost three fourths of the variation in game-by-game attendance is explained by the current set of variables. The findings for the main variables of interest are similar, but smaller, than those found in Table 3.2.

As in previous studies of annual attendance, the American League attracts 5,000 fewer fans, all else equal. Increases in the Fan Cost Index decrease the number of fans attending games, although the result isn't significant.[26] As in Scully (1974a), black pitchers face customer discrimination at the gate of about 2,000 fans for the home team pitcher, while Latino and Asian pitchers increase demand above and beyond their skills, as compared to white pitchers. As expected, this effect is less important for the visiting pitcher than for the home pitcher.[27]

The home team pitcher's career wins and losses have unexpected signs, even though the percentage of games played is included as a control for the normal increase in these variables that occurs over the course of the season. Greater career losses increases demand and greater career wins decreases it. However, there is a correlation between career and season wins and losses. Subsequent analysis shows that net career winning percentage works as expected. The visiting pitcher's career wins and losses follow the

Table 3.2[a]
Regression Results of the Demand Specification Analysis

Dependent Variable: Game Attendance	$A > B > 0 > C$[b]	Optimal Prob. with Odds Data	Optimal Prob. with Winning Percentage Data[b]
Adjusted R-squared	0.631	.603	0.64
F-value	37.82	55.23	40.86
Number of Observations	1102	2193	1102
Home Team Current Win Percentage	55560	-	-
	(7.202)		
Visiting Team Current Win Percent	12804.6	-	-
	(1.578)		
Square of the Difference in Win Percents	-33429	-	-
	(-1.827)		
Prob (Home Team Wins): Odds Data	-	42201	-
		(1.821)	
Prob (Home Team Wins): Squared	-	-31452	-
		(-1.748)	
Prob (Home Team Wins): Win Percents	-	-	48266
			(2.256)
Prob (Home Team Wins): Squared	-	-	-34219
			(-1.885)
Optimal Probability Home Team Wins	-	0.671	0.70
Percent of Games Played by Home Team	69924	63613	8824
	(2.446)	(3.026)	(0.286)
Percent of Games Played by Visiting Team	-71549	-99846	-62322
	(-2.486)	(-4.447)	(-1.937)
Percent of Games Played * Win Percent (H)	54957	59583	62017
	(3.450)	(5.767)	(4.385)
Percent of Games Played * Win Percent (V)	20913	22504	-15998
	(1.548)	(1.770)	(-0.523)
Games Behind Leader * Pct Games Left (H)	17238	15359	-6938
	(1.594)	(1.695)	(-0.245)
Games Behind Leader * Pct Games Left (V)	1812	1924.4	12920
	(0.916)	(0.188)	(0.348)
Intercept	-41335	-36269	-18234
	(-2.079)	(-2.178)	(-0.678)
Home Team Wins in Last 10 Games	227.8	-43	119
	(0.913)	(-0.259)	(0.484)
Visiting Team Wins in Last 10 Games	-226.8	-254	-293
	(-1.016)	(-1.620)	(-1.345)

Table 3.2 continued

Home Team Runs in Last 10 Games	187	-43	113
	(0.595)	(-0.208)	(0.354)
Visiting Team Runs in Last 10 Games	303	205	368
	(1.042)	(0.953)	(1.311)
American League Dummy	-4683	-4914	-4701
	(-5.079)	(-6.415)	(-5.16)
Fan Cost Index	-42	-46.8	-42
	(-0.886)	(-1.22)	(-0.903)
Home Team Pitcher Is Asian	14585	16190	14593
	(6.972)	(9.683)	(6.941)
Home Team Pitcher Is Black	-2061	-1283	-2221
	(-2.323)	(-1.998)	(-2.664)
Home Team Pitcher Is Latino	2844	1635	2667
	(3.378)	(2.637)	(3.184)
Visiting Team Pitcher Is Asian	6933	3959	6477
	(2.704)	(2.439)	(2.696)
Visiting Team Pitcher Is Black	-1960	-1115	-1731
	(-2.153)	(-1.622)	(-1.869)
Visiting Team Pitcher Is Latino	500	1247	518
	(0.674)	(2.204)	(0.712)
Home Pitcher's Career Losses	60	40.8	56
	(2.570)	(2.409)	(2.429)
Visiting Pitcher's Career Losses	-9.5	-19.8	-12.4
	(-0.501)	(-1.327)	(-0.653)
Home Pitcher's Career Wins	-37	-26.8	-34
	(-1.928)	(-1.886)	(-1.826)
Visiting Pitcher's Career Wins	16	24.4	18.5
	(1.140)	(2.028)	(1.328)
Home Pitcher's Season Wins	302	141	241
	(4.194)	(2.131)	(3.355)
Visiting Pitcher's Season Wins	-26	70	-33
	(-0.427)	(1.165)	(-0.544)
Home Pitcher's Season Losses	-461	-327	-443
	(-5.663)	(-4.682)	(-5.551)
Visiting Pitcher's Season Losses	-101	-141	-93
	(-1.274)	(-2.174)	(-1.185)
The Game Is Played at Night	-489	-588	-551
	(-1.104)	(-1.706)	(-1.248)
The Game Is Played on the Weekend	5055	5735	5036
	(9.89)	(15.93)	(9.309)
Percentage Black in the Local CMSA	-8528	-17738	-7517
	(-1.152)	(-3.205)	(-1.043)
Percentage Latino in the Local CMSA	-30927	-37419	-31358
	(-5.818)	(-8.94)	(-5.9810
Population of the Local CMSA	0.000800	0.000854	0.000802
	(4.257)	(5.764)	(4.32)

Table 3.2 continued

Unemployment Rate of the Local CMSA	-1441	-1352	-1393
	(-4.475)	(-5.615)	(-4.349)
Recreation Index of the Local CMSA	-18	-29	-21
	(-0.17)	(-0.366)	(-0.2010
Temperature at Game Time	1394	327	1090
	(3.454)	(1.608)	(2.665)
Temperature at Game Time Squared	-8.9	-1.40	-6.9
	(-3.344)	(-0.969)	(-2.587)
Stadium Capacity	0.33	0.21	0.35
	(4.247)	(3.725)	(4.451)
Stadium Built Within Last Decade	16913	16547	16855
	(15.044)	(18.86)	(15.293)
Classic Stadium	10544	5966	10794
	(6.077)	(4.628)	(6.470)
Opening Day	-	11962	-
		(3.465)	
Home Team's Previous Season's Wins	161	292	149
	(3.146)	(7.637)	(3.017)
Visiting Team's Previous Season's Wins	59	103	54
	(1.579)	(3.511)	(1.474)

Note: t-stats are in parentheses.
[a] These regressions have robust corrected standard errors for the cluster correlation problem.
[b] This analysis is performed using only data from the second half of the season to allow for the winning percentages to become stable.

expected pattern, but are generally not significant.

The home and visiting pitcher's season wins and losses follow the expected pattern of having positive and negative effects on attendance, respectively. An extra win for the home team pitcher increases attendance by about 250 spectators. Again, the home pitcher's numbers are more important to the home town fans with respect to demand than the visiting pitcher's. The effect of night games is unexpectedly negative, but only marginally significant.

Perhaps work or school nights account for some of this result. A weekend game draws an extra 5,000 fans to the park. Thus, the owners are correct to fill all weekend days with games, and allow the breaks in the season to occur during the week. Opening day attracts almost 12,000 additional fans to the stadium. Warmer temperatures increase fan attendance by about 900 fans per 1° Fahrenheit increase, but the effect is decreasing as temperatures rise (the negative coefficient on temperature squared).[28]

Cities with relatively large black and Latino populations have lower attendances, all else equal. Brent Staples (1987) claims that about 93% of ticket buying fans are white. This may explain the city racial composition effect. It also may explain the discrimination effect against blacks, although not the attendance premium afforded Latino players. The population effect is extremely consistent. An increase in the local

Table 3.3[a]
Fixed Effects Regression Results of the Demand Specification Analysis

Dependent Variable: Game Attendance	$A > B > 0 > C$[b]	Optimal Prob. with Odds Data	Optimal Prob. with Winning Percentage Data[b]
Adjusted R-squared	0.74	0.72	0.75
F-value	80.14	168.49	83.11
Number of Observations	1102	2193	1102
Home Team Current Win Percentage	35187	-	-
	(2.622)		
Visiting Team Current Win Percent	10849	-	-
	(1.819)		
Square of the Difference in Win Percents	-18429	-	-
	(-1.524)		
Prob (Home Team Wins): Odds Data	-	26332	-
		(1.949)	
Prob (Home Team Wins): Squared	-	-22435	-
		(-1.875)	
Prob (Home Team Wins): Win Percents	-	-	28751
			(2.100)
Prob (Home Team Wins): Squared	-	-	-20841
			(-1.911)
Optimal Probability Home Team Wins	-	0.59	0.69
Percent of Games Played by Home Team	6673	13149	7123
	(0.266)	(0.724)	(0.313)
Percent of Games Played by Visiting Team	-11500	-40246	-19374
	(-0.455)	(-2.174)	(-1.128)
Percent of Games Played * Win Percent (H)	32151	35031	43589
	(3.010)	(3.246)	(2.315)
Percent of Games Played * Win Percent (V)	21917	25494	-43010
	(1.421)	(3.593)	(-2.357)
Games Behind Leader * Pct Games Left (H)	3211	4236	-31482
	(0.594)	(0.614)	(-0.217)
Games Behind Leader * Pct Games Left (V)	1243	-2371	54979
	(0.805)	(-0.320)	(2.096)
Intercept	-41335	-10332	-3820
	(-2.079)	(-0.836)	(-0.182)
Home Team Wins in Last 10 Games	146	-227	155
	(0.701)	(-1.799)	(0.799)
Visiting Team Wins in Last 10 Games	-96	-186	-130
	(-0.589)	(-1.604)	(-0.815)
Home Team Runs in Last 10 Games	127	-236	38
	(0.556)	(-1.559)	(0.171)

Table 3.3 continued

Visiting Team Runs in Last 10 Games	-130	-302	-34
	(-0.534)	(-1.880)	(-0.144)
Home Team Pitcher Is Asian	6105	5718	5990
	(1.954)	(3.480)	(1.959)
Home Team Pitcher Is Black	-1047	-1055	-1267
	(-1.696)	(-2.230)	(-2.103)
Home Team Pitcher Is Latino	351	-126	218
	(0.579)	(-0.264)	(0.354)
Visiting Team Pitcher Is Asian	3681	3231	3817
	(3.668)	(2.765)	(3.653)
Visiting Team Pitcher Is Black	-1583	-1250	-1434
	(-2.129)	(-2.294)	(-1.908)
Visiting Team Pitcher Is Latino	729	1223	764
	(1.291)	(2.883)	(1.371)
Home Pitcher's Career Losses	25	6	20
	(1.323)	(0.418)	(1.092)
Visiting Pitcher's Career Losses	3.5	-14	1.5
	(0.214)	(-1.183)	(0.088)
Home Pitcher's Career Wins	-20	-2	-16
	(-1.287)	(-0.161)	(-1.028)
Visiting Pitcher's Career Wins	3	15	6
	(0.243)	(1.492)	(0.471)
Home Pitcher's Season Wins	168	127	131
	(2.697)	(2.294)	(2.093)
Visiting Pitcher's Season Wins	-6	3.7	2
	(-0.113)	(0.071)	(0.038)
Home Pitcher's Season Losses	-235	-186	-245
	(-3.565)	(-3.259)	(-3.747)
Visiting Pitcher's Season Losses	-101	-88	-128
	(-1.622)	(-1.657)	(-1.977)
The Game Is Played at Night	-616	-772	-654
	(-1.587)	(-2.651)	(-1.684)
The Game Is Played on the Weekend	5364	5608	5353
	(11.89)	(16.30)	(12.041)
Temperature at Game Time	934	106	694
	(2.875)	(0.535)	(2.076)
Temperature at Game Time Squared	-6.3	-0.07	-4.7
	(-2.901)	(-0.051)	(-2.110)
Home Team's Previous Season's Wins	388	340	388
	(2.568)	(3.237)	(2.543)
Visiting Team's Previous Season's Wins	65	96	66
	(2.340)	(5.127)	(2.355)

Note: t-stats are in parentheses.
ᵃ These regressions have robust corrected standard errors for the cluster correlation problem. The team specific fixed effects vaiables are left out of the table.
ᵇ This analysis is performed using only data from the second half of the season to allow for the winning percentages to become stable.

population by one million is associated with an increase in attendance by about 850 fans per game.

As expected, larger stadiums allow for more fans to attend games. On average, five more seats are associated with an increase in attendance of one more fan per game.[29] This result is smaller than the result from Rascher (1998) using NBA data. Because NBA games are 95% filled to capacity, an additional seat at an NBA game has a higher marginal effect than one at a baseball park. Thus, the finding here is not surprising.

The most significant factor of demand is the new stadium effect. A new stadium attracts an extra 16,000 fans to the park per game.[30] Apparently, there is more to attending a baseball game than the quality of the teams on the field.

The two classic stadiums increase attendance by about 8,000 fans. To capture both of these effects at the same time, the last few new stadiums built have been designed to look like the classic ballparks of the past.

Each team's number of wins from the previous season has a lasting effect on the current season. For each extra win the home team had in 1995, about 300 additional fans per game showed up to watch a baseball game during the 1996 season. The effect is predictably smaller for the visiting team. Also, the second half of the season, as expected, is less affected by this phenomenon.

Using columns 2 and 3 of Tables 3.2 and 3.3, we see that either pre-game odds data or converting winning percentages into probabilities gave similar results regarding the *ex ante* optimal probability that the home team wins a particular game. The attendance maximizing probability is between 60% and 70%.[31] Home town fans want their team to have about twice the chance to win the game as the visiting team.

Surprisingly, the wins and runs scored in the last ten games by both the home and visiting teams appear to be ineffective predictors of attendance. Overall team winning percentage and pitcher quality may overshadow these effects.[32]

The interaction between the percentage of games played and the team's winning percentage is predictably positive. Wins are more important with respect to attendance as the season progresses.

Similarly, the interaction of games behind the leader and the percentage of games left in the season for a particular team is positive. If there are a lot of games left in the season, the further behind the leader a team is, the less effect it has on attendance. However, these coefficients are barely marginally significant in only a few of the regressions.

As expected, the odds data provided a superior forecast of game outcome than the probability using winning percentage. The Chi-square statistic for the former was 13.14, and for the latter, 7.55 for a probit analysis of outcomes on probabilities.

CONCLUSION

This chapter contains an empirical investigation of one aspect of the sports league model in Rascher (1997). It shows that fans are more sensitive to changes in the player quality level of the home team than of the visiting team, and that they prefer close contests, but still want to see the home team win. Thus, there exists empirical support for the notion of a positive production network externality in professional sports.

An original data set is collected that contains many potential factors of demand for baseball games. Questions of customer discrimination, marketing ability, marginal productivity, and public financing of stadiums can be addressed using this data set.

The assumptions of the demand specification are empirically verified in both a fundamental model and a team fixed effects model. The *ex ante* optimal probability that the home team wins is about 66%. Thus it is between 0.5 and 1.0 as assumed by the model. The answer to the quote "Are the Bulls so good they're bad for the NBA?" is a cautious yes. If the optimal probability that the home team wins is similar in basketball to baseball, and if the Chicago Bulls were to continue dominating, then fans across the NBA would likely stop coming to games. As Danny Ainge, coach of the NBA's Phoenix Suns, puts it "it'll be better when the Bulls break up. More teams will feel they have a chance to win it all." Further, the fans will realize this as well and begin showing up at the gate again.

This analysis also reconfirmed Scully's findings of customer discrimination against black pitchers, and found owners are correct in their use of weekend games and new stadiums to attract additional fans. The probability of the home team winning using odds data outperforms a similar variable using winning percentage as both predictors of attendance and of winning.

NOTES

The author would like to thank Severin Borenstein, Clair Brown, Ken Chay, Elizabeth Gustafson, Larry Hadley, Terry Kennedy, and Jimmy Torrez for helpful comments. However, the usual caveat applies.

1. The previous literature failed in this respect (see the next section for details). Additionally, imagine two sets of teams. One set contains a high-quality and a low-quality team. The other set consists of two teams each having equal amounts of player quality, but whose player quality sums to the total player quality of the teams in the first set. Previous models of demand for games within the two sets had the same quantity demanded. The current model allows for the closeness of the game between the teams in the second set to have a positive effect on demand.

2. It is possible for each team to have a greater than 50% chance of winning its home games because of home field advantage. In fact, it is in the interest of sports leagues (given the findings here) to create a home field advantage for each team in their league.

3. See Cairns et al., 1986, for a brief summary of long run demand studies of professional team sports.

4. Interestingly, these studies have had problems getting a negative sign on the ticket price variable. Some have concluded that owners are not profit maximizers when setting ticket prices. Likely, it is because of a lack of proper control variables or a simultaneity problem.

5. Domazlicky and Kerr (1990) find similar results using a limited baseball data set.

6. Of the 2,267 games, 51 were sellouts.

7. The power of the internet was evident in the creation of this data set. Every variable came directly off of an internet web page for free except the pitcher race variable.

8. The source of the team wins variables and the score variables is www.usatoday.com. They had a listing by team of each game played and the score.

9. These data were found at www.sportsfaxnews.com.

10. This information was found at www.totalbaseball.com.

11. These last three variables came from the in-depth boxscores at www.usatoday.com

12. This data came from Stats Inc. Incidentally, they created this data set for video game companies who want the pitchers to appear ethnically correct.

13. Because winning percentage is not linear in wins, it is necessary to correct for the high volatility of winning percentage at the beginning of the season by interacting it with the percentage of games played in the season. This essentially creates a variable that is linear in wins.

14. Betting on spreads, say in basketball, usually follows an 11-for-10 rule, meaning that a bet of $11 gets a chance to win $10 because the bookie keeps the vigorish of $1. In spread betting, the bettor can bet on either side of the spread with the same payoff structure.

15. If T_i and T_j are the playing strengths of team i and j, then the probability that team i beats team j is

$$Prob(i \text{ beats } j) = \frac{T_i}{T_i + T_j}.$$

Assuming that each team in the league plays every other team an equal amount of times, the expected winning percentage of team i when playing an average team is ·

$$w_i = \frac{T_i}{T_i + \dfrac{n\bar{T} - T_i}{n-1}},$$

where $\bar{T}$ is the average strength of each team in the league, and n is the number of teams in the league. Solving for T_i and T_j leads to

$$T_i = \frac{n\bar{T}w_i}{(n-1)-(n-2)w_i},$$

and

$$T_j = \frac{n\bar{T}w_j}{(n-1)-(n-2)w_j}.$$

Plugging back into the probability equation and letting n go to infinity yields equation (5).

16. These were found at www.wwcd.com.

17. This was sent to me by Doug Pappas from the Society for the Advancement of Baseball Research (www.sabr.com).

18. One potential reason for ticket prices being ineffective predictors of attendance may be that owners set them artificially low or neutral and set concessions, parking, and merchandising prices to maximize profit.

19. This data was obtained from www.census.gov and www.bls.gov for the U.S. teams, and from www.statcan.ca for Toronto and Montreal.

20. Both variables were found on the web at www.wwcd.com

21. This data came from the *Places Rated Almanac*, but was found on one of the author's (George Loftus) web pages, weber.u.washington.edu/~gloftus.html, at the University of Washington. I thank David Boyd for the idea to use this variable.

22. The table of correlations is available upon request from the author.

23. The data for the second half of the season will be used in analyses using winning percentage because of the excessive volatility present in this variable at the beginning of the season.

24. Some of the control variables were left out of the analysis because of collinearity problems (the cloudiness index with temperature, the ticket price data with Fan Cost Index). Others were removed because of low explanatory power in the spirit of stepwise regression.

25. The levels of significance for A, B, and C are 1%, 10%, and 6%, respectively.

26. Even if it were statistically significant, the implied elasticity would be near -0.20, and thus not be very important anyway.

27. The Asian pitcher variables are somewhat misleading because both Asian pitchers in the league pitch for the Los Angeles Dodgers. Statistically, this variable is related to a team fixed effect variable for the Dodgers. Thus, it is hard to separate out the Los Angeles effect from the Asian pitcher effect. In fact, in the fixed effect regressions in Table 3.3, Los Angeles and one other variable (St. Louis) had to be removed to avoid singularity. Of course, one fixed effect variable has to be removed because of singularity and is used as the comparison variable for the other fixed effect variables.

28. This appears to be quite a large effect. Perhaps a control for month of the season interacted with temperature might explain the result.

29. The causality of this result is uncertain given that many new stadiums have been built recently, perhaps reacting to the excess demand that already existed.

30. A back of the envelope analysis shows that this leads to an extra 1.3 million fans for the season for a particular team. If each fan spent $15 at the game, that leads to almost $20 million in extra revenues. Most stadiums cost $100– $200 million. Thus, their costs could be recovered in five to ten years (excluding the real interest rate).

31. Assuming a quadratic relationship between probability and attendance leads to an equation of the form $Y = aP + bP^2$. Taking the derivative with respect to P further leads to $a + 2bP = 0$. Next, solving for P gives $P = -(a/2b)$.

32. The correlation table shows that there is an association between some of these variables.

Section III

THE LOCATION OF TEAMS AND STADIUMS

4

Emerging Markets in Baseball: An Econometric Model for Predicting the Expansion Teams' New Cities

Thomas H. Bruggink and Justin M. Zamparelli

Recent expansion in Major League Baseball (MLB) and announced plans for future expansion have created interest in the selection process for the host cities. According to the Major League Expansion Committee, the three criteria for evaluation of applying cities are: (1) market factors, (2) the financial backing of an investment group, and (3) stadium plans.[1] This study is concerned with the ultimate factor for long term franchise success under the current financial arrangements. Although location of business expansion has long been a topic of interest, the baseball industry has unique elements that force one to re-examine traditional location theory.

In this chapter we build an econometric model that uses market data on current and potential franchise locations to identify those metropolitan areas that are most deserving of inclusion in the next round of expansion.[2] Although we use this market viability model to identify emerging markets, it can also evaluate current problems in "small market" cities. A market viability model can also identify current home cities in which the teams are predicted to do poorly. Thus it can be used in conjunction with a revenue sharing plan to distribute revenue among the teams.

BACKGROUND ISSUES

MLB owners and officials must consider market demand when making an expansion location decision. There are a variety of factors that contribute to this demand, including population, consumer incomes, corporate financial backing, identity as a sports town, and distance from other existing teams. This last factor is somewhat unique to professional sports given the monopoly positions of sports leagues. In MLB, an expansion team will not be permitted to locate in a metropolitan area that is considered to be part of an existing team's territory even if the other factors indicate an attractive location opportunity.

Hotelling's retail location model (1932) is based on the assumption that consumers shop at the nearest firm. Competition among retailers will therefore result in any relocation that moves in the direction of a rival's territory while protecting one's own original base of customers. In contrast, MLB, as a legal cartel, turns the Hotelling theory upside down since new franchises will locate *outside* of the territories of existing teams. This way, existing teams will not have to face competition, and the league can still capture a new portion of the population that is not currently exposed to major league baseball. Thus, expansion should be understood as market extension rather than competition with existing teams.

For example, the two additions to MLB in the early 1990s, the Colorado Rockies and the Florida Marlins, represented entry into new geographic regions with no encroachment issues. On the other hand, New Jersey is unlikely to obtain its own MLB team despite having four metropolitan areas with a population of over one million. The New York Yankees and Mets and Philadelphia Phillies owners will not allow such an entry.[3]

Territorial issues aside, another qualification is noted by Quirk and Fort (1992). It is not the objective of the current league owners to place a team in every deserving city. "In an era in which teams play in publicly owned stadiums, there are obvious strategic advantages for league members in having cities available that lack league teams but are capable of supporting a team" (p. 299). Therefore, it is in the interests of owners to always have at least one viable city in waiting to make the threat of "build it or we'll move" credible.

Very little research has been done on this topic of the location of expansion teams in professional sports. Most studies focus on the public's role in subsidizing the construction of sports stadiums.[4] Because these are mostly concerned with efforts to retain or relocate existing teams, our model does not build on this work.

EMPIRICAL MODEL

The award of a franchise is based on market viability, financial resources, and stadium plans. The empirical model developed below will select the leading contender cities based on market factors. In the next section we will analyze this group to identify the two most likely selections.

The empirical model is represented below:

$$MLB = \beta_0 + \beta_1 POP + \beta_2 GROWTH + \beta_3 INCOME \\ + \beta_4 SPORTS + \beta_5 COMP + \beta_6 TV + \beta_7 DIST + \epsilon, \tag{1}$$

where ϵ is the random error. The dependent variable is MLB which records the number of MLB teams in the metropolitan area (0, 1, or 2).

The first predictor variable is POP. There is no better measure of the existing/potential demand for a MLB franchise than the population of a metropolitan area (the 1994 population estimate published by the U.S. Census Bureau, in millions). The larger the population of a metropolitan area, the greater the potential attendance and the better the area is suited to support a MLB franchise.

GROWTH, the second predictor variable, is the percentage growth rate of population for a metropolitan area. It is another measure of existing/potential demand for a MLB franchise. This variable attempts to measure the effect of an emerging major metropolitan area. For metropolitan areas that already have a franchise, this variable was measured as the growth rate for the ten years prior to acquiring a professional baseball franchise. For the candidate metropolitan areas, the growth rate was measured for the ten years prior to 1994. Historically, the growth rate of metropolitan areas has been a significant part of the emergence of new MLB franchises. This can be seen as early as the movement of teams into California in the 1950s, and as recently as the franchise awarded to Phoenix. On the other hand, if a city has a sufficient population to support a team but also exhibits stagnant or declining growth, their long term viability may be in doubt.

The third predictor variable is INCOME, and it is measured as the per-capita income of a metropolitan area ($1,000s). Metropolitan areas with above-average incomes possess a greater ability to support MLB via a greater demand for entertainment goods. In essence, the average income can be considered an estimate of the relative strength of the area's economy that directly effects the residents' ability and desire to spend entertainment dollars on MLB among other things. Another predictor variable is SPORTS, which is the number of major league teams from other sports located in the metropolitan area. Franchises in other sports are viewed as complements to MLB teams rather than substitutes because the seasons generally do not overlap and the price structure for baseball is much lower than other professional sports. We believe that other professional franchises in the area may increase the likelihood of obtaining a MLB team because they offer proof that there is spectator interest in major league sports. Another predictor variable, COMP, is the number of Fortune 500 company headquarters located in a metropolitan area. This is an additional measure of a city's ability to support MLB. It is useful in measuring the potential for an ownership group as well as the potential demand for luxury suites that are crucial to the success of a MLB franchise.

TV measures the number of households with televisions in a metropolitan area. Since the television explosion of the mid-twentieth century, MLB has obtained a larger portion of its revenue from TV contracts. A larger potential viewing audience will increase a team's exposure as well as the value of TV contracts. However, the measurement of television audiences nearly coincides with population in most cities (POP and TV are correlated at 0.94), making TV potentially redundant. Including both POP and TV in the estimation of our model resulted in a slightly lower adjusted R-squared than estimation with only POP. Since it has little impact on prediction ability, TV is dropped from our equation to simplify the model.

DIST, the last predictor variable in our model, measures the distance to the closest MLB franchise. Within baseball, the owners exercise veto power over any expansion selection. Given their presumed desire to preserve their territorial monopolies, this veto power may be the most influential location factor. Among all professional sports, only baseball has been successful in preventing the formation of rival leagues. Existing owners of MLB franchises will not accept the addition of a new franchise that could compete with their own. The greater the distance of a city from all existing MLB franchises, the greater the liklihood that MLB will support a new franchise in that city. Descriptive statistics for all variables are presented in Table 4.1.

Table 4.1
Means and Standard Deviations of Variables

VARIABLE	MEAN	STANDARD DEVIATION
MLB	0.55	0.64
POP	2.54	2.15
GROWTH	20.9	15.5
INCOME	22.7	3.30
SPORTS	1.43	1.20
COMP	4.78	7.63
TV	1.22	0.94
DIST	212.0	150.3

ESTIMATION OF THE MODEL

Our sample of metropolitan areas includes the 54 largest primary metropolitan statistical areas based on the 1994 population estimates published by the U.S. Census Bureau. These 54 metropolitan areas include only those with a population of greater than one million. There is symmetry in this sample in that twenty-six of these metropolitan areas have a MLB franchise and twenty-eight do not. Due to data limitations, no consideration is given to the existing or potential Canadian and Mexican markets.

Some of the original fifty-four metropolitan areas were merged to form combined markets. First, the Los Angeles and Orange County (Anaheim) metropolitan areas were joined to form a single metropolitan area supporting two teams. This was due to the minimal distance between the two franchises and the overlapping fan interest. Thus the populations of the separate areas would not necessarily be a fair estimate of the division of the fan base.

This same reasoning was applied to the combination of the Oakland and San Francisco metropolitan areas since the franchises are only eight miles apart. The Dallas and Fort Worth/Arlington metropolitan areas are also combined. The Texas Rangers have their stadium in the Fort Worth/Arlington area. However, they are effectively a Dallas team as well as a Fort Worth team. Dallas is only twenty-five miles away from the stadium and has no expectations of getting its own team.

Finally, the Washington, DC and Baltimore areas are merged, due to the short forty-mile distance and the potential for overlapp in the fan base if Washington were awarded a franchise. In order to justify expansion into the DC area, our empirical model must forecast the combined metropolitan area as capable of supporting two teams.

We use ordinary least squares regression analysis to estimate equation (1). It has several advantages over the logit model. First, it easily accommodates those metropolitan areas that have more than one team or have the potential to support more than one team. Second, the theoretical functional form in this relationship is additive rather than the S-shaped curve of the logit model. For example, a contender city with twice the population of another city should have that difference reflected. Although the logit technique does offer an error term with properties more likely to validate hypothesis testing, this advantage is inapplicable if the sample is viewed as the entire population.

The OLS estimation of our model generates the following:[5]

$$MLB = -0.695 + 0.127\ POP + 0.0041\ GROWTH + 0.154\ INCOME$$
$$\quad\ (0.41)\quad (0.037)\qquad (0.0034)\qquad\qquad (0.0166)\qquad\qquad\qquad (2)$$

$$\quad + 0.173\ SPORTS + 0.0119\ COMP + 0.00085\ DIST$$
$$\quad\ \ (0.060)\qquad\qquad (0.0086)\qquad\quad (0.00035)$$

R-squared = 0.76
Adjusted R-squared = 0.73
F-statistic = 23.6
Standard errors are in parentheses.

The overall fit shows that 76% of the variation in the dependent variable is explained by the predictor variables. All coefficients have the expected signs, exhibit reasonable magnitudes, and are statistically significant.

DISCUSSION OF RESULTS

The dependent variable, MLB, provides an estimate of the expected number of franchises that each city could support according to the market factors in the model. Predicted values for MLB are presented in Table 4.2. The predicted value for NYC exceeds two and ranges to a low of zero for Monmouth County, New Jersey among others.

All cities that are predicted to have at least one team currently do have a team. Several existing teams are in cities that are predicted to have far less than one team (Milwaukee, San Diego, Cincinnati, and Kansas City are predicted to have 0.35 teams or less!). This indicates problems for small market teams.

Cities that want to win a team in the next round of expansion are keenly interested in what they can do to increase their market viability. To this end we use standardized coefficients to look at the variables that have the most impact on market viability:

These coefficients show the change in the dependent variable, in units of standard deviations, for a one standard deviation change in each predictor variable. For example, a one standard deviation change in POP will increase the expected number of franchises by 0.44 standard deviations of the MLB variable. It is no surprise that POP has, by far, the biggest impact on the market viability of a city. The next largest

Table 4.2
Predicted Values for MLB

	Metropolitan Area	No. of Teams	Predicted No. of Teams
1	Los Angeles/Orange County	2	1.97
2	New York	2	2.30
3	Chicago	2	1.61
4	Philadelphia	1	1.13
5	DC/Baltimore	1	1.60
6	Detroit	1	1.03
7	Houston	1	1.11
8	Atlanta	1	1.09
9	Boston	1	0.92
10	Riverside/San Bernardino	0	0.27
11	Dallas/Ft. Worth	1	1.21
12	Minneapolis	1	0.88
13	Nassau/Suffolk, NY	0	0.36
14	San Diego	1	0.37
15	St. Louis	1	0.74
16	Phoenix/Mesa	1	0.76
17	Pittsburgh	1	0.65
18	Cleveland/Lorain/Elyria	1	0.43
19	Seattle/Bellevue/Everett	1	1.12
20	Oakland/San Francisco	2	1.46
21	Tampa/St. Pete	1	0.61
22	Miami	1	0.72
23	Newark	0	0.04
24	Denver	1	1.02
25	Portland/Vancouver	0	0.28
26	Kansas City	1	0.32
27	Cincinnati	1	0.35
28	San Jose	0	0.21
29	Southern VA	0	0.07
30	Sacramento	0	0.22
31	Milwaukee/Waukesha	1	0.34

Table 4.2 continued

32	Indianapolis	0	0.33
33	Columbus, OH	0	0.00
34	San Antonio	0	0.22
35	Orlando	0	0.23
36	Ft. Lauderdale	0	0.05
37	New Orleans	0	0.24
38	Bergen/Passaic, NJ	0	0.00
39	Charlotte, NC	0	0.47
40	Buffalo/Niagra Falls	0	0.19
41	Salt Lake City	0	0.59
42	Harford	0	0.15
43	Providence	0	0.00
44	Greensboro/Winston-Salem	0	0.10
45	Rochester	0	0.02
46	Middlesex/Somerset/Hunt, NJ	0	0.00
47	Las Vagas	0	0.26
48	Memphis	0	0.04
49	Nashville	0	0.07
50	Monmouth/Ocean City, NJ	0	0.00
51	Oklahoma City	0	0.00

impact is the number of other sports teams. The placement of other professional teams establishes the city as "major league." The third most important factor is the distance to the next major league city. This variable reflects the monopoly power of the existing team owners, who will deny any proposal for a new team that infringes on their territory.[6] The remaining factors are quite small relative to the first three.

The market viability aspect of the baseball owners' decision to locate expansion teams leaves little opportunity for affecting the outcome. Local government officials

Variable	Standardized Coefficient
POP	0.44
SPORTS	0.32
DIST	0.19
COMP	0.14
GROWTH	0.10
INCOME	0.08

and private investor groups can do little, if anything, to alter the outcome of the variables used in this model. Their input, however, is crucial to the final decision which will be illustrated by our analysis of the next round of expansion.

CHOOSING THE NEXT EXPANSION TEAMS

The fitted values of the dependent variable in our location model act as a market viability index, indicating the expected number of teams per city capable of being supported by market factors. The city-by-city outcomes for the top ten metropolitan areas are shown in Table 4.3. The ten cities were chosen based on the size of the market viability index and the presence of an existing professional sports team in football, basketball, or hockey. As the index number for a given city approaches one, the city can be identified as having the market to support a franchise.[7] As noted earlier, this number could approach or exceed two in large and combined metropolitan areas.

Only three cities appear to be in contention for the two locations: Washington, DC, Salt Lake City, and Charlotte. Realistically, the actual choice will be based not only on the market viability index and presence of other sports franchises, but will be supplemented with information on corporate backing and stadium plans. Next, we consider each city using all location criteria.

Washington, DC

This city was one of the first in the United States to have a baseball franchise. It received its initial franchise in 1899 when the National League expanded to twelve teams. They occupied the Baltimore/DC market alone until 1954 when the Baltimore Orioles were created from the old St. Louis Browns franchise. Eight years later, DC lost its team to Minneapolis, but it was immediately replaced with an expansion team. However, that team soon moved to Texas, and the city has been without a team since 1972.

Despite this ignoble history, this location has a number of advantages. First, it scored the highest on the market viability index.[8] Second, it has an investment group to finance the entry fee and team development (Ringolsby, 1997). Third, the funding is in place for a 45,000 seat stadium in Northern Virginia that would cost $250 million (Lipton and Markey, 1995). Finally, Northern Virginia has the seventh largest media market in the country and Fairfax County has one of the highest median incomes

(Nakamura, 1994).

Disadvantages include the loss of two teams in the past thirty years and the close proximity to Baltimore. Possible territorial problems are mitigated by plans to locate the stadium outside of Washington, DC in Northern Virginia, and to have the team join the National League.

Table 4.3
Viability Index for Top Ten Cities

	Contender City	Viability Index
1	Washington, DC	0.60
2	Salt Lake City	0.59
3	Charlotte	0.47
4	Indianapolis	0.33
5	Portland	0.28
6	New Orleans	0.24
7	Orlando	0.23
8	Sacramento	0.22
9	San Antonio	0.22
10	Buffalo	0.19

Salt Lake City

This city ranked second in the market viability index, but there is no investment group committed to bringing a team to this city. Furthermore, the population density falls off rapidly outside the city, and this makes the television thin (forty-first in the nation).

An advantage is the absence of infringement on a competitor's territory. On the other hand, the general region of the noncoastal western United States is already covered with teams in Denver and Phoenix. Although this might not make much of a difference for professional basketball and football, the attendance demands of baseball are far greater (basketball has forty home dates with 20,000 seat arenas, football has eight home dates with 50,000 seat stadiums, but baseball has eighty-one home games in 40,000 seat parks).

Charlotte

This city ranks a close third based on the market viability index. Also, they have a willing financial group led by the owner of the professional basketball team and the AAA minor league baseball team in Charlotte. The newly built minor league stadium is expandable to 35,000 in order to support a major league franchise. Disadvantages include nearness to the competing baseball cities of Atlanta (240 miles) and Washington, DC (300 miles—assuming they receive the first expansion slot).

Based on this analysis, the Washington, DC/northern Virginia is the leading candidate for expansion, unless owners want to leave this site open to add credibility to "threats to move" when negotiating with cities for the public financing of new stadiums. The newly emerging baseball markets are Charlotte and Salt Lake City. However, it appears that Salt Lake City has taken itself out of contention, leaving Charlotte as the other top candidate. Whether Salt Lake City can amend this outcome, or even if it wants to, is not known at this time.

Buffalo, Orlando, and Sacramento have expressed interest in an MLB team, but the results of our econometric model do not offer encouragement. Indianapolis and Portland have higher viability indices, and international sites in Mexico (Monterey) and Canada (Vancouver) would probably be more viable than these three cities.

CONCLUSIONS

Our market viability model for predicting leading candidates for MLB expansion has identified the top three cities for the next round of expansion. Consideration of investor groups and stadium plans make Salt Lake City appear to be the third choice behind Washington, DC and Charlotte. Other cities that have expressed interest such as Orlando, Buffalo, and Sacramento do not come close to our top three.

There are a number of existing teams in cities for which our linear model generates low predicted values for market viability (expected number of teams). These include San Diego at 0.37, Cincinnati at 0.35, Milwaukee at 0.34, and Kansas City at 0.32. In these cities, teams can survive financially only via good management that balances the competing goals of minimizing payroll and maximizing team performance. Nonetheless, the market factors are not favorable, and this fact must be considered when revenue sharing allocations and requests for relocation are reviewed. Taxpayers and public officials in cities with a low viability index should carefully review an owner's demands for public funding of a new stadium as a condition for keeping the team in the area. If market conditions are not favorable, then large public subsidies may be required to support such teams because expected attendance goals are unlikely to be met.

The quantitative factors that determine market viability offer little opportunity for city officials to increase their viablity since they are unable to directly manipulate the important factors. However, stadium plans and the ability of local governments to provide public subsidies does offer a policy tool that can make a difference, provided the city is already a leading candidate.

The results of our econometric model could be factored into a revenue sharing allocation that helps teams in vulnerable markets. However, this must be done with great care because our econometric model does not account for differences in the popularity of baseball between specific cities. Even with revenue sharing, teams located in cities with low viability may be unable to retain talented players once they become free agents. On the other hand, preserving competitive balance in baseball must be based on something more substantial than the willingness of star players like

Tony Gwynn to choose to remain in small markets and be underpaid.

NOTES

The authors thank Rodney Fort and John Fizel for comments on earlier drafts of this chapter.

1. These criteria are set by the Major League Baseball Expansion Committee (Nakarmura, 1994). Twenty-one of the twenty-eight owners must approve the idea of expansion, and then a vote on the cities takes place.

2. The history of Major League Baseball has revealed several recent periods of expansion. The American and National Leagues consisted of 16 teams in 1968, but as the year 2000 approaches, there are thirty teams with homes in the United States and Canada, and two more expansion franchises, although not yet announced, appear inevitable some time after the two newest teams begin play in 1998.

3. Up until 1980, individual team owners had veto power to prevent the incursion of new or relocated teams, but this has now been replaced by a three-fourths majority vote. However, in practice, "expansion into an existing territory can be blocked by one or at most three existing team owners" (Quirk and Fort, 1992, p. 300).

4. For example, see the studies by Baade and Dye (1988, 1990).

5. The results from the logit model are available upon request from Bruggink. All estimated models exhibit a good fit and correct signs on the coefficients.

6. The Baltimore/Washington, DC area is an exception to this rule because the Baltimore Orioles originally infringed on the Washington Senators' territory when the former relocated from St. Louis. Because DC has since lost its team through relocation, MLB officials have acknowledged its potential for rebirth of a franchise.

7. For a city to increase the "expected number of teams" from 0.3 to 0.5 (which would move it from a wannabee to a real contender), it would have to increase its population by 1.5 million or move itself 222 miles further away from its current location.

8. For the combined Baltimore/Washington, DC market, the expected value of (MLB - 1) will be used to make predictions for the Washington, DC/northern Virginia market. The -1 represents the Orioles.

5

Mega-Sports Events as Municipal Investments: A Critique of Impact Analysis

Philip K. Porter

INTRODUCTION

Faced with the tax bill for sponsoring mega-sporting events, taxpayers, at least those who are not fans, are asking why they should be forced to pay for an event that most locals do not attend. To answer this criticism, sponsors and providers of events like the Olympics, the Super Bowl, the NCAA Basketball Tournament, even Grand Prix Racing, and the PGA Golf Tour point to the indirect (spillover) benefits implicit in regional multipliers. "You may not go the event," they say, "but those who do bring hundreds of millions of dollars into the community and that, in turn, generates several times as much spending in subsequent months as those enriched in the first wave of spending spend their new-found wealth." This argument has been offered by proponents for the subsidy of mega-sporting events.[1]

This chapter takes a critical look at regional impact analysis as it is applied to sporting and other entertainment events. I have chosen Super Bowls for the empirical part of the chapter because they are annual and reasonably uniform events (although the locations differ), they generate huge direct and indirect returns that after the fact can be compared to recorded activity, and there are several impact studies available for critique. The results are shocking. For each of the six events studied in three different locations, there is no measurable impact on spending associated with the event. The projected spending and spillover benefits of regional impact models never materialize.

Several sources of error have been discussed in the literature that might tend to moderate the projected impact. These include investigator bias, error in measurement, unanticipated leakages from the region, substitution in consumption, diminishing returns in production, and crowding out (capacity constraints). What we find here is that a combination of these sources, albeit in unique and unanticipated forms, combines to eliminate any measurable impacts from Super Bowl events and, it is anticipated, from other mega-sporting events as well.

This chapter follows the format of a mystery novel. The following section presents a review of impact analysis and possible sources of error in this methodology. Particular emphasis is placed on event studies and who is paying for them. The next section, "Super Bowl Impact Studies," sets the stage and introduces the mystery. Three Super Bowl Impact Studies (1991 Tampa Superbowl, 1995 Miami Super Bowl, and 1996 Phoenix Super Bowl) as well as conventional wisdom predict huge windfalls for the communities that host Super Bowls. But, in these and every other instance studied (Miami in 1976 and 1979 and Tampa in 1984) no windfall materializes. Who stole Super Bowl prosperity? The section "Near-Perfect Complements and Capacity Constraints," solves the mystery. Capacity constraints and input complementarily that heretofore has not been contemplated and cannot be identified or measured by impact study methodology accounts for the discrepancy. Regional hotel and motel prices steal Super Bowl prosperity. The chapter's conclusion offers suggestions for further study.

IMPACT ANALYSIS

Economic impact projections are based on input-output analysis, developed and formalized by Wassily Leontief (1936). Leontief was inspired by the eighteenth-century French economist Francois Quesnay's work *Tableau Economique*, which first introduced the idea of industry interdependence through a rudimentary illustration of a French market. Armed with a growing data base and increased calculating capacity, Leontief and others began to construct tables detailing the relation of inputs to outputs within an economy. Armed with modern high-speed calculators, input-output analysis has become one of the most widely used economic tools and has been adapted to explain interregional flows of products (Miller and Blair, 1985, p. 2).

The Model

An input-output table quantifies the interdependent relation between industries in a region. To illustrate, consider a region with two interdependent industries. Industry i produces output X_i and sells some amount to industry 1, z_{i1}, and some to industry 2, z_{i2} as inputs, and the rest to final consumers, inventories, government, and industries outside the region, Y_i.[2] Thus, for the two industry region,

$$X_1 = z_{11} + z_{12} + Y_1$$
$$X_2 = z_{21} + z_{22} + Y_2. \tag{1}$$

The technical coefficient, $a_{ij} = z_{ij} / X_j$, is the value of industry i's sales used to produce a dollar of industry j's sales. Substituting $a_{ij} X_j$ for z_{ij} and rearranging equation (1) yields

$$\begin{bmatrix} 1-a_{11} & -a_{12} \\ -a_{21} & 1-a_{22} \end{bmatrix} \begin{bmatrix} X_1 \\ X_2 \end{bmatrix} = \begin{bmatrix} Y_1 \\ Y_2 \end{bmatrix} \text{ or } AX = Y. \tag{2}$$

Assuming A has an inverse, A^{-1}, with coefficients m_{ij}, write the output demand system is

$$\begin{bmatrix} X_1 \\ X_2 \end{bmatrix} = \begin{bmatrix} m_{11} & m_{12} \\ m_{21} & m_{22} \end{bmatrix} \begin{bmatrix} Y_1 \\ Y_2 \end{bmatrix} \ or \ X = A^{-1}Y. \tag{3}$$

As the region's sales are $X_1 + X_2$, equation (3) shows that an exogenous increase in the demand for industry 1's output (e.g., increased government spending) equal to dY_1 will have a total impact on the region of $(m_{11} + m_{21})dY_1$. The term $m_{11} + m_{21}$ is the regional multiplier. The multiplier is always greater than one. To see this, note that when industry 1 sells an additional unit of output, regional sales increase by 1. This is the direct effect of the increase in demand. To support this increase in sales, industry 1 is expected to purchase an additional a_{11} from its own industry and a_{21} from industry 2. Thus, $a_{11} + a_{21}$ is the indirect, first-round effect of the new unit of sales.[3] In turn, to support the first-round indirect effect on industry 1 of a_{11}, industry 1 is expected to purchase an additional $a_{11} a_{11}$ from itself and $a_{11} a_{21}$ from industry 2, and to support the first-round indirect effect on industry 2 of a_{21}, industry 2 is expected to purchase an additional $a_{21} a_{22}$ from itself and $a_{12} a_{21}$ from industry 1. These are the second round indirect effects. This process continues until the indirect effects, the ripples of increased sales, diminish to negligible amounts. The sum of the direct and indirect effects per unit of output is the multiplier.

Sources of Error[4]
Implicit in the above presentation is a set of assumptions that, were they not maintained, would change the nature and magnitude of the calculated multiplier. In what follows, we concentrate on systematic, rather than random error as the source of overestimated impacts. Not the least source of systematic error is bias. Spending and costs for events are easily measured so that the promoter can price to maximize profit. Thus, the promoter has no need for an impact study except when awareness of the indirect (spillover) effects is used as justification for public subsidy for the event. Fixed public subsidies do not alter the price of the event. Rather they serve to increase the profits of the promoter. Thus, the buyers of event studies are event promoters seeking subsidies and the government agencies that wish to support them, and the audience is composed of taxpayers and government representatives. These studies are seldom criticized and seldom published where they might be subjected to scholarly review. With a rationally ignorant audience and concentrated special interest support, bias is likely. One outlet for investigator bias is the choice of the multiplier. Some practitioners of event impact analysis generate multipliers from their own model of the regional economy while others prefer instead to purchase one of several regional I-O models of the economy like Micro IMPLAN and RIMS II, a product of the U.S. Department of Commerce. Increasing degrees of refinement of the regional I-O models exist. There are, therefore, many multipliers from which to chose: one for each I-O model. Each has a national, regional, state, and perhaps county or MSA level of

aggregation. Also, each has choices of industry aggregation like tourism or recreation and sports activities that might be reasonably chosen to reflect the activity under study. The practitioner can chose from several industries, i, each with different m_{ij}'s calculated from different specifications and using different regional data. Because the promoters and government sponsors pay the practitioners to do the studies, and because the taxpaying audience is rationally ignorant, one would expect high multipliers to drive out low multipliers in the market for impact studies.

A second outlet for investigator bias is the choice of the impact area. Smaller areas yield more exogenous spending changes (larger dY), because new spending can be generated only from residents outside the area who are drawn in by the event, but should imply lower multipliers, because more of the inputs needed to support the new spending will be purchased from outside the study area (lower a_{ij}). However, in many impact applications, because multipliers are calculated at regional levels different from the impact area, dY grows as the area is reduced without a corresponding decrease in the multiplier. This bias leads impact conscious practitioners to choose small impact areas.

Data measurement is never exact, and at the level of regional I-O models reliance on different sources of data leads to the menu of multipliers from which the practitioner chooses. At the level of the impact study, data measurement error can be significant and can have profound impacts on the findings. In event studies, survey data, drawn from those attending the event, are extrapolated to estimate exogenous spending increases (dY). Legions of interviewers are sent forth to ask of those attending the event: "Why are you here? Where are you from? Who did you bring with you? and How much will you spend?" Survey data have their own measurement problems, but if properly conducted, they are at least unbiased.[5] Biased error arises because of the "but for" assumption. The survey technique readily identifies and samples those who, but for the event, would not be in the area and declares their spending as net new (exogenous) spending. What the survey technique cannot identify and sample are those not in the area that, but for the event, would have been. If the foxes held their convention in the hen house, this survey technique would attribute positive impacts to the foxes and never notice that all the hens were gone.

The multipliers generated by an I-O model portray accurate impacts only when the underlying production functions and the set of industrial relations are invariant with respect to demand. When these change, which is a clear possibility, the effect is almost always to reduce the indirect effects. Diminishing marginal returns in the short run and decreasing returns to scale in the long run imply that increasing output to meet demand raises costs and prices. This reduces impacts as buyers seek substitute products and inputs. When an expanding industry's demand for inputs is not met by local suppliers and the industry increases its imports, a_{ij} falls and the realized multiplier is less than that predicted from the previous relation among industries. Even if the industrial relations within the area are maintained, when there are binding capacity constraints somewhere along the line, increased demand must crowd out some other activity, blunting the net impact.[6]

Finally, the reliance on dollar measures is problematic. When capacity constraints push prices up, the appearance of a gain is illusory. Sales appear to increase because prices rise but local residents with higher incomes face higher prices. The measured impact is not real.

SUPER BOWL IMPACT STUDIES: PROJECTIONS VS REALIZATIONS

I use the term projected impacts because the methodology of impact analysis does not describe the time path of secondary effects. The practitioner's estimate of direct impacts from surveys is usually in time with the event while secondary impacts are still to come. We look at the historical sales data from a vantage point at least several months in the future to see what was realized. Interestingly, the lag in completing and submitting reports would permit such a retrospective look. When this is done, the practitioner is left explaining why his or her findings were not realized. Nonetheless, government supporters and event promoters consistently use the higher projections rather than the lower reality when next they stump for public support for an event.[7]

Projected Impacts

I have been able to secure three Super Bowl Impact studies: those for the 1991 Tampa Bay Super Bowl, the 1995 Miami Super Bowl, and the 1996 Phoenix Super Bowl.[8] A summary is presented in Table 5.1.

Table 5.1
Super Bowl Impact Summaries

Super Bowl	Sponsor of Analysis	Direct Impact	Indirect & Total Impact	Multiple
1991 Tampa	NFL	$44.1m from visitors $15m from organizers	$58.7m $117.8m	1.99
1995 Miami	SB Host Committee (the NFL)	$176.0m from visitors $28.5m from organizers	$160.3m $364.8m	1.78
1996 Phoenix	Office of Tourism & SB Host Committee	$108.7m from visitors $53.5m from organizers	$143.6m $305.8m	1.89

Note: m = million.

These three Super Bowls are recent and span a time of relatively low inflation. Yet, the estimated impacts range from $117.8 million to $365.8 million and the multipliers range from 1.78 to 1.99 with no evident logical explanation.[9] In part this reflects underlying assumptions about the size of the impact area, what constitutes net new spending, and adjustments for crowding out. That is, each investigator can offer explanations for the differences when asked. While these findings offer no insights into impact analysis, they do indicate that choices are made by investigators that affect the outcomes of these studies. In the critique that follows, it is enough to note that a trend, statistically fit to the historical sales records, is so accurate that if only a small fraction of the predicted impacts had been realized in the host counties, it would have been obvious after the fact.

A Historical Review

The Department of Revenue in Arizona and in Florida were kind enough to supply me with a historical record of sales by months in each of the Super Bowl host counties. In Florida, the data cover January 1978 to June 1996 and in Arizona, the data cover January 1986 to May 1997. It is expected that these records are reasonably accurate, as each state relies heavily on sales taxes for revenue. In addition, such records are the source of much of the regional data used in the I-O models to calculate multipliers. Dade County (Miami), Florida hosted three Super Bowls within the time span of the data set (1979, 1989 and 1995; the 1969 Super Bowl III was outside the data set) and Hillsborough County (Tampa), Florida hosted two Super Bowls (1984 and 1991). Thus, tests can be implemented for the impacts of six Super Bowl events with the available data. In each of the impact studies the area of projected impact was greater than the host county, so care must be taken when comparing projected impacts to the historical record.

For each county the following equation was estimated using ordinary least squares estimation technology.

$$SALES_t = \beta_0 + \beta_1 SB + \beta_2 STATE_t + \beta_3 STATESQ_t + \beta_4 SEASON + \beta_5 X + \epsilon_t. \quad (4)$$

Here:

$\beta_0 - \beta_4$ are coefficients,
β_5 is a vector of coefficients,
$SALES_t$ is host county real sales at time t,
SB is a dummy variable equal to 1 during the month(s) of anticipated Super Bowl impacts,
$STATE_t$ is state-wide real sales at time t,
$STATESQ_t$ is state-wide real sales at time t squared,
$SEASON$ is average monthly real county sales / average annual real county sales,
X is a vector of control variables, and
ϵ_t is the error term.

Control variables included in every regression were time, T, and time squared, T^2, to capture trends in county sales that differ from trends in state-wide sales. In the two Florida counties, a control variable, $SERVICE$, equals 1 for each month in the period July 1987 to February 1988 when a tax on services was in place. This variable was introduced into equations estimating taxable sales to capture service sector effects in these counties that might differ from state-wide effects. Finally, in Hillsborough County a control variable, $STORM$, equal to 1 for each month in the period August 1990 to April 1991 was introduced to capture the effects of Operations Desert Shield and Desert Storm. Hillsborough County is home to McDill Air Force Base, which housed the U.S. Southern Command in charge of these operations. Super Bowl XXV was held there in January 1991. The explanatory power of these models was consistently high (R^2 = 0.88 in Dade County, 0.96 in Hillsborough County and 0.94 in Maricopa County). *STATE*, *SEASON*, *T*, and *SERVICE* were consistently and uniformly significant explanatory variables in these equations.

The Super Bowl dummy variable, *SB*, took on three different characterizations in separate regressions. In the first regression *SB* was set equal to 1 for the Super Bowl month of January in the appropriate county regression. In the second regression *SB* was set equal to 1 for the Super Bowl month of January and the next month, February. As the Super Bowl comes late in the month and there is no known time profile of the secondary effects predicted in impact analysis, this characterization of *SB* would capture spillovers in spending and/or accounting and some indirect spending effects. In the third regression, continuing the logic of the second regression, *SB* was set equal to 1 for January, February, and March of the Super Bowl year. Table 5.2 presents the impact on real host county sales of each of the six Super Bowl events yielded by regression analysis as the coefficient (together with the standard error) of *SB*.

Table 5.2
Regression Results in Selected Super Bowl Host Counties
(values in millions)
Dependent Variables: Country Real Sales (standard errors in parentheses)

	January Impact	January-February Impact	January-March Impact
1979 Super Bowl	-.058 (.274)	-.250 (1.978)	-.319 (1.656)
1984 Super Bowl	1.279* (.579)	.460 (.409)	.241 (.336)
1989 Super Bowl	-5.607 (2.728)	-2.278 (1.946)	-1.724 (1.604)
1991 Super Bowl	.030 (.614)	-.146 (.459)	-.319 (.403)
1995 Super Bowl	-9.916 (3.383)	-2.750 (2.150)	-1.895 (1.733)
1996 Super Bowl	57.497 (52.506)	40.679 (36.866)	11.691 (30.635)

*Positive and significant at α - .05.

Only one of the eighteen Super Bowl dummies had the anticipated sign and was significantly different from zero. Two others were negative and significant and the rest were insignificant. In the Florida Super Bowls the coefficients never exceeded $10 million. In the Maricopa County, Arizona regression the estimated impacts were in the neighborhood of $50 million or less. None of the estimated impacts come close to the projections of impact analysis and all fail miserably a t-test of the difference between observed and projected impacts. Consider each of the three Super Bowls for which impact studies are available. The base year for the Consumer Price Index used to compute real sales is July-August 1983 so that real impacts are in 1983 dollar values. The real impact projected for the 1991 Super Bowl ($117.8 million 1991 dollar values) would be $87.4 million (1983 dollar values). The standard error of the estimator for Super Bowl effects from the regression equation ranges from $400,000 to $600,000. If only 10% of the projected impacts ($8,470,000) had been realized in the host county, it would have been evident. Similarly, the projected real impact of the 1995 Super Bowl was $242.2 million compared to the standard error of the estimator from the regression equations of between $1.7 million and $3.4 million. The projected impact of the 1996 Super Bowl was $197.7 million compared to the standard error of the estimator from the regression equation between $30 million and $52 million. Such huge projections, were they even remotely correct, could not go unnoticed.[10]

To put this in another light, consider that Hillsborough County averaged real taxable sales in January of $160 million per week and the direct spending impact of its 1991 Super Bowl was estimated to be $43.8 million ($59.1 in 1991 dollar values). Winter is the height of tourist season in Florida; its roads, restaurants, malls and attractions are used at near capacity. Direct spending impacts all come in the week of the Super Bowl. If they were strictly in addition to existing spending, they would have created gridlock. Yet there was no report of increased congestion or problems of crowding. Evidence presented in the next section offers an explanation for these results.

NEAR-PERFECT COMPLEMENTS AND CAPACITY CONSTRAINTS: THE FOX IN THE HEN HOUSE

For an increase in demand to have any real effect, the sector directly impacted must have excess capacity. At full capacity, supply is perfectly inelastic and any increase in demand has price consequences only. The direct impact is only nominal, but the untrained practitioner mistakenly confuses increased sales value with an increase in sales quantity. Rents in the impacted sector will rise with the increase in prices, but so too does the cost to locals for consumption goods bought from this sector. Since the impacted sector does not produce any additional output, there will be no new purchases from input suppliers and, hence, no secondary (indirect) impacts. It is possible to realize an induced secondary impact if the owners of the businesses in the impacted sector are local residents. That is, the economic rents generated will induce directly affected owners to increase personal consumption, creating a second round of impacts. If the entrepreneurial talent is imported (if the owners do not reside within the impact area) there will be no induced effect.

With respect to Super Bowls and other mega sporting events, if one event crowds out another, the net impact is zero. Similar to the problem of interviewing the hens at a fox convention, it is nearly impossible for the impact study practitioner to ascertain that the local stadium would otherwise have been vacant on the event date, but one thing is certain: *if it weren't for the event in question the stadium would have been available for another event.* Most large cities have tourist and visitor's bureaus and sports authorities that promote the area and its amenities to interested groups. It is the function of these agencies to see that the community's infrastructure is efficiently utilized. When an area's amenities are not being used these agencies will increase marketing activities and offer discounts to increase demand.[11] In addition to the work of local government, hotel and resort interests also seek business to utilize their capacity. We witness this in the seasonal cycle of prices—low prices during off-peak periods and higher prices during peak periods of demand—and in the increased promotional efforts made to attract customers to off-peak periods. To the extent government and private interests are successful in attracting business to fill a void, the net impact of an event singled out for study is reduced.

Still most stadiums are not fully utilized, so excess capacity exists. And government agencies do not entirely quit promoting the area when a given level of demand is reached. Super Bowl events should show some economic impact albeit, as the biases outlined above suggests, less than impact analysis would predict. What mechanism works to reduce it to immeasurable levels? Besides the stadium and facilities required to stage a mega sporting event, one needs hotel and other visitor accommodations to make it successful. Direct new spending, the engine of impact analysis, is realized only if visitors stay and spend money in the area. In the process of creating impact, hotel rooms and Super Bowl seats are perfect complements. If there is a capacity constraint for hotel rooms, the impact of a Super Bowl will not be realized.

Smith Travel Research is a private company that collects and distributes data on hotel and motel utilization and prices. The data are collected by sampling the hotels and motels in an area and are used in the industry to, among other things, set rates and plan for seasonal fluctuations in demand. I have data from Smith's giving hotel and motel occupancy and average prices for Hillsborough County (Tampa), Florida and Dade County (Miami), Florida for each month from January 1988 to December 1996. Three Super Bowls are covered in this data set: The 1989 and 1995 Miami events, and the 1991 Tampa event. In each instance ambient hotel and motel real prices rose significantly while occupancy rates did not change appreciably in the month of the event. Compared to the average for the January months one year before and one year after each event, real prices rose 11.26%, 19.83%, and 4.44%; while occupancy rose only 1.24%, 2.29%, and 4.35% for the 1989, 1991, and 1995 Super Bowls, respectively.

Of course, these simple comparisons can be misleading since they are not subject to tests of significance, and the other relevant data on prices and occupancy (in other months) is ignored. To utilize all of the information we estimate the following linear relationships using an OLS model.

$$OCC_t = \beta_0 + \beta_1 BOWL + \beta_2 SEASON_{OCC} + \beta_3 T + \epsilon_t, \text{ and}$$
$$RATE_t = \gamma_0 + \gamma_1 BOWL + \gamma_2 SEASON_{RATE} + \gamma_3 T + \varepsilon_t. \quad (5)$$

Here:

β_0–β_2 and γ_0–γ_2 are coefficients,
β_3 and γ_3 are vectors of coefficients
OCC_t is the hotel and motel occupancy rate at time t,
$RATE_t$ is the real average price of a hotel or motel room at time t,
$BOWL$ is a dummy variable equal to 1 during the month of a Super Bowl (there are two $BOWL$ dummies in the Dade County regression) and zero otherwise,
$SEASON_i$ is average monthly i / average annual i ($i = OCC, RATE$),
T is a vector of time variables including time in months from January 1988, its square and its cube, and
ϵ_t and ε_t are the error terms.

The explanatory power of this simple model is quite high. The occupancy equations explained 95% of the variation in monthly occupancy rates for Hillsborough County and 67% for Dade County. The rate equations explained 94% of the variation in real monthly rates in both counties. The coefficients for BOWL from the regressions are presented in Table 5.3. In each case, occupancy did not rise by a significant magnitude, confirming that Super Bowl demand (the foxes) merely squeezed out normal demand (the hens). The mechanism by which the increase in demand is blunted is hotel price increases which showed significant increases for the Super Bowl month in every equation.

Table 5.3
Hotel Price and Occupancy Regression Results
(t-statistics in parentheses)

	Dependant Variable	
	OCC	RATE
1989 Super Bowl	-0.8339	7.1099*
	(-0.18)	(3.99)
1991 Super Bowl	1.1148	8.6770*
	(0.47)	(9.63)
1995 Super Bowl	1.7193	3.9761†
	(0.38)	(2.24)

*significant at $\alpha = .01$; † significant at $\alpha = .03$

If there are no real changes surrounding a Super Bowl event, does the sales model of equation (4) fail because it does not pick up the nominal changes that occur as a result of hotel price increases? Smith's reports the room revenue in its survey and these can be analyzed using the standard error of the coefficient estimates of the dummy variable *SB* for significance. First, we calculate the real room revenue in the host county for each of three months: the January of the Super Bowl, the January one year previously, and the January one year after the Super Bowl. Using the average of real room revenue in the January before and the January after the Super Bowl, we interpolate a real room revenue base as the expected January real room revenue if there had not been a Super Bowl. Actual real room revenue less expected real room revenue is a measure comparable to the coefficient of *SB* under the null hypothesis that there are no real effects of the Super Bowl. These calculations together with the standard errors from the sales regression are presented in Table 5.4.

Table 5.4
Real Room Revenue Increases: Compatibility with Sales Regression Results
(values in millions of 1983 dollars)

Super Bowl	Real Room Revenue Increase (ΔR)	Percent Increase ($\Delta R/R$)	Standard Error of SB	H_0: $\Delta R \geq 0$
1989 Miami	6.749	13.2%	2.728	Fail toReject
1991 Tampa	2.795	22.9%	.614	Fail to Reject
1995 Miami	4.660	8.5%	3.383	Reject

Constant dollar sales increases resulting from increases in room prices with little or no increase in occupancy range from $2.8 million to $6.7 million. These findings clearly are much closer to the results of the real sales regression that find little and no effect of a Super Bowl than to the findings of the impact analysis practitioners who estimate impacts on sales of $118 million to $365 million. Still, as Table 5.4 shows, even these small effects should have shown up as statistically significant in at least two of the samples. What happens to reduce Super Bowl effects even further?

One explanation is offered by the booking behavior of hotels in Super Bowl cities. Upon announcing the award of the January 2002 Super Bowl to Tampa, Florida, national travel agencies, local agencies of government and affiliates of the NFL booked 35,000 premium rooms for that week. This represents about 8% of the current supply of rooms for rent in Hillsborough County (including rooms of all qualities). If one makes the assumption that only the top 20% of rooms for rent in Hillsborough County are suitable to these advanced purchasers' tastes, 40% of the supply is already taken. Faced with this advanced demand, hotels insist that reservations be made for extended periods even if the guest is only staying a few nights. Thus, reported occupancy and room revenues overstate the actual real occupancy and impact on the area. That is, if one Super Bowl visitor rents a room for a week, thus crowding out a typical tourist for that week, and the Super Bowl visitor stays only four days, then room occupancy does not appear to decline. But impacts from other spending (restaurants, shopping, etc.) would decline. The net effect could be negative!

CONCLUSION

Super Bowls and other mega-sporting events have received plenty of attention from sponsors and the media. Reports of huge impacts from such events are used as justification for municipal expenditures to keep or lure a team to an area, to build stadiums, or to make bids for future Olympic or NCAA games. One result is citizen complaints about inconveniences suffered when the event takes place. This study has taken a critical look at real-time impact analysis through the looking glass of historical, realized sales. These sales are found to be greatly overstated at best, and total fabrications at worst.

Investigator bias, data measurement error, changing production relationships, diminishing returns to both scale and variable inputs, and capacity constraints anywhere along the chain of sales relations lead to lower multipliers. Crowding out and price increases by input suppliers in response to higher levels of demand, and the tendency of suppliers to lower prices to stimulate sales when demand is weak lead to overestimates of net new sales due to the event. These characteristics alone would suggest that the estimated impact of a mega-sporting event will be lower than impact analysis predicts. When there are perfect complements to the event (like hotel rooms for visitors) with capacity constraints and/or suppliers who raise prices in the face of increased demand, impacts are reduced to zero. Today's Super Bowl visitor (the fox) drove away yesterday's and tomorrow's visitor (the hen), not with threats, but with a greater willingness to pay for space.

NOTES

1. See Noll and Zimbalist (1977), p. 1.

2. Ideally, input and output numbers are real measures. However, aggregating industry values necessitates using a common metric like dollars of value. As we will see later, this is one source of bias in impact analysis.

3. The inclusion of a household sector, which, in effect, produces labor, creates an additional indirect effect, commonly called an induced effect, because new labor income increases the demand for output.

4. Detailed discussion of the technical errors (other than bias and mistake) can be found in Carter and Brody (1970a, 1970b) and in Miller and Blair (1985) and in Mills (1993).

5. One interviewer for a study of a college Spring break beach party conducted fifty interviews, all of them of women.

6. In events sponsored by local governments, budget constraints imply that spending for the event must necessarily reduce spending for other government activities or increase taxes and reduce spending by resident taxpayers. Interestingly (perhaps tellingly), impact practitioners seldom apply (or at best, are not asked to apply) multipliers to tax increases.

7. See "Economic Impact Analysis of Super Bowl XXV on the Tampa Bay Area," Appendix D, where the authors write, "Super Bowl XXV could not have occurred at a worse economic time, with an economic contraction led by a downturn in consumer spending during the month of the Super Bowl, total seasonally adjusted general sales *fell* by 4.1%." The impact projection rather than the reality was widely touted in 1996 when the NFL promised Tampa another Super Bowl if they used taxpayer money to build a new $200 million stadium.

8. "Economic Impact Analysis of Super Bowl XXV on the Tampa Bay Area" reports an estimated impact of the 1984 Super Bowl XVII on the Tampa Bay area of $88 million. This study could not be located.

9. For example, simple inflation would explain greater impacts in later Super Bowls, yet the estimated impact falls from 1995 to 1996.

10. These regressions reflect total sales in the area. In Florida where the data are further refined as taxable and nontaxable sales, regressions showed the same pattern of results for the taxable subset of all sales with the exception that there were no positive and significant Super Bowl effects. It is perhaps most appropriate to use taxable sales to test for direct effects since nearly all visitor sales are taxable. Indirect effects may reflect significant purchases of non-taxable items by local residents.

11. Private discussions with personnel at the New Orleans Tourist and Visitor's Bureau revealed that the Sugar Bowl and the Super Bowl, both in January 1997, were enough to "let us ignore January and get to work on February."

6

Baseball and Basketball Stadium Ownership and Franchise Incentives to Relocate

Gerard C. S. Mildner and James G. Strathman

INTRODUCTION

Over the past four years, seven major league sports franchises have moved and several more relocations have been proposed.[1] This mobility of sports franchises has created a political uproar in the cities that have lost their sports teams and has led to calls in Congress to regulate the location of teams (Vader, 1995; Malkin, 1997; Norton, 1995). Cities desiring to acquire or retain sports franchises have invested millions of dollars in building stadiums, constructing parking facilities and other infrastructure, and even guaranteeing ticket sales to make their city more attractive to potential teams.

These investments and subsidies represent a transfer of resources from city taxpayers for the dubious benefit of supporting a segment of the entertainment industry and maintaining a city's "major league" reputation (Federal Reserve Bank of Cleveland, 1991). In fact, analysts have concluded that the net economic benefits for a city to have sports franchises are much more limited than voters and political leaders have assumed (Baade and Dye, 1988, 1990).

A different set of studies have looked at the motivation of sports franchises to relocate and the role that local governments play in attracting and retaining teams (Shropshire, 1995; Euchner, 1993). What is clear from these studies is that stadium ownership plays an important role in the decision to relocate.

In an earlier paper, we examined the factors leading Major League Baseball franchises to relocate using data from 1950 to 1995 (Mildner and Strathman, 1996). In this chapter, we extend our analysis to look at the National Basketball Association from 1960 to 1995. Our intent is to extend this line of research to cover the other major league sports, but we present here the data for these two sports along with some location data for professional hockey and football. The chapter proceeds as follows: our model of the team relocation decision process is specified; our data set is described; the analysis of that data presented; and a final section concludes.

MODEL

In our model, there are three agents in the decision to relocate: the franchise owner, the stadium owner, and the local government. We assume that the franchise owner is primarily concerned about the net revenues of his sports team, and that the goal is profit maximization. The key determinants of net revenues are players' salaries, stadium rent, television income, ticket revenue, capital gains from franchise value, and subsidies from the local government. The stadium owner is also primarily concerned about net revenue for this facility which includes stadium rent, concession revenue, and capital gains from stadium value. Local governments are concerned about two things: the presence of the team and the cost of subsidies to the taxpayer.

Franchise relocation is analyzed using a logit model of the following structure:

$$P(M_i = 1) = Z_i B_n + B_1 S_i + e_i. \tag{1}$$

The probability of decision to move in year I, M_i, depends upon a variety of franchise factors Z_i (metropolitan population growth, annual attendance growth, team's winning percentage, and league-wide team expansion, among others), and municipal stadium/arena ownership, S_i, where $S_i = 1$ if the city owns the stadium and $S_i = 0$ otherwise. Our expectation is that the coefficient on S_i would be positive indicating an increased likelihood of moving relative to city ownership. Other variables test alternative hypotheses to predict the incentive to move, such as falling attendance, losing seasons, declining metropolitan economies, or stagnant metropolitan population.

Franchise Factors

In sports, where a significant source of team revenue comes from ticket sales and local or regional broadcast revenue, owners will prefer to locate in large and growing metropolitan areas. Larger metropolitan areas allow the team to have greater ticket sales (or higher ticket prices) for a given stadium capacity. Given the rise and fall of various regional economies, franchises will tend to follow the nation's long-run shifts in population, with owners moving when the expected rise in net revenues exceeds the costs of relocation.

Mitigating the movements suggested by this franchise migration model has been the tendency of sports leagues to increase the number of teams and locate those new teams in markets without teams. Expansion by leagues has been seen as a mechanism to capture monopoly rents by existing owners and prevent the formation of competing leagues (Quirk and Fort, 1992). Because these expansion decisions reduce the opportunity set of underserved markets, they tend to reduce the relocation probability of any one franchise.

A final group of factors that might reduce franchise mobility is team success and popularity. An owner will be more likely to relocate his franchise when the team has a losing tradition or when fan loyalty (measured by attendance) is weak. Conversely, a small metropolitan area could retain a franchise by higher than anticipated attendance. Thus by including either attendance or winning percentage, the model can test whether franchise success inhibits mobility.

Stadium Factors

In our model, there are three possible institutional arrangements: either the stadium is owned by government, the sports franchise owner, or by a third party. Our hypothesis is that stadium ownership by local government leads to subsidies being a given to local franchises *and* leads to a greater likelihood of team relocation. Because local government officials exaggerate the economic benefits of the presence of a sports franchise and discount the costs of subsidies paid by taxpayers, they are likely to be held hostage by the sports franchises with threats to move. When the local government is also the stadium or arena owner, they have greater opportunities to make those subsidies in a way that is hidden from taxpayers: below market rent payments, subsidized loans, low-cost transportation facilities, tax abatements, or below market value tax assessment, among others. Thus, one reason that sports franchises operating in municipally owned facilities are more mobile is the "stadium subsidy mechanism" that municipal ownership allows.

When the stadium owner is also the sports franchise owner, the owner now has a large incentive not to relocate. He owns the same sports facility that his team uses and the relocation decision will mean that the stadium will lose value. Since in many cases, the value of the stadium equals or exceeds the value of the franchise, the owner will only leave a city when the value of the stadium is already very low or the increase in net revenue from moving to a larger market is very high.[2] Hence the second reason that municipal ownership of stadiums leads to more franchise mobility is the "stadium value motive."

We would expect sports franchises that own their own stadiums to have a lower likelihood of moving. For the intermediate case where stadiums are owned by a third party, we would expect to see a level of mobility that ranks between franchise ownership of their own stadiums and municipal stadium ownership. In this intermediate case, the franchise owner does not have the stadium value motive to stay, but the threat to leave will likely result in reduced stadium rent or a revenue-sharing arrangement with the stadium owner. Since the local government does not have the stadium subsidy mechanism, the threat to leave does not easily generate offers from local government to prevent the move.

In practice, third-party ownership has become rather rare. Our previous paper (Mildner and Strathman, 1996) indicated that third party ownership had the same effect as team ownership for baseball franchises. Hence, for our model, we estimate the effect of public ownership alone. No data are currently available that allows us to measure the tax subsidy issue directly. Instead, we will follow the franchise relocation decision alone.

DATA

Franchise Data

For this research, we have developed two data sets: one for Major League Baseball (MLB), 1950–1995, and one for the National Basketball Association (NBA), 1960–1995.[3] The baseball data set has 1,026 observations of team-years, while the basketball data set has 681 observations. Data were collected on team performance, attendance, metropolitan population, franchise ownership, stadium/arena characteristics, and stadium/arena ownership.

The data for the two sports are summarized in Table 6.1 by decade, along with the first six years of the 1990s. As can be seen in the growth of franchise years, both sports underwent a significant expansion between the 1960s and the 1970s, although by comparison baseball is a relatively established sport. The growth in franchise years per decade for baseball was 24% for 1950–1969 and for 1960–1979, and slowed down to 6% for 1970–1989. The comparable numbers for the NBA are 86% for 1960–1979 and 23% for 1970–1989. The growth in the 1970s also reflects the merger of the NBA with the American Basketball Association in 1976.

The relative stability of baseball is also demonstrated in long metropolitan tenure, as well as ownership and stadium use. Since the NBA was founded in 1947, the opportunity to establish metropolitan tenure is not the same as baseball. Nevertheless, the difference (or at least the percentage difference) in each of these "tenure" measures has been reduced, indicating reduced rates of ownership tenure in basketball, and the end of basketball's rapid expansion years.

Stadium age and stadium capacity data indicate two important trends in both sports. First, the late 1960s and 1970s were an era for new stadium construction (and hence declining age) and rising stadium capacity, with basketball arenas tending to be much smaller and newer than baseball facilities. Between the 1960s and the 1990s, baseball stadiums grew by 0.47% per year in capacity, while basketball arenas grew by 1.0% per year, more than twice as fast.

One reason for the slow growth in baseball stadium capacity is that unlike the other sports, baseball has always had a significantly higher capacity than average attendance, so that capacity growth has a lesser impact on team attendance. Of course, the popularity of each sport and the physical limitation on human eyesight also play a role.

Average baseball stadium age declined from thirty to twenty years in the 1970s as a host of new stadiums and new franchises were established. By the 1990s the average age has risen to twenty-eight years. The rising average age of stadiums in the 1990s may explain why team owners are presently clamoring for local governments to build new stadiums. Baseball stadiums today are approaching the average age experienced in the 1950s, an era of owner discontent and franchise movement and a time when teams abandoned old stadiums such as Braves Field, the Polo Grounds, Ebbets Field, Sportsman's Park, and Shibe Park. In addition to the unattractiveness of an older facility for fan attendance, owners have an additional incentive to demand new facilities. The rising demand for "luxury boxes" that offer close viewing, catering, and other amenities at a premium price cannot be satisfied by older stadiums with more

Table 6.1
Franchise and Stadium Trends in Baseball and Basketball

		1950s	1960s	1970s	1980s	1990s
Franchise Years	MLB	160	198	246	260	162
	NBA		91	192	236	162
Average Metro	MLB	5.4	5.3	5.4	5.6	6.0
of Franchise (millions)	NBA		5.8	4.6	5.2	5.4
Average Owner Tenure	MLB	16.6	13.0	15.2	11.6	14.0
(years)	NBA		7.3	7.3	8.5	11.2
Average Stadium Tenure	MLB	37.7	27.5	20.2	27.0	28.7
(years)	NBA		7.7	7.6	13.0	15.3
Average Stadium A0	MLB	30.0	24.7	19.7	26.2	28.3
	NBA		18.6	14.2	17.1	18.1
Average Stadium	MLB	42.0	45.5	48.9	51.9	51.6
Capacity	NBA		13.8	15.9	17.1	17.9
Stadium Owned—Third	MLB	0.025	0.06	0.065	0.04	0.04
	NBA		0.22	0.16	0.09	0.06
Stadium	MLB	0.788	0.50	0.22	0.20	0.25
	NBA		0.18	0.18	0.17	0.30
Stadium Owned—	MLB	0.188	0.44	0.71	0.76	0.70
Publicly	NBA		0.60	0.66	0.74	0.64
Adjusted Average Annual	MLB	1.09	1.14	1.34	1.76	2.07
Attendance (millions)	NBA		0.285	0.405	0.499	0.663
Attendance as Percent of	MLB	32.0	30.9	33.8	41.9	49.5
Stadium Capacity	NBA		50.4	62.1	71.1	90.3
County Move Probability	MLB	0.031	0.020	0.008	0.000	0.000
	NBA		0.055	0.031	0.013	0.000
Metro Move Probability	MLB	0.031	0.015	0.008	0.000	0.000
	NBA		0.055	0.026	0.008	0.000

"democratic" seating arrangements. League rules that exclude luxury box revenue from the revenue sharing with the visiting team also encourage the development of new stadiums.

The trends in stadium ownership are very different for each sport. The development of new baseball stadiums in the 1960s and 1970s ended a long tradition of team ownership of facilities. Public ownership of stadiums rose from 19% in the 1950s to 70% in the 1990s. For basketball, franchise ownership of arenas has always been the exception. During the early years of the sport, many teams played in publicly owned arenas, arenas owned by National Hockey League teams, and college facilities. In the last few years, however, teams such as Chicago, Philadelphia, Phoenix, Portland, Sacramento, and Utah have built their own new arenas. The owner of the Washington Wizards franchise (formerly the Bullets) is even moving from a team-owned arena to a downtown facility that he will also own. There has even been a modest revival of baseball teams building their own facilities, including the Texas Rangers and the Cleveland Indians franchises.

Attendance per team has risen significantly for both sports, especially basketball. Baseball attendance has risen 2.2% per year between 1960–1995, while basketball attendance has risen by 3.2% per year. Thus, whereas the average baseball team in the 1960s had four times the annual attendance of the average basketball team, by the 1990s the multiple has fallen to three. Given that baseball teams have approximately twice as many home dates and three times the stadium capacity, this means that average per game attendance at baseball is only 50% greater, despite having stadiums with almost three times the capacity.

The rise in the popularity of basketball is also noted by looking at attendance in relation to stadium capacity. According to our data, basketball attendance in the 1990s was running at 90.3% of arena capacity, while for baseball, the figure was 49.5%. Both capacity figures are significantly higher than during previous decades, although the trends are different.

For baseball, the takeoff in capacity utilization has occurred entirely in the last twenty years. Until the 1970s only one-third of baseball seats were occupied on average, whereas today the number is one-half. For basketball, the rise in attendance/capacity ratio has been strong in each of the decades surveyed, from 50% to 62% to 71% to 90%. Whether due to the development of prominent stars or good promotion, basketball has developed a large fan base.

One possible explanation for the rise in baseball attendance might be the construction of smaller single-use facilities. These new stadiums, including the Ballpark at Arlington, Camden Yards in Baltimore, Coors Field in Denver, and Jacobs Field in Cleveland, have been acclaimed by architects and baseball enthusiasts and have stimulated attendance. In three of these four cases, the new stadium replaced a larger multiple-use stadium whose configuration was judged poor for baseball viewing.

Franchise Moves

Finally, the variable indicating the number of moves per franchise year is measured in two ways. County move probability view any movement in franchise location from one county to another as a move, including, for example, a team moving from a downtown arena to a suburban arena. The second measure, metro move probability, only records a move from one metropolitan statistical area to another. In practice, there is very little difference, and we focus on the metro move variable for our analysis.

For both sports, franchise relocation is rare. In Table 6.2, we show the number of moves per franchise year and find it declining for both sports over time. For baseball, there were a flurry of moves in the 1950s, when the Braves, Browns, and Athletics each left their hometown (which they shared with another team) to a smaller metropolitan area where they were the only team in town. And in 1958, the Dodgers and the Giants both left the New York metropolitan area, reestablishing their rivalry in California. The advent of airplane travel in the 1950s made long-distance traveling by teams more feasible and increased the set of possible team locations.

Moves in baseball became somewhat rarer in the 1960s and 1970s, perhaps in part because expansion soaked up the demand for franchises in growing parts of the country. Washington, DC lost both the original Senators and the expansion Senators to Minneapolis and Dallas, respectively. The Braves and Athletics continued the movement to new locations, and the ill-fated Pilots left Seattle for Milwaukee, partly because Seattle had a poor stadium and partly because they finished thirty-three games out of first place.

For basketball, many of the early moves in the league reflected the maturation of a business enterprise that was founded in small cities like Fort Wayne, Rochester, Syracuse, Minneapolis, and Waterloo, Iowa. The Lakers' move west in 1960 was soon followed by the Warriors. The Warriors move opened up the Philadelphia market for Syracuse. Another of the original NBA franchises that has made several moves is the Royals/Kings franchise, which was originally based in Rochester, moved to Cincinnati in 1957, transferred to Kansas City, played some of its home games in Omaha, and has finally settled in Sacramento.

As the league expanded in the 1960s and 1970s, many new franchises suffered from poor attendance and losing records, and moved after a few years. The failed Packers/Zephyrs franchise in Chicago left for a new arena in Baltimore, and moved to a new arena in suburban Washington, DC eight years later. The Rockets left San Diego for Houston after four seasons, and the Jazz left New Orleans for Salt Lake City after 5 seasons. The Braves/Clippers franchise has made two moves and as the secondary franchise in Los Angeles may move again.

But for both sports, the likelihood of moving has been declining. In the 1950s, the probability that a baseball team would move in a given year was 3%, which was cut in half by the 1960s and in half again by the 1970s. No baseball team has moved since the Senators left for Texas in 1972. For basketball, the likelihood of moving in the 1960s, 5.5%, fell to 2.6% in the 1970s, and no team has moved since 1985.

Metropolitan Markets

Another key determinant of franchise moves is the absence of franchises in large metropolitan areas. For both baseball and basketball (and unlike football which only

Table 6.2
Inter-Metropolitan Franchise Move

Sport	Year	Franchise	MSA of Origin	MSA of Destination
Baseball	1953	Braves	Boston	Milwaukee
	1954	Browns/Orioles	St. Louis	Baltimore
	1955	Athletics	Philadelphia	Kansas City
	1958	Dodgers	New York	Los Angeles
		Giants	New York	San Francisco
	1961	Senators/Twins	Washington, DC	Minneapolis
	1966	Braves	Milwaukee	Atlanta
	1968	Athletics	Kansas City	Oakland
	1970	Pilots	Seattle	Milwaukee
	1972	Senators/Ranger	Washington, DC	Dallas
Basketball	1960	Lakers	Minneapolis	Los Angeles
	1962	Warriors	Philadelphia	San Francisco
	1963	Zephyrs/Bullets	Chicago	Baltimore
		Nationals/76ers	Syracuse	Philadelphia
	1968	Hawks	St. Louis	Atlanta
	1971	Rockets	San Diego	Houston
	1972	Royals/Kings	Cincinnati	Kansas City
	1973	Bullets	Baltimore	Washington, DC
	1978	Braves/Clippers	Buffalo	San Diego
	1979	Jazz	New Orleans	Salt Lake City
	1984	Clippers	San Diego	Los Angeles
	1985	Kings	Kansas City	Sacramento

has a national television contract), the incentive to move to a larger metropolitan area is considered crucial for individual team owners. As Quirk and Fort (1992) have pointed out, sports leagues have a collective interest in insuring that the largest metropolitan areas have franchises, so as to preclude competitive leagues and thus capture the monopoly rents that come from being the sole professional league.

In Table 6.3, we show how franchises in the four sports leagues are distributed by metropolitan areas, ranked in order of population. The second column provides an indicator of how "saturated" each metropolitan area is by calculating a metropolitan population per franchise indicator.

In general, sports teams locate in large metropolitan areas. The five metropolitan areas above six million in population each have five or more franchises whereas franchises between two and six million people have between two and four franchises. Below two million, no franchise has more than two franchises.

Among the various sports, widely different location strategies are chosen. For baseball, where local attendance and television markets are paramount, all the large metropolitan areas have teams. A baseball team has eighty-one home dates, plays in a large facility, and has home games every other day during the six month season. By comparison, hockey and basketball have half as many games, have stadiums one-third the capacity, and play much less frequently.

All twenty-six U.S.-based baseball franchises are located in metro areas ranked in the top twenty-five. The only top twenty-five metro areas without a baseball team are Phoenix, Tampa, and Portland, and the leagues will be establishing new franchises in Phoenix and Tampa. In a previous paper (Mildner and Strathman, 1996), we demonstrated that the movement of baseball franchises to the Midwest and Western cities in the 1950s resulted from the development of airplane travel and the rise of those metropolitan areas in population.

For basketball and hockey, the loss for being located in smaller metropolitan areas is less severe due to the fewer number of dates and smaller seating capacity. And because the seasons for the two sports almost perfectly overlap, teams are reluctant to locate in the same city hosting a team in the other sport, presumably for fear of saturating the market for fall and winter indoor sports. This reluctance is somewhat remarkable given that hockey teams and basketball teams can experience economies of scope by sharing sporting facilities and have developed scheduling arrangements that avoid same night event conflicts.

Thus, while ten of the eleven largest metropolitan areas in the United States have both hockey and basketball franchises, for metropolitan areas ranked 12 through 29, only Phoenix (#18) and Denver (#20) have franchises in both sports. Those anomalies may be explained both by fast population growth in those metro areas and anticipation that they will become larger markets in the long run.

The table also offers some insight on where possible future sports expansions might take place for hockey and basketball. Houston (#10), Atlanta (#12), and Seattle (#13) stand out as large metropolitan areas that might be ready for hockey, their second fall-winter indoor sport. Atlanta was recently awarded a new NHL franchise, and is building a new basketball/hockey arena. An offer from Houston was rejected in the recent NHL decision on new franchises largely because of the age of the current arena, whereas Seattle completed its 17,000 seat Key Arena in 1995.

The only medium size metropolitan areas with hockey but not basketball are St. Louis (#17), Pittsburgh (#19), and Tampa (#21). St. Louis and Pittsburgh are slow-growing metropolitan areas that seem likely to fall in size rankings over time. More attractive candidates might be San Diego (#16), Cincinnati (#23), Kansas City (#24), or Norfolk (#27), which stand out as large metropolitan areas without either hockey or basketball. San Diego and Norfolk both have the advantage of being fast-growing metropolitan areas, however San Diego has the dubious distinction of attracting and losing two basketball franchises (Rockets and Clippers).

Perhaps the most likely candidate, now that Toronto and Vancouver have received NBA franchises, would be Montreal. With a metropolitan population of 3.32 million, Montreal would rank as high as Atlanta in our U.S. metro population table. It has a newly built indoor arena, and would have a natural rivalry with the Toronto franchise.

For football, the need to locate in large metropolitan areas is a league concern and not a significant team owner concern. This is because fans are willing to drive longer distance for weekend football games (hence, the market is regional, not metropolitan) and because of the importance of national television contract in team revenue. Thus, teams are able to survive in small metropolitan areas such as Green Bay and Jacksonville, and teams can make franchise shifts to smaller markets, such as the Rams' move from Los Angeles to St. Louis, or the Oilers' move from Houston to Memphis (and ultimately to Nashville). In those cases, the desire to reduce stadium rents and increase luxury box and concession revenue were more important factors.

The NFL's concern for franchise location is much greater than individual owners. Failure by a league to have a presence in major television markets can lead to new league formation and a loss of monopoly rent. This has happened twice before to the NFL, most recently when the American Football League established franchises in the then under-served markets of Boston, New York, Houston, Denver, and Buffalo, and later expanded to Miami.

Thus, Table 6.3 exposes a potential market for a rival football league as the large metropolitan areas of Los Angeles, Houston, and Cleveland currently have no franchise, and two major markets, New York and Chicago, may be considered underserved. We suspect, however, that this gap is really a temporary disequilibrium and the league will undergo expansion to these cities in upcoming years. Nevertheless, the failure of the league to control franchise mobility (as baseball and hockey have done) represents an important weakness in league structure.

STATISTICAL ANALYSIS

Table 6.4 reports the logit regression estimates of our single-equation model specified by equation (1). Separate regression equations are estimated for baseball and basketball teams moving between metropolitan areas. The only two statistically significant variables in the baseball equation are the negative time trend and the positive effect of public stadium ownership on teams moving to a new city. This result lends support to our hypothesis that public ownership of stadiums contributes to greater team mobility.

Of the other variables reaching low levels of statistical significance, team winning percentage (three-year moving average) was weakly negative and team attendance was weakly positive. The winning percentage result is intuitive (that winning teams stay put) but the attendance figure is not. One possibility is that the teams leaving the highly attended New York region may skew this result. Of course, that begs the

Table 6.3
Sports Franchises by Metro Areas, 1997
Ranked by Population, 1994

	Metro Areas	Pop. (m)	Pop. Per Team	MLB	NBA	NHL	NFL	Total
1.	New York	19.80	2.20	2	2	3	2	9
2.	Los Angeles	15.30	2.55	2	2	2		6
3.	Chicago	8.53	1.71	2	1	1	1	5
4.	Washington, DC	7.05	1.41	1	1	1	2	5
5.	San Francisco	6.51	1.09	2	1	1	2	6
6.	Philadelphia	5.96	1.49	1	1	1	1	4
7.	Boston	5.50	1.38	1	1	1	1	4
8.	Detroit	5.26	1.32	1	1	1	1	4
9.	Dallas	4.36	1.09	1	1	1	1	4
10.	Houston	4.10	2.05	1	1			2
11.	Miami	3.41	0.85	1	1	1	1	4
12.	Atlanta	3.33	1.11	1	1	a	1	3
13.	Seattle	3.23	1.08	1	1		1	3
14.	Cleveland	2.90	1.45	1	1			2
15.	Minneapolis	2.69	0.90	1	1	a	1	3
16.	San Diego	2.63	1.32	1			1	2
17.	St. Louis	2.54	0.85	1		1	1	3
18.	Phoenix	2.47	0.82	a	1	1	1	3
19.	Pittsburgh	2.40	0.80	1		1	1	3
20.	Denver	2.19	0.55	1	1	1	1	4
21.	Tampa	2.16	1.08	a		1	1	2
22.	Portland	1.98	1.98		1			1
23.	Cincinnati	1.89	0.95	1			1	2
24.	Kansas City	1.65	0.83	1			1	2

Table 6.3 continued

Metro Areas	Pop. (m)	Pop. Per Team	MLB	NBA	NHL	NFL	Total
25. Milwaukee	1.64	0.82	1	1			2
26. Sacramento	1.59	1.59		1			1
27. Norfolk	1.53	na					0
28. Indianapolis	1.46	0.73		1		1	2
29. San Antonio	1.44	1.44		1			1
Columbus	1.42	na			a		0
Orlando	1.36	1.36		1			1
New Orleans	1.31	1.31				1	1
Charlotte	1.26	0.43		1		1	2
Buffalo	1.19	0.60			1	1	2
Salt Lake City	1.18	1.18		1			1
Greensboro	1.11	1.11			1 b		1
Nashville	1.07	na			a	b	0
Memphis	1.06	1.06				1 b	1
Raleigh	0.97	na			b		0
Jacksonville	0.97	0.97				1	1
Green Bay	0.20	0.20				1	1
Total Cities			26	27	20	30	103
Canadian Cities			2	2	6	0	10

a. The table reflect 1998 expansions by the MLB in Tampa and Phoenix, and proposed expansion by the NHL in Nashville, Atlanta, Minneapolis, and Columbus, Ohio.
b. The Houston NFL franchise and the Hartford NHL franchise played the 1997 seasons in Memphis and Greensboro, respectively, in anticipation of moves to Nashville and Raleigh.

question of why an owner would leave a high attendance city.

The basketball equation showed no effect of public ownership. One possible explanation is that indoor arenas have a value for hosting musical events and other sports, whereas baseball stadiums are highly specialized facilities. Hence, the "salvage value" of abandoned arenas means that a basketball team that owns a stadium might have less of a mobility constraint than a baseball team. Short of attempting additional specifications and constructing other variables, we conclude that stadium ownership does not seem to be a significant factor in determining movements by basketball franchises.

Table 6.4
Determinants of Inter-Metropolitan Franchise Movement
Logit Regression

Variable	Coefficient (t-ratio)	
	Baseball	Basketball
Constant	0.375 (0.17)	-0.036 (-0.02)
Time	-0.158 (-4.114)	0.033 (0.481)
Average Winning Percentage (three-year moving average)	-9.15 (-1.749)	3.85 (0.977)
Number of New Franchises in Year	-0.218 (-0.467)	
Metro Population	-0.376 E-07 (-0.410)	-0.842 E-06 (-2.142)
Owner Tenure	-0.20 E-01 (-0.436)	0.051 (0.551)
Publicly Owned Stadium	3.37 (2.636)	0.257 (0.299)
Stadium Capacity	-0.197 E-01 (-0.640)	-0.337 E-04 (0.280)
Adjusted Annual Attendance	0.923 E-06 (1.32)	-0.167 E-04 (-2.81)
Log Likelihood	-60.8	-68.2
Log Likelihood (B)	-41.7	-55.1
Likelihood Ratio Statistic (8 d.f.)	38.3	26.3
McFadden's R2	0.32	0.19
N	1,026	681

Table 6.5
Determinants of a Public Stadium Ownership
Logit Regression

Variable	Coefficient (t-ratio)	
	Baseball	Basketball
Constant	0.807 (1.86)	1.75 (3.86)
Time	0.243 (6.68)	0.069 (1.61)
Time Squared	-0.223 E-02 (-3.19)	-0.006 (-0.59)
Adjusted Annual Attendance	-0.588 E-07 (-3.92)	-0.233 E-05 (-3.28)
Metropolitan Tenure	-0.051 (-13.56)	0.012 (1.04)
Owner Tenure	-0.057 (-6.98)	-0.063 (-4.32)
Metro Population	3.37 (2.636)	0.131 E-06 (6.30)
Log Likelihood	-649.2	-429.9
Log Likelihood (B)	-338.7	-364.8
Likelihood Ratio Statistic (8 d.f.)	620.9	130.2
McFadden's R2	0.48	0.15
N	1,026	681

Unlike baseball, metropolitan population and average annual attendance were important factors in basketball team moves. Thus, teams in small or declining metropolitan areas and low attendance are the franchises that would most likely be candidates for moving.

A related question that we investigated is what conditions determine public ownership of stadiums and arenas. Table 6.5 reports the results of logit regressions on the probability of public ownership of stadiums for baseball and for basketball. This model performs much better than the relocation equation, with similar results for both sports.

First, we find a general trend toward public ownership over time, although this is only significant for baseball. Second, we find that teams with low annual attendance are in public stadiums. This may reflect the idea that expansion teams are more likely in public stadiums and their poor performance may be associated with low attendance. Third, teams that have only been located in a metropolitan area for a short period of time are more likely to be in publicly owned stadiums. This may reflect the pattern that only cities that build public stadiums attract new franchises. Finally, recent acquisition of the franchise by a new owner is associated with playing in a publicly owned stadium. Each of these results points to the importance of municipal ownership in attracting new teams.

Lastly, we examine the determinants of annual attendance, viewing that as a proxy for team net revenue. In Table 6.6, we present a regression equation that predicts the log of "adjusted" annual attendance. For baseball, we adjusted for the effect of strike years and for both sports, we adjusted for the increase in the number of games per season.

Results for the two sports are very similar. Stadium age is negatively correlated with fan attendance, however the pattern of causation isn't entirely clear. Fans may prefer new ballparks and arenas, but it's also true that high fan attendance may generate the revenues required to support new stadium construction. Fan attendance rises with a winning record (again, there is a weak case for reverse causation). Larger cities have higher attendance, and attendance is rising over time in both sports.

Metropolitan tenure, which we interpret as a tradition effect, has a significant impact in baseball but not in basketball. This may reflect the relatively recent popularity of basketball and the high frequency of team moves in earlier years. Note that the absolute value for the coefficient on metropolitan tenure for baseball is much smaller than the coefficient on stadium age. This indicates that a team moving to a new metropolitan area will likely gain more attendance from the playing in a new stadium effect than they lose from the loss of tradition effect. This may explain why so many long-established franchises like the Giants and Dodgers were willing to leave long established homes for the sake of a new, attractive ballpark.

A second key difference in the two attendance equations is the significance of the capacity variable for basketball and not for baseball. As discussed earlier, basketball arenas have consistently been playing to higher capacity utilization levels than baseball, with the current level at 90%. Under those conditions, the team with the higher attendance is the one with more seats. The need to upgrade facilities to meet rising demand may also explain why basketball arenas are so much newer than baseball stadiums. Baseball, on the other hand, requires the additional seating capacity to meet the higher demand on weekends or when a particularly good match-up occurs.

Table 6.6
Determinants of Attendance
Dependent Variable: Log of Annual Adjusted Attendance

Variable	Coefficient (t-ratio)	
	Baseball	Basketball
Constant	12.28 (47.89)	7.04 (16.44)
Log Stadium Capacity	0.050 (1.06)	0.53 (11.81)
Stadium Age	-0.091 (-7.18)	-0.050 (-5.35)
Log Winning Percentage	0.678 (13.19)	0.381 (13.54)
Log Metro Percentage	0.120 (7.90)	0.043 (3.37)
Time	0.020 (22.49)	0.027 (21.82)
Metropolitan Tenure	0.115 E-03 (2.85)	0.002 (1.59)
SEE	0.34	0.23
R2	0.49	0.71
N	1,026	681

CONCLUSIONS

The results of this research will help inform officials about the feasibility of using subsidized stadium development as a means of attracting and maintaining sports franchises. For baseball franchises, team ownership of a stadium makes the franchise less likely to move. Cities with publicly owned facilities may want to explore privatization.

The best prospects for cities seeking to attract a new baseball franchise are teams currently playing in public facilities. Even teams that own their own facilities might be attractive if a city has a new facility and the land occupied by the current stadium has a high alternative use. A second consideration would be to identify teams that had poor winning records since they are somewhat more likely to move. That may sound attractive, but it assumes that the objective is to win a team, not just a winning team.

For basketball-seeking cities, the advise is less clear. We do not yet have a useful model of franchise relocation. We know that teams are playing next to capacity. We also know, from our equation, that teams draw better in large metropolitan areas with new stadiums. Part of the reason for the poor performance of the relocation equation may be the number of expansion franchises in recent years. This suggests a different model for future research that will predict where a league will expand its membership.

Finally, we want to exercise a word of caution to city officials who see economic development and political gains from attracting new franchises. As others have noted, sports is just one of many entertainment outlets. Consultants' estimates of the multiplier effect of sports expenditures are frequently exaggerated. While making investments in new facilities may influence some team location decisions on the margin, we suspect these effects are small and the benefits are fleeting.

NOTES

1. The moving franchises (and their destination city) are the Cleveland Browns (NFL, Baltimore), the Los Angeles Raiders (NFL, Oakland), Los Angeles Rams (NFL, St. Louis), the Winnipeg Jets (NHL, Phoenix), the Quebec Nordiques (NHL, Colorado), the Minnesota North Stars (NHL, Dallas), and the Hartford Whalers (NHL, Greesboro-Charlotte). In addition, the Houston Oilers (NFL) are scheduled to move to Memphis and later to Nashville.

2. Estimates of franchise values are reported in Quirk and Fort (1992). The highest values for each of the major leagues are for basketball, the Boston Celtics, $120 million (1986); for baseball, the New York Mets, $100 million (1986); and for football, the New York Giants, $150 million. As for hockey, the NHL recently announced four new expansion teams, with the entry price set at $80 million. By comparison, seven new sports stadiums and arenas have been built in Baltimore, Cincinnati, Cleveland, Nashville, San Francisco, St. Louis, and Seattle for between $250 million and $525 million (Malkin, 1997).

3. The reason for the difference in time periods is that professional basketball was an unstable business enterprise until the early 1960s. The NBA merged with other leagues in the late 1940s and early 1950s and clearly had a less prominent place in the public eye than college basketball. In addition, data for the NBA prior to 1960, particularly on attendance, are very difficult. Thus, while the baseball data are comprehensive, there are twelve missing team-year observations for basketball, largely due to missing data on team attendance. Finally, pro basketball in the 1950s was frequently played in neutral cities or in doubleheaders where attendance and stadium data become less meaningful. The missing observations are the St. Louis Hawks, 1960–1967; the Syracuse Nationals, 1960–1961, and the Chicago Packers/Zephyrs, 1961–1962. The year refers to the beginning year of the season.

Section IV

MANAGERIAL DECISIONS: INPUTS AND OUTPUTS

7

Alternative Econometric Models of Production in Major League Baseball

Elizabeth Gustafson, Lawrence Hadley, and John Ruggiero

INTRODUCTION

Major League baseball (MLB) is a uniquely suited industry for empirical analysis of production. The industry generates data that directly measure outputs and inputs. Existing empirical analyses of baseball production typically select team winning percent (or the ratio of wins to losses) as the output produced.[1] The selection of team inputs varies between studies. Porter and Scully (1982) selected slugging percent and the pitching staff's ratio of strikeouts to walks to measure team inputs.[2] Other analyses use the ratio of runs scored to opposition runs scored as the only input in the production function.[3] Finally, Kahn (1993a) and Ruggiero, Hadley, and Gustafson (1995) provide a more comprehensive list of team inputs that includes slugging percent, earned run average, and stolen bases, among others.

While the selection of inputs has differed in the existing production analyses, there has been little deviation in the selection of output. The goal of managers and teams is to win baseball games in order to qualify for the playoffs, and ultimately, win the World Series. As a result, the existing baseball production models have selected the winning percent as an output. This assumes that the only objective of management is to maximize the probability of winning. In developing a team, however, management may have other goals that are indirectly related to winning ball games. For example, general managers may attempt to develop a team that will increase attendance in order to increase team revenues. It is common to assume that the primary interest of owners in any industry is the financial success of their business. However, in the case of professional team sports, it is plausible that owners are also interested in the success of their team as a sports entity. Our contention is that, *a priori*, MLB owners pursue a dual objective that includes the financial success and the sports success of their business (team). This raises the question of whether ignoring the revenue output and modeling only winning percent may lead to misspecification of the production function.

For example, suppose that a team's season attendance proxies its financial success and that the team's winning percent proxies its baseball success. Suppose further that management improves the quality of the team's inputs by adding superior hitters (as measured by slugging percent) to the team's roster. We expect that this would simultaneously increase the team's attendance and its winning percent.[4] *Ceteris paribus*, fans attend a baseball game to observe superior hitting (and pitching), and, at the same time, superior hitting wins baseball games. It is plausible, therefore, to model baseball as a joint or multiple production process. In this chapter, we relax the assumption of one output and investigate ways of modeling baseball production as a joint or multiple production process where teams produce winning percent and attendance.

There are three basic ways to model production of more than one output by the same firm. One can use separate production functions for each output, a single joint production function, or simultaneous production functions for the outputs. Chizmar and Zak (1983) suggest that both the relationship among the outputs and the issue of input exhaustion must be considered in determining which modeling technique is appropriate. Input exhaustion is complete if using an input to produce one output completely exhausts that input so that it cannot also be used to produce another output. When the outputs are produced by separate production processes with complete input exhaustion and no causal relationship among the outputs, then it is clear that treating each output separately with its own production function is appropriate.

In baseball the input "baseball talent" is not completely exhausted by its role in producing winning percent but is also able to contribute to attendance. We describe this as incomplete input exhaustion. In such a case, writing separate production functions requires determining how much of the input is used for each output. This is generally difficult. A preferred model for incomplete exhaustion of inputs is a joint production function that can be estimated by Vinod's (1976) methodology based on canonical correlation analysis. However, if inputs are shared with no exhaustion at all, as may be the case in MLB, then the entire amount of the input can be used in each one of the separate production functions. Another difficulty with joint production functions arises because some, but not all, of the inputs in baseball production are shared. Certainly, increasing an input like slugging percent will tend to increase both winning percent and attendance. However, while increasing city population will cause attendance to rise, there is no expected effect on the team's winning percent. The joint production function implies that all inputs are shared in a similar way.

While a joint production function can handle the problem of incomplete input exhaustion, it cannot model a causal relationship among the outputs. If there is a causal relationship among the outputs (e.g., increased winning percent leads to increased attendance), then a simultaneous equations model is appropriate. Since the simultaneous equations model has one equation for each output, each equation must include the input amounts used for that output. Such a model can not deal with the incomplete exhaustion of inputs mentioned above.

This discussion raises some questions and problems regarding the proper way to model baseball production when two outputs, winning percent and attendance, are considered. Reasonable arguments can be made for a variety of modeling approaches. This chapter compares estimates of baseball production using Ordinary Least Squares (OLS) on separate equations, canonical regression of a joint production function, and Three Stage Least Squares (3SLS) on a simultaneous equations model. A single equation model for winning percent is also estimated using generalized least squares to correct for the correlation between disturbances caused by the requirement that average winning percent is always 0.5 in a closed sports league.

The rest of the chapter is organized as follows. The next section introduces the inputs of the production processes and the OLS models. The following two sections introduce the joint production model and the simultaneous equations model. This is followed by empirical analysis using MLB data for the 1990–1992 seasons. The last section presents conclusions.

SEPARATE PRODUCTION FUNCTIONS

Traditionally, the production function for winning percent (*WP*) has been modeled as a single equation using team talent as inputs. Similarly, attendance (*ATT*) has been shown to depend on team talent as well as variables describing the market and the price. We can write the two separate production functions as:

$$WP = f(Y) + e_1 \tag{1}$$

$$ATT = g(Z) + e_2, \tag{2}$$

where Y and Z are vectors of variable inputs that each contain some of the same variables. We use the Cobb-Douglas form for the two production functions.

The Y vector includes team slugging percent (*SLG* = total bases/total at-bats), total team stolen bases (*SB*), team earned run average (*ERA* = [total earned runs*9]/[total innings pitched]), and lagged winning percent (*WP$_{-1}$*), which is included to capture unmeasured features of the team that may carry over from the previous season. The performance variables (*SLG, SB,* and *ERA*) are each measured as a ratio to the league average for the season in order to account for possible differences in the level of play in different leagues and different seasons.

The Z vector includes all of the Y inputs as well as average ticket price (*TP*), the population of the team's metropolitan area (*POP*) and a dummy which is one for American League teams (*AL*) to account for different ways of measuring attendance in the two leagues. An alternative model for *ATT* replaces the three performance variables with *WP*. These models are estimated using OLS to provide a benchmark for comparison with the joint production and simultaneous production models (see below).

Chapman and Southwick (1991) pointed out that the league average winning percent must be 0.5 in any season, which implies that there is correlation between the disturbances for different teams in a league. Under these circumstances OLS will yield inefficient estimates. They determine that the correlation between the disturbances for any two teams in the same league and season can be approximated by

$$\frac{\sigma^2}{(n-1)},$$

(3)

where σ^2 is the variance of the disturbances for the WP equation and n is the number of teams in the league. The WP equation is corrected for this form of correlation among the disturbances using Generalized Least Squares (GLS) for increased efficiency.

A JOINT PRODUCTION FUNCTION

Assuming that both team attendance (ATT) and team winning percent (WP) are produced using m inputs ($X = x_1, \ldots x_m$) the production function can be written as:

$$g(WP, ATT) = f(X),$$

(4)

where the vector X includes all the input variables in Y and Z so that all inputs are included. Specifying the production function in extended Cobb-Douglas form, we have:

$$WP^{\alpha_1} ATT^{\alpha_2} = \beta_0 x_1^{\beta_1} x_2^{\beta_2} \ldots x_m^{\beta_m}.$$

(5)

Specifying equation (5) in log-linear form we have:

$$\alpha_1 \ln WP + \alpha_2 \ln ATT = \sum_{k=1}^{m} \beta_k \ln x_k + \ln \beta_0.$$

(6)

Vinod (1968) provided a methodology based on canonical correlation analysis to estimate multiple output joint production functions. This method, canonical regression analysis, estimates joint production functions consistently. Vinod showed that if the joint production in equation (6) is the correct specification of the model then the application of OLS to individual equations produces biased coefficient estimates while canonical regression analysis does not. Chizmar and Zak (1984), Gyimah-Brempong and Gyapong (1991) and Ruggiero (1995) applied canonical regression to analyze joint production in the provision of educational services. Canonical regression creates two variates, U and V, consisting of linear combinations of the outputs and inputs, respectively (specified in log form). This can be represented mathematically as:

$$U = a_1 \ln WP + a_2 \ln ATT$$

(7)

and

$$V = b_1 \ln x_1 + b_m \ln x_m. \tag{8}$$

The weights $A \equiv (a_1, a_2)$ and $B \equiv (b_1, \ldots b_m)$ are chosen so that the correlation between variates U and V is maximized, in other words,

$$\rho^* = \underset{A,B}{Max}\ Corr(U,V), \tag{9}$$

leading to estimates $A^* = (a_1^*, a_2^*)$ and $B^* = (b_1^*, \ldots b_m^*)$. Recognizing that

$$U = \rho^* V, \tag{10}$$

an estimate of equation (6) is obtained by substituting equations (7) and (8) into equation (10), and evaluating the resulting equation with A^* and B^* yields:

$$a_1^* \ln WP + a_2^* \ln ATT = \sum_{k=1}^{m} \rho^* b_k^* \ln x_k + \epsilon. \tag{11}$$

Following Gyimah-Brempong and Gyapong (1991), the marginal output elasticity of input k in the production of winning percent is:

$$ME(WP, x_k) = \frac{\partial \ln WP}{\partial \ln x_k} = \frac{\rho^* b_k^*}{a_1^*}, \tag{12}$$

and the marginal elasticity of input k in the production of attendance is:

$$ME(ATT, x_k) = \frac{\partial \ln ATT}{\partial \ln x_k} = \frac{\rho^* b_k^*}{a_2^*}. \tag{13}$$

The marginal elasticities provide estimated relationships of the joint production process. The canonical regression technique, developed to estimate joint production, has been proved by Vinod (1968)[5] to be maximum likelihood (assuming normality) and to provide consistent estimates of the slope parameters (even without assuming normality).

SIMULTANEOUS PRODUCTION FUNCTIONS

Modeling production of WP and ATT in a simultaneous system allows us to incorporate the idea that increased WP leads to increased ATT. The simultaneous system is:

$$\ln WP = \delta_1 + \delta_2 \ln SLG + \delta_3 \ln SB + \delta_4 \ln ERA + \delta_5 \ln WP_{-1} + e_1 \tag{14}$$

$$\ln ATT = \gamma_1 + \gamma_2 \ln WP + \gamma_3 \ln WP_{-1} + \gamma_4 \ln TP$$
$$+ \gamma_5 \ln POP + \gamma_6 AL + e_2 \tag{15}$$

$$COV \ (e_1, \ e_2) \neq 0. \tag{16}$$

Equation (16), which states that the disturbances of the two equations are assumed to be contemporaneously correlated, causes this otherwise recursive model to be simultaneous. If equation (16) is not true (the covariance between the disturbance terms equals zero), then OLS will yield unbiased estimates for equations (14) and (15). A test for significant correlation between the disturbances of equations (14) and (15) can serve as a test for simultaneity in this case. We might expect the disturbances of these two equations to be correlated due to omitted effects that may cause a team to win more games than predicted and also cause that team to have greater attendance than predicted. For example, the presence of charismatic players might have such an effect. Three-Stage Least Squares (3SLS) should provide consistent and asymptotically efficient estimates of this model.

EMPIRICAL ANALYSIS OF THE THREE MODELS

We estimate our models for MLB using data from the 1990–1992 seasons. In our opinion, these three seasons represent a relatively stable period in the industry. Unlike 1994–1995, these three seasons were played in their entirety. They predate the recent turmoil in the industry regarding revenue sharing, salary arbitration, and the negotiation of a new collective bargaining agreement.

The output variables in our model are team winning percent and annual attendance for the current season. Team performance variables measuring the baseball inputs in our model include team slugging percent (total bases/total at-bats), total team stolen bases, team earned run average ([total earned runs*9]/[total innings pitched]), and lagged winning percent equal to the team's winning percent from the previous season. The first three team performance variables are measured as ratios to the league average for the season. The data for all of these variables were obtained from *The Baseball Encyclopedia* (9th edition), and the 1991, 1992, and 1993 issues of the *National League Green Book* and the *American League Red Book*.

Population of each team's metropolitan area, the average ticket price, and a binary variable identifying each team's league (American League equals one) were entered as control variables in our model. Population data were obtained from the U.S. Bureau of the Census and average ticket price data were supplied by Don Coffin. Table 7.1 presents summary statistics for all variables in our model.

Table 7.2 presents the estimated elasticities for the winning percent models described earlier. The results for the attendance models are shown in Table 7.3. In each table an additional OLS model is included for comparison with the canonical regression model. The canonical regression marginal elasticities shown in column three of Tables 7.2 and 7.3 are calculated using equations (12) and (13), and the canonical regression parameter estimates used in equations (12) and (13) are reported in Table 7.4. The marginal elasticities have no standard errors reported, so Tables 7.2 and 7.3 do not indicate statistical significance for these estimates. Standard errors for the canonical regression parameter estimates in Table 7.4 are found using the jackknife technique.

Table 7.1
Descriptive Statistics

Variable	Mean	Standard Deviation
Winning Percent	500	59
Attendance	2,147,562	648,649
Lagged Winning Percent	500	58
Slugging Percent	0.382	0.020
SLG/(League Ave SLG)	1.00	0.048
Stolen Bases	124	42
SB/(League Ave SB)	1.00	0.310
Earned Run Average	3.83	0.037
ERA/(League Ave ERA)	1.00	0.083
Ticket Price	8.22	0.66
Population (thousands)	6,165.536	5,186.913

*The variables were calculated from data taken from the 1990–1992 seasons. Sample size is 78. We would like to thank Don Coffin for providing ticket price data.

Looking first at the winning percent models in Table 7.2, we see that the coefficients and significance test results are very similar for all models except the canonical regression model. Column one shows the single equation results. The GLS model in column two corrects that model for correlation among disturbances due to the season league average winning percent always being 0.5. Our data includes two leagues over three seasons, and this requires omitting six observations to avoid having a singular covariance matrix for the disturbances. Randomly choosing teams to omit, we excluded data on the Atlanta Braves and the Baltimore Orioles. Both OLS and GLS show significant and correctly signed coefficients on the three performance statistics, and the coefficients of those variables are almost identical. Only the lagged winning percent variable has appreciably different coefficients in the OLS and GLS models and these coefficients are highly insignificant under both estimation techniques.

Column three of Table 7.2 shows the marginal elasticities for winning percent obtained from the joint production canonical regression model and, for comparison, column four shows results from an OLS model that uses the same variables. No t-statistics are presented for the canonical regression marginal elasticities, but the joint model in Table 7.4 presents jackknifed t-statistics for the canonical regression coefficients. The most striking result is that the canonical elasticities for the performance variables are quite different from the other models. This model necessarily includes ticket price and population as determinants of winning percent despite the fact that the OLS model indicates that these variables are insignificant in explaining baseball success. It is true that we sometimes expect big cities to have teams which can afford superior players, but the model already controls for player quality.

Column five of Table 7.2 shows the three stage least squares estimates for the winning percent equation. Again, there is very little difference between this model and the OLS model in column one. The causal model presented earlier can be considered recursive except for the possibility of correlation between disturbances of the two equations. Thus, testing for simultaneity, we estimate the correlation between the disturbances of the WP and ATT equations to be -0.199, which is not significantly different from zero at the 0.05 level of significance. This result suggests that there is no reason to use a simultaneous estimation method.

The attendance equation results are shown in Table 7.3. The first and second columns show the two OLS models proposed earlier. Model one uses performance statistics to represent team quality and Model two uses winning percent in place of the performance statistics. Both models show that current team performance is significant and that there is a significant lagged effect of WP on attendance as well. Population positively affects attendance and attendance levels are significantly higher for teams in the AL, other things constant. This result for attendance is expected because the leagues report attendance figures differently. In the AL, attendance is measured by total ticket sales. In contrast, attendance for National League (NL) teams is measured by the actual number of fans that enter the stadium. Game-day attendance will always be less than ticket sales due to no-shows. Ticket price has no significant impact on attendance.

Column three of Table 7.3 shows the marginal elasticities for attendance from the canonical regression, again presented without t-statistics. The AL dummy could not be used in the canonical regression, so an OLS model with the same variables is shown in column four for comparison purposes. The canonical marginal elasticities show a much smaller effect of lagged WP (0.23 instead of 0.78) and much larger effects of ERA (-2.74 instead of -1.54) and population (0.64 instead of 0.15). Lagged winning percent and ticket price are not statistically significant in the joint canonical regression equation shown in Table 7.4. Vinod has shown that when a joint production function is the true function, OLS estimation leads to bias and inconsistency. The large differences in these estimates could be attributed to such bias if we believe that the joint production function is the true function.

Column five of Table 7.3 presents the 3SLS model, which includes the same variables as the OLS regression in column two. The coefficients show some small

Table 7.2
Winning Percent Regression Results*
All performance statistics are measured relative to their league average for that year.

Variable (all variables in logs except AL)	Dependent Variable = ln WP (Parentheses contain t-statistics.)				
	1 OLS Elasticities	2 GLS Elasticities	3 Canonical Regression Marginal Elasticities (no t-stats)	4 OLS Elasticities (Canonical comparison)	5 3SLS Elasticities
Constant	6.34** (16.06)	6.27** (14.78)		6.40** (15.10)	6.34** (16.60)
Lagged WP	-0.021 (-0.33)	-0.010 (-0.15)	0.065	-0.023 (-0.363)	-0.021 (-0.34)
Slugging Average	1.44** (9.33)	1.44** (8.76)	0.720	1.51** (9.29)	1.45** (9.91)
Stolen Bases	0.045* (1.89)	0.044* (1.73)	0.167	0.058** (2.25)	0.042* (1.88)
Earned Run Average	-0.96** (-10.13)	-0.96** (-9.50)	-0.795	-0.97** (-10.15)	-0.96** (-10.69)
Ticket Price			-0.081	0.014 (1.25)	
Population			0.185	0.014 (1.25)	
Adjusted R^2	0.712			0.712	0.712
Sample Size	78	72	78	78	78

*Significance at the 0.05 and 0.10 levels are indicated, respectively, by ** and *.

Table 7.3
Attendance Regression Results[a]

All performance statistics are measured relative to their league average for that year.

			Dependent Variable = ln ATT (Parentheses contain t-statistics.)		
Variable (all variables in logs except AL)	1 OLS Elasticities Model 1	2 OLS Elasticities Model 2	3 Canonical Regression Marginal Elasticities (no t-stats)	4 OLS Elasticities (Canonical comparison)	5 3SLS Elasticities
Constant	6.75** (4.56)	-1.65 (-0.91)		6.74** (4.48)	-3.21* (-1.70)
Win Percent		1.26** (5.68)			1.58** (6.18)
Lagged WP	0.78** (3.49)	0.87** (3.95)	0.23	0.78** (3.42)	0.82** (3.76)
Slugging Average	2.38** (4.19)		2.48	2.37** (4.11)	
Stolen Bases	0.032 (0.36)		0.57	0.025 (0.28)	
Earned Run Average	-1.54** (-4.61)		-2.74	-1.54** (04.57)	
Ticket Price	-0.33 (-1.01)	-0.23 (-0.74)	-0.28	-0.29 (-0.85)	-0.33 (-1.11)
Population	0.15** (3.90)	0.13** (3.48)	0.64	0.15** (3.83)	0.15** (4.28)
American League	0.092* (1.80)	0.091* (1.77)			0.092* (1.93)
Adjusted R^2	0.466	0.458		0.449	0.442
Sample size	78	78	78	78	78

[a] Significance at the 0.05 and 0.10 levels are indicated, respectively, by ** and *.

differences, especially for WP and lagged WP, and the explanatory power is smaller (0.442 instead of 0.458).

CONCLUSIONS

We have explored the idea of modeling baseball production under the assumption that winning percent and attendance are multiple or joint outputs as alternatives to modeling each production function separately. The same data set and set of inputs was used in three production models so that estimates from those models can be compared.

Estimation of two separate production functions using OLS implies that we expect no causal relationship between the outputs that would lead to simultaneity. Also, it implies that inputs are not shared, that they are shared with no exhaustion, or that we have correctly entered the amount of input used by each output. If we assume that increased team performance, measured by winning percent, has a causal effect on attendance, but increased attendance does not cause increased winning percent, then the model is recursive. The exception is contemporaneous correlation between the disturbances of the two equations. Theoretically we expect a positive correlation between the disturbances because omitted variables may affect winning percent and attendance in the same direction. However, our estimate of this correlation is negative and insignificant. We conclude that there is no need to use a simultaneous estimation method. The fact that our 3SLS estimates are very similar to the OLS estimates confirms this conclusion.

Canonical regression was used to estimate a joint production function model that allows inputs to be shared by the two outputs. The estimates of marginal elasticities from this model are quite different from the elasticities estimated by the OLS and 3SLS models, and, upon closer examination, we find some possible explanations of these differences. One drawback of the joint production function model for baseball production is that all inputs must be assumed to be used in the production of all outputs. This is not true in the case of baseball. In our model, we expect ticket price and population to affect attendance but not winning percent. When using a joint production function, all inputs must be included, but they cannot yield zero marginal elasticities for the output they are not expected to effect. In fact, for each input, the ratio of its marginal elasticity in the WP equation to its marginal elasticity in the ATT equation must be the same.

The joint production model implies that each input contributes in the same proportion to production of the two products. We can see this implication by considering the marginal elasticities from this model given in equations (12) and (13). Using these marginal elasticities we find that

$$\frac{ME(WP, X_k)}{ME(ATT, X_k)} = \frac{a_2}{a_1} \tag{17}$$

for all $k = 1, 2, \ldots, m$. This fixed relationship between the marginal elasticities means that it is not possible for one input to have a large impact on WP and a small impact on ATT while a different input has a large impact on ATT but a small impact on WP.

Table 7.4
Canonical Regression Results[a]

Variable	Parameter Estimate
Outputs	
Winning Percent	0.855
Attendance	0.247
Inputs	
Lagged Winning Percent	0.056 (0.096)
Slugging Percent	0.612** (0.077)
Stolen Bases	0.142** (0.071)
Earned Run Average	-0.675** (0.084)
Ticket Price	-0.069 (0.063)
Population	0.158** (0.077)
American League	0.043 (0.071)
ρ^*	0.869

[a] The parameter estimates were obtained using canonical correlation analysis assuming an extended Cobb-Douglas production function. All variables other than the league dummy were measured in logarithms. Standard errors, calculated by jackknifing, are reported in parentheses.
** Indicates statistical significance at the 0.05 level.

The fixed ratio of marginal elasticities for all inputs also occurs when using the translog production function to represent joint production.

In baseball production it is reasonable to assume that the inputs are not at all exhausted by production of either output. This implies that it is reasonable to use the entire amount of each relevant input in each production function separately rather than estimating a joint production function. If one is interested in effects of inputs on one of the products, such as winning percent, then it seems preferable to estimate an individual production function instead of using the marginal elasticities from a joint production function, given their peculiar restrictions.

Our research provides some insight on the choice of models for estimating baseball production functions. Keeping in mind the theoretical issues of causal relationships between outputs, sharing of inputs, and correlation between disturbances, we conclude that none of the more complicated estimation techniques is clearly superior to using OLS to estimate the separate equations for winning percent and attendance. We examined a causal model that is simultaneous only if disturbances are contemporaneously correlated and our empirical results do not support the simultaneity. Regarding our canonical regression joint production model, both theoretical and empirical considerations suggest the possibility of misleading estimates. We used GLS to correct the OLS model of winning percent for the baseball reality that average winning percent must always be 0.5. That correction requires the omission of one observation for each league each season, but the estimates are basically unchanged.

The existing baseball literature on production, winning percent, and attendance is mostly comprised of single-equation models that use OLS estimation techniques. Despite the theoretical and econometric problems that have often been raised in discussions among those who do research on the economics of baseball, our empirical results give these previous studies a relatively clean bill of health.

NOTES

1. See Porter and Scully (1982), Kahn (1982) and Ruggiero, Hadley, and Gustafson (1995) for examples of baseball production that use winning percent as the only output. Horowitz (1994) and Scully (1994) use the ratio wins to losses as the output measure.

2. Whether these two inputs capture all is debatable. In particular, slugging percent captures the hitter's batting average and power, but potentially ignores their ability to drive in runs. Also, team speed and fielding percent is ignored. The ratio of strikeouts to walks perhaps captures pitcher's control, but does not necessarily measure the ability of pitchers to prevent runners from scoring. Kahn (1993a) and Ruggiero, Hadley, and Gustafson (1995) provide a more complete list of inputs.

3. Horowitz (1994) invokes the so-called "Pythagoras Theorem" to evaluate the performance of managers. The underlying basis for the analysis is a production relationship. Horowitz uses the wins-losses ratio as output and the runs-opposition runs ratio as the input. In fact, both variables are proxies for winning percent.

4. In the literature on baseball attendance, existing models include performance (winning percent) as a determinant of attendance. In the context of these demand models, inclusion of winning percent as an exogenous variable is appropriate. See Coffin (1996) for a further discussion. In a production framework, both attendance and winning percent are endogenous and are jointly produced.

5. It should be pointed out that the parameter estimates obtained in the solution of the canonical regression are not unique. All parameters could be multiplied by a positive constant without affecting the canonical correlation. The elasticity measures, however, are unique.

8

Technological Change and Transition in the Winning Function for Major League Baseball

Thomas H. Bruggink

INTRODUCTION

Successful competitors acquire strategic resources ahead of their rivals. This behavior is most telling when the business environment changes. Major League Baseball (MLB) provides an opportunity to observe this response to change. With this research we will examine the golden age of baseball, from 1901 to 1940, when the playing style of baseball changed from emphasizing speed and defense to emphasizing power hitting. Changes in rules, stadium configurations, and the physical composition of the ball during these two eras had substantive effects on what it takes to win ball games. This study attempts to measure the changes in the team winning function due to policy changes that affect the technical aspects of the game.

In most industries, the lack of detailed data on different qualities of inputs limits the study of the adjustment to change. However, the statistics available in MLB allow a more complete specification of input-output relationship. Therefore the diffusion process can be unraveled.

Modern professional baseball began with the new century. After decades of short-lived leagues and high turnover of teams and players on those teams, the American and National Leagues emerged in 1901 to form the cartel that exists to this day. Prior to this time, the baseball rules and equipment underwent several transformations. By 1901, the major conditions of the game, such as the length between bases, the length of the pitcher's mound to home plate, number of strikes for an out, and so on, had been settled. Nonetheless, other aspects of the game remain dynamic. For example, as the second and third decades of modern baseball unfolded, several small but substantive opportunities for changes in the winning function occurred: (1) the liveliness of the ball,[1] (2) legal pitching practices,[2] (3) the distance from home plate to the outfield wall in each stadium.[3]

The golden age of baseball is divided into two eras—the deadball era and the lively ball era. In the first era, society's traditional beliefs in individualism, self-reliance, and competition were well-represented in the national pastime. A dirt-stained uniform was the medal awarded to aggressive base runners and fielders. The archetypical hero was Ty Cobb. He hit for high average but not for power, while stealing bases at unprecedented rates (with spikes up). The Georgia Peach said it best himself: "It's a struggle for supremacy, a survival of the fittest" (Ward, 1994).

What made this style successful? In part, the answer lies with the technology of the game. The ball lacked resiliency, but the balls were seldom replaced. As the innings wore on, the hitters were swinging at a softened, discolored ball. This favored pitchers, especially those with "trick" pitches (cut ball and spit ball). With pitchers having the upper hand, base running and fielding also became more important.

In an effort to draw back the fans from the World War I slump in attendance, the owners favored changes in rules and technical aspects that would create the same kind of excitement on the playing field that was generated by the Roaring Twenties culture. In this era people yearned for heroes that were capable of prodigious feats. The home run is the most heroic act in baseball. The mightier the home run, the greater the hero. Babe Ruth was the mightiest of them all: "I swing big, with everything I've got. I hit big or I miss big. I like to live as big as I can" (p. 170, Ward, 1994). Ruth's big bang playing style, made possible by the new rubber-center ball, was popular with the fans, who came back in droves.

HYPOTHESES

Power hitting displaced speed as the Babe Ruth era approached. Outlawing trick pitches (spit ball), a new baseball, and closer outfield stadium walls placed new weights on the old winning function. The 2–1 pitching duel turned into a 10–7 slugfest. The teams that acquired more of these power hitting inputs early on relative to others were more successful, just as those teams that acquired more speed relative to others were more successful in the Ty Cobb era. Early success by teams with these power hitters led to the widespread adoption of the new playing style, as hitters learned to be sluggers. Specific hypotheses are:

1. Due to rule and other technical changes in the winning function for baseball, we expect higher absolute levels for power hitting and lower levels for speed as we go from the Ty Cobb era to the Babe Ruth era.
2. Teams that acquire power inputs more quickly than others will be more successful as the winning function changes. After any change that favors power hitting, the coefficients for relative power should rise over time (in annual league production functions) and then stabilize as other teams catch up and team levels begin to converge to the average.
3. Given their fundamental importance, hitting for average and pitching should play approximately the same role in both eras in a winning function that measures relative inputs, even though the average values of these two inputs changed.

REVIEW OF LITERATURE

Winning functions first appeared in Scully's seminal work (1976) on the measurement of players' marginal revenue products. The first equation of his two-equation system was a winning function employing one variable for hitting and one for pitching. The functional form was additive. He also included variables for teams that are in contention or out of contention for league championships to reflect intensities of play. In the many subsequent studies on free agency, the post-Scully winning functions changed as the earned run average is substituted for the strikeout-to-walk ratio, and relative values replaced absolute levels. The hitting and pitching indices are calculated by dividing team values by the league averages [Cassing and Douglas (1980), Sommers and Quinton (1982), Raimondo (1983), Hill (1985), and Bruggink and Rose (1990)]. Although researchers differed on their choice of hitting and pitching factors, none included variables for speed, fielding, and managerial ability, nor did any attempt to separate power hitting from hitting for average.

Winning functions also appear outside the Scully methodology. In his study on customer discrimination in attendance, Irani (1996) estimated an additive winning function that included variables for speed and fielding in addition to the standard post-Scully specification.

In a similar vein, several studies have attempted to measure managerial quality, output elasticities, and technical efficiency in baseball using the Cobb-Douglas production function [Zech (1981), Porter and Scully (1982), Singell (1993), Kahn (1993), and Ruggiero, Hadley, and Gustafson (1995)]. Winning percent remains the dependent variable and the core predictor variables include slugging average, earned run average, stolen bases, and fielding average. This literature is dominated by the issues in specifying managerial input, and alternative approaches to estimating efficiency.[4]

EMPIRICAL MODEL

In this chapter I follow the post-Scully tradition for specifying the winning function, with two differences: (1) offense is separated into hitting for average and "isolated" power hitting (the essential difference between the two eras), and (2) variables for speed and fielding are included.

The technical relationship between team inputs and winning is measured by relative, not absolute, levels because a successful baseball team needs to acquire more hitting or pitching inputs *relative to its opponents*.[5] This performance relationship is measured by the following variables:

Dependent Variable
WIN_{it} = winning percentage[6] of team i in year t;
Explanatory Variables
$MAVG_{it}$ = team i batting percentage in year t divided by the league average (American or National League) the same year;
$MPOWER_{it}$ = team i slugging percentage minus batting percentage in year t divided by the league average the same year;
$MERA_{it}$ = team i earned run average in year t divided by the league average the same year;

$MSPEED_{it}$ = stolen bases plus triples for team i in year t divided by the league average the same year;

$MFIELD_{it}$ = team i fielding percentage in year t divided by the league average for the same year.

METHODOLOGY

This study will first identify the trends in the absolute changes in baseball inputs over time and then focus on changes in relative importance of these inputs.

1. The major league means and standard deviations for batting, power hitting, earned run average, speed, and fielding percentage will be measured annually from 1901 to 1940 to discern changes in the magnitudes of these inputs over time.
2. A performance relationship (called a production function in the economics of sports literature) for each era will be estimated. The Ty Cobb era (1901–1919) will be a pooled sample of sixteen teams each year for a total of 304 observations. This will be compared to an identical sample construction for the Babe Ruth era (1920–1940), consisting of 336 observations.
3. Within each era, a performance relationship for every overlapping five-year period will be estimated using the index values discussed above. A five-year moving average will be employed to smooth out year-to-year fluctuations. Therefore, fifteen samples of 80 observations will be generated for the Ty Cobb era (1901–1919), and seventeen samples of the same for the Babe Ruth era (1920–1940).

RESULTS

In going from the Ty Cobb era to the Babe Ruth era, the year-to-year means for power hitting, contact hitting, and fielding all increased while the mean for speed fell (see Figures 8.1– 8.3). As a consequence of the increased hitting, the means for the earned run average also rose.

In comparing the winning functions for the Ty Cobb and Babe Ruth eras, the index variables allow one to measure the impact on winning percentage for a team that has, for example, a 10% higher value than the league average. The coefficient for the power hitting index increased from 0.0948 to 0.1572 while the coefficient for speed fell from 0.0545 to 0.02122. The coefficients for frequency hitting and pitching remained essentially the same for the two eras (0.7029 versus 0.7022 for hitting and -0.3937 versus -0.4184 for pitching). Even though the absolute levels for hitting and pitching changed, the quality of being 10% better than average had the same impact on winning.

Ty Cobb Era 1901–1919

$$WINNING = -1.44 + 0.70 \text{ MAVG} + 0.095 \text{ MPOWER} - 0.39 \text{ MERA} \qquad (1)$$

$$\text{(t-ratios)} \quad (9.04) \qquad (3.97) \qquad\qquad (-20.4)$$

$$+ 0.055 \text{ MSPEED} + 1.48 \text{ MFIELD}$$

$$(3.32) \qquad\qquad (3.06)$$

R-squared = 0.797   Adjusted R-squared = 0.793   F = 233.7

Babe Ruth Era 1929–1940

WINNING = -3.52 + 0.70 MAVG + 0.157 MPOWER -0.42 MERA   (2)
(t-ratios)   (13.0)   (11.7)   (-25.5)
          + 0.021 MSPEED + 3.55 MFIELD
          (2.54)   (7.32)
R-squared = 0.887   Adjusted R-squared = 0.886 F = 520.0

Figure 8.1
Year-to-Year Means for Batting Average
and Power Percentage

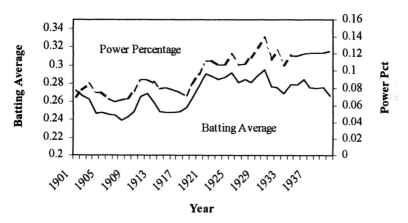

Figure 8.2
Year-to-Year Means for ERA and Fielding Percentage

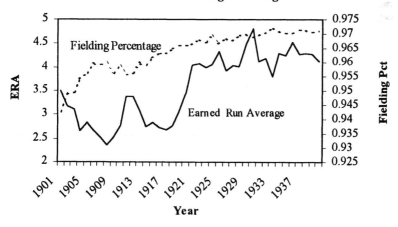

Figure 8.3
Year-to-Year Means for the Speed Variable

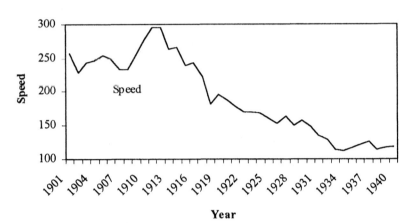

The coefficient for fielding percentage greatly increased although it was expected that fielding would become less of an impact factor as all teams approached mastery. This result is suspect, however, due to the high covariance between its coefficient and the coefficient of the intercept term. During the same time the intercept term moved in the opposite direction.

The change in the two winning functions did not take place instantaneously. To see the transition, regression equations were estimated based on overlapping five-year time periods (see Figures 8.4– 8.8). The results for the coefficients based on the five-year moving averages show that the coefficients for speed and power change dramatically during the Ty Cobb era and eventually stabilize in the Babe Ruth era at new levels. The coefficients for batting average rise but less dramatically than power hitting. Of course the coefficients for pitching go in the opposite direction and then stabilize.

If we consider the five-year moving averages as samples, the t-statistics for the regression coefficients can be used to make additional conclusions: (1) the speed coefficient ceases to be statistically significant in the sample centered on the year 1913,[7] (2) the power coefficient begins to be statistically significant in the sample centered on year 1906, and (3) all other coefficients, except the ones for fielding, are statistically significant for all estimates in both eras.

CONCLUSIONS
Policy changes in some of the technical aspects of baseball during the early days have resulted in changes in the performance relationship for winning. This study provides numerical content to those changes. Power hitting displaced speed as

baseball moved from the Ty Cobb era to the Babe Ruth era. The emphasis on power hitting began earlier than most observers acknowledge; substantive changes in the winning function were noted halfway through the first era. The typical pattern for the coefficients of power hitting and speed over time is the following: winning was more and more impacted by relative changes in team power hitting and less impacted by relative changes in team speed as the Ty Cobb era unfolded. Then the coefficients of these inputs stabilized at new levels throughout the Babe Ruth era. The methodology employed here also revealed another interesting result: even though absolute levels for frequency hitting and pitching changed between the two periods, the relative role played by each input remained the same. In other words, if a team had a batting average 10% higher than the rest of the league in a given year, the impact on the winning percent for that team was identical in both eras.

Figure 8.4
Regression Coefficients for the Batting Index in the
Five-Year Moving Average Winning Function

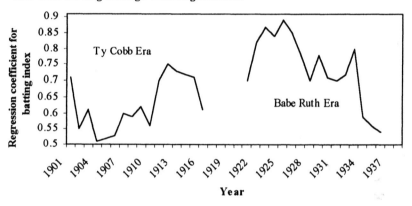

Baseball owners and officials that contemplate changing the rules or technical aspects of the game (e.g., using aluminum bats in place of wood, or changing the size of the strike zone) can anticipate measurable differences in the style of play. Whether the desired outcomes match the measured outcomes is another issue worthy of study.

Future research in this area can estimate changes in the winning functions in other baseball eras. The influx of African American and Latin American players provides another example of the diffusion of change that is potentially as significant as any rule or equipment change. A more recent example is the difference in playing style between the National and American Leagues due to variations in the designated hitter rule and umpire interpretation of the strike zone.

Figure 8.5
Regression Coefficients for the Power Index in the Five-Year
Moving Average Winning Function

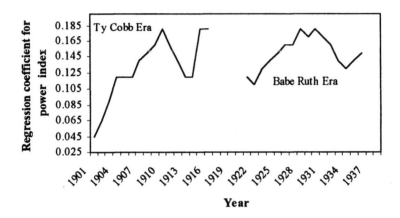

Figure 8.6
Regression Coefficients for the Pitching Index in the
Five-Year Moving Average Winning Function

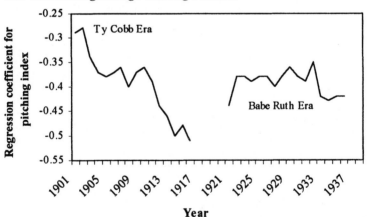

Figure 8.7
Regression Coefficients for the Fielding Index in the
Five-Year Moving Average Winning Function

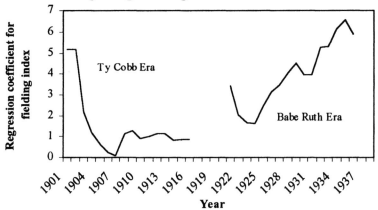

Figure 8.8
Regression Coefficients for the Speed Index in the
Five-Year Moving Average Winning Function

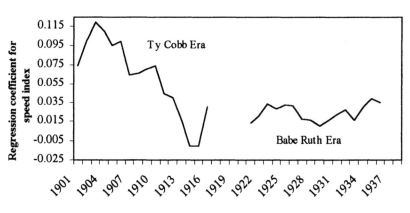

NOTES

Special recognition goes to Jason Desser and Sebastian Crapanzano, who provided crucial assistance in the early stages of this chapter. Their contributions are greatly appreciated. I also thank James Eaton, Larry Hadley, Scott Feuss, Dan Rascher, and Nellie Fox for their helpful comments.

1. In 1911, cork replaced wood in the center in baseball, and in 1920 rubber replaced cork.

2. Starting in 1920 new balls were required at the start of each game and were not allowed to be discolored by rubbing in the dirt, etc. The same year outlawed the spitball and other trick pitches (a special roster of spitball pitcher allowed to finish their careers).

3. The following three stadiums provide examples of how the home run distance changes over time:

Fenway Park		Tiger Stadium		Braves Field	
324 feet	(1921)	345 feet	(1921)	403 feet	(1915)
320	(1926)	340	(1926)	404	(1922)
318	(1931)	339	(1930)	320	(April 1928)
312	(1934)	367	(1931)	354	(July 1928)
315	(1935)	339	(1934)	340	(1930)
		340	(1938)	354	(1931)
		324	(1939)	359	(1933)
				354	(1934)
				368	(1936)
				350	(1940)

Source: Total Baseball (1996).

4. See pages 191–92 in Ruggiero, Hadley, and Gustafson (1995) for a review of the literature on these topics.

5. A sports league is a closed system in which one team's success can only increase at the expense of another tema. Thus when one team's output (winning percentage) goes up sharply, one or more teams winning percentage must fall, even if the absolute level of inputs (batting average, etc.) improves. This is why relative measures are used in this paper. As such it may not be appropriate to label the winning equation as a "production function," although this is the practice in the literature.

6. Winning percent is stated as a proportion, the common practice in the media and record books. It should be noted that since the league average for winning percent is always 0.500, the stated winning percentages already reflect relative performance.

7. The speed coefficient is briefly significant statistically for the samples centered on years 1926–1928.

9

Streak Management

Rodney Fort and Robert Rosenman

INTRODUCTION

We are interested in how resources are allocated in the presence of perceived streaks in professional sports. Other works have searched for streak-related inefficiencies in sports betting markets,[1] but we look directly at daily game outcomes in Major League Baseball (MLB) over the 1989 and 1990 seasons. We find that team winning and losing streaks are, by and large, random occurrences. However, there is evidence that *some* managers may be better than others at extending winning streaks and ending losing streaks (holding win percentage constant, as detailed below) or what we refer to as "streak management." In addition, we find that winning streaks increase attendance while losing streaks negatively impact the gate for baseball teams.

This leads us to wonder whether or not managers might have an incentive to portray themselves as streak managers and allocate talent inefficiently. That *some* managers, namely, successful streak managers, allocate talent differently than other managers can be consistent with efficient resource use, given our results. However, if *all* managers act as if they are successful streak managers, there is the potential for misallocation. Our only evidence that this may be occurring is from managerial efficiency analysis. We find that streaks are not managed according to the quality of a given manager's team; streak management strategies that are on net valuable to a winning team may be devastating to a losing team, but some managers practice them regardless of winning record.

We offer no explanation of how some managers may be able to manage streaks. But the scenario that is consistent with our findings is as follows. A given manager sets the pitching rotation and rest intervals for fielders, yielding daily lineups that maximize owner profits. Effective streak management involves a plan that results in wins that occur in streaks (or quickly ended losing streaks). Of course, the costs that must enter into the streak management decision concern how changes in pitching rotations, use of relief pitchers, and reduced rest periods for regular players effect performance throughout the rest of the season. If another manager is not an effective streak manager, then altering the pitching rotation to end a losing streak will reduce that rotation's effectiveness for no reason. If the streak was really just a random occurrence, then the best pitchers were overutilized to end the streak. Even though we provide no model, it is this decision-making process that can be reasonably termed "streak management."

THE RANDOM NATURE OF STREAKS

We define a winning streak as successive wins and a losing streak as successive losses. We investigate the randomness of streaks with runs tests and spectral analysis. For runs tests, the expected number of streaks is

$$\frac{2n_1 n_2}{n_1 + n_2} + 1, \tag{1}$$

where n_1 is the number of wins and n_2 is the number of losses (Freund, 1971). The test statistic is the difference between the calculated mean number of streaks and the actual number of streaks, divided by the standard deviation. This ratio conforms to the student t distribution. Since the mean depends on team performance, a look at each team in each year is dictated; we make no assumption that teams with different observed win percentages conform to the same distribution of streaks.[2]

It is important to note that the runs test detects successive wins or losses that are *different than a team's win percentage would indicate*. Thus, if a team is playing 0.333 ball, a streak pattern of WLLWLLWLL . . . will not be detected by the runs tests just described. But this also means that team performance is controlled for in the analysis of streaks, an important control that we attempt to maintain throughout the chapter. Thus, using the runs test, we look for streaks that differ from what the team's win percentage would lead us to expect.

Table 9.1 shows the results of runs tests. At the usual 5% level of significance, streaks are non-random for San Francisco in 1990. At the 10% level of significance, California and Oakland in 1989 and Pittsburgh in 1990 can be added to the list of teams with significantly non-random streaks. The conclusion appears to be as follows. By and large, streaks are random; across the entire sample, randomness seldom is rejected. But there is evidence that winning streaks are extended and losing streaks are ended in a non-random way for some managers.

Turning to spectral estimates of streak frequency requires formulation of cumulative periodograms (Durbin, 1969).[3] Table 9.2 shows the results. Again, at the 5% level of significance, random streaks are rejected for California and Detroit in 1989 and for the New York Yankees, Oakland, New York Mets and Pittsburgh in 1990. At the 10% level, Minnesota and Los Angeles in 1989 and Cleveland, Seattle, San Francisco, and St. Louis in 1990 would be added to the list of teams with non-random streaks. The conclusion is similar to the one for runs testing: by and large, streaks are random, but some managers may be streak managers. Table 9.3 summarizes the results of runs and spectral analysis and brings other team descriptives together for the analysis that follows.

Table 9.1
Runs Tests for Streaks

	Calculated Runs Test Statistic[a]	
Team	1989	1990
American League		
Baltimore	0.546	0.895
Boston	−0.939	0.603
California	−1.723	0.323
Cleveland	0.023	0.333
Chicago	−1.307	−1.119
Detroit	−1.026	0.566
Kansas City	0.079	−1.481
Milwaukee	−0.158	−0.314
Minnesota	−1.417	−0.973
New York	0.481	−1.506
Oakland	1.825	0.091
Seattle	0.763	1.631
Texas	0.008	0.080
Toronto	0.763	−0.857
National League		
Atlanta	0.600	−0.742
Chicago	−0.842	−0.917
Cincinnati	−0.564	−0.443
Houston	−0.426	−1.039
Los Angeles	1.130	1.388
Montreal	−0.631	−0.225
New York	−0.722	−0.519
Philadelphia	0.718	0.347
Pittsburgh	−1.016	−1.942
San Diego	−0.670	−0.925
San Francisco	0.240	−2.023
St. Louis	1.465	1.525

[a] Approximate two-tail critical value (level of significance): 1.645 (10%), 1.960 (5%), 2.576 (1%).

Table 9.2
Cumulative Periodogram Analysis for Streaks

Team	Maximum Deviation from White Noise[a]	
	1989	1990
American League		
Baltimore	0.0779	0.0938
Boston	0.0776	0.0662
California	0.1503	0.0512
Cleveland	0.0608	0.1183
Chicago	0.0989	0.0920
Detroit	0.1607	0.0677
Kansas City	0.0574	0.0941
Milwaukee	0.0694	0.0763
Minnesota	0.1090	0.0935
New York	0.0657	0.1595
Oakland	0.0859	0.1337
Seattle	0.0686	0.1172
Texas	0.0621	0.0607
Toronto	0.0954	0.0558
National League		
Atlanta	0.0648	0.0845
Chicago	0.1012	0.0856
Cincinnati	0.0828	0.0708
Houston	0.0629	0.0785
Los Angeles	0.1079	0.0989
Montreal	0.0578	0.0529
New York	0.0765	0.1344
Philadelphia	0.0623	0.0638
Pittsburgh	0.1059	0.1589
San Diego	0.0881	0.0865
San Francisco	0.0424	0.1096
St. Louis	0.0699	0.1168

[a]Approximate two-tail critical values (levels of significance): 0.1078 (10%), 0.1202 (5%), 0.1441 (1%).

Table 9.3
Non-Random Streaks and Win Percentages
(Summary from Both Runs and Periodogram Tests)

				Streaks	
Team	Win %	Finish	Relative Efficiency*	Longest (W,L)	Ave. Win Streak (Std.Dev.)
1989					
Cal.**	0.562	Third	+0.188	+7, -7	2.71 (1.71)
Det.**	0.364	Last	+0.085	+7, -12	1.69 (1.21)
LA*	0.481	Fourth	-0.105	+5, -5	1.75 (0.96)
Min.*	0.494	Fifth	+0.117	+6, -8	2.26 (1.48)
Oak.*	0.611	First	-0.122	+7, -4	2.13 (1.29)
1990					
Clev.*	0.580	Second	-0.079	+6, -5	1.83 (1.15)
Mets*	0.562	Second	-0.001	+11, -5	2.45 (2.27)
Yanks**	0.414	Last	+0.144	+6, -8	1.89 (1.21)
Oak.**	0.636	First	+0.014	+7, -4	2.78 (1.51)
Pit.**	0.586	First	+0.132	+7, -6	2.85 (2.00)
SF**	0.525	Third	+0.088	+9, -6	2.50 (2.06)
Seat.*	0.475	Fifth	-0.145	+5, -5	1.65 (0.91)
StL.*	0.432	Last	-0.135	+4, -7	1.56 (0.80)

*Calculated as ln(actual average streak length)–ln(predicted streak length); positive numbers indicate above average efficiency while negative numbers indicate below average efficiency. *Significant at the 10% level. **Significant at the 5% level.

STREAK MANAGEMENT AND MANAGERIAL EFFICIENCY

Our primary interest is the behavior of managers toward streaks. If there are no streaks but managers act as if there are, then resource misallocation follows. Here, we examine the relationship between managerial efficiency and streak management in order to see if effective managers also manage streaks. We use ideas from Porter and Scully (1982) and Scully (1989) to examine the relative efficiency of managers identified in Table 9.3. The idea is to regress average streak length on number of wins (both measured in logarithms). This regression provides an estimate of the overall league efficiency in transforming wins into win streak length. We then compare the subset of managers in Table 9.3 to the league predictions. The results for 1989 and 1990 are as follows, with standard errors in parentheses (all coefficients were significant at the 5% level):

1989: ln(average streak) = −3.052 + .856 ln(wins),
                           (.079)   (.124)
Observations = 26, R^2 = 0.664,

$$(2)$$

1990: ln(average streak) = −4.146 + 1.106 ln(wins),
                           (.088)   (.153)
Observations = 26, R^2 = 0.685.

A one-tailed test failed to reject that the coefficients on ln(wins) are equal to one in each regression (5% significance level), implying that league-wide streak averages are unit elastic with respect to wins. Overall, a 1% increase in wins increases the average win streak length by about 1%.

Comparing among managers, above average managerial efficiency is indicated when actual streak lengths exceed the streak length predicted from the regression; below average managers will have actual streak lengths below their model prediction. Recalling that Table 9.3 only includes managers with non-random streaks, relative managerial efficiency is shown only for streak managers. For differences significant at the 5% level, all streak managers are above average in terms of their managerial efficiency.

Another comparison in Table 9.3 reveals that the value of transforming wins into streaks varies (1) for teams with different win percentages holding streak length constant and (2) for teams with different streak lengths holding win percentage constant. To see this, suppose the expected streak length is 1.5 for each of two teams, one playing 0.667 ball and the other playing 0.333 ball (the former streak might be WWLWWL . . . , while the latter streak might be WLLWLL . . .). But our results show that the 0.667 team has longer streaks than the 0.333 team, on average! Whether winning causes non-random streaks, or vice versa, remains unresolved but a potential implication is that the probability of streaks being non-random is greater for really good and really bad teams. As a result, better teams do better winning in streaks while bad teams do worse losing in streaks. Better teams should strive to put their wins together in streaks while worse teams should spread their wins out.

Given this outcome, the relative efficiency coefficients should be positive for winning teams and negative for losing teams. But in 1989 and 1990, managers of Detroit, Minnesota, and the New York Yankees, poor teams all, did not manage their streaks in accord with the quality of their team. Streaks were too long for these poor teams. From this perspective, the propensity for Yankees owner George Steinbrenner to fire managers is well-founded and the question becomes just why Tigers owner Mike Ilitch (and his predecessors) kept Sparky Anderson around for so long. Anderson appears to have done well with a good team (the Cincinnati Reds of the 1970s and the early 1980s Tigers), but his management technique resulted in streak lengths detrimental to the final win percentage of poorer Tigers teams.

Thus, it appears that streak managers are above average in terms of managerial efficiency. However, a few streak managers for poorer teams had streaks that were too long. We wonder why, and extend our curiosity to the possibility that even managers that are not streak managers may try to behave as if they were! If there is an incentive to try, or act as if you can manage streaks, even though you can't, then there is an additional reason to suspect a misallocation of talent during the season. We show in the next section that there may well be such an incentive to try to be a streak manager.

STREAKS AND ATTENDANCE

If fans enjoy streaks, then the profit-maximizing owners and the managers they hire find them a valuable occurrence as well. In all models of attendance, fans are attracted to games by increased chances that the home team will win and the chance to see a close contest, while the rest of fan demand follows the usual development including prices, income, and other tastes and preferences (Noll, 1974; Thomas and Jolson, 1979; Siegfried and Eisenberg, 1980; Drever and McDonald, 1981; Becker and Suls, 1983; Schofield, 1983; Medoff, 1986). We extend this past development to include the potential for streaks to effect the chances that fans will attend:

$$A = A(P, S, I; T), \tag{3}$$

where A = attendance (0 = no, 1= yes), P = price of a game, S = substitute entertainment alternatives, and I = income. The vector T covers "taste" variables, like home team favoritism, on-field competitiveness, and streaks.

The following description of the variables used in the empirical analysis follows the structure summarized in Table 9.4, where descriptive statistics also are listed. Absent observations at the individual level, daily attendance is measured as the historical odds of attending a game. Taking attendance to be logarithmically distributed, the logarithm of the ratio of attendance to stadium capacity shows the aggregate odds that a given fan can attend; the numerator shows that they did, while the denominator controls for the chances that they could. This logit is estimated by OLS, using White's correction for heteroscedasticity.

Turning to the independent variables, price must measure both ticket price and opportunity costs, so we include whether or not the game occurred on a weekend versus a weekday. Substitutes and scale effects can be captured by population. Including an income measure will determine whether baseball attendance is a normal or inferior good.

In the "tastes" vector, we dummy whether or not the game is against a divisional rival. Comparative win percentages between the two teams on any given day are used to capture preferences for both close contests and home-team chances. Finally, it can be expected that fans prefer new stadiums as measured by stadium age.

Streak lengths of the two teams are added to the "taste" vector as the model extension of interest here. Consistent with our previous treatment, streaks are entered as successive wins or losses on the day that a game is played. Since we are looking at team streaks, each team's season-long set of streaks is taken as a draw from that team's streak distribution. Thus, if we observe team i, with a four game winning streak, playing team j with a three game losing streak, we take this to be one observation of a winning streak for team i and one observation of a losing streak for team j.[4]

Other controls are included. East versus west rivalry, stadium capacity, the month that a game is played (to control for games that are closer to the pennant race and playoffs), whether the observation is a double-header, and any potentially unspecified visiting team appeal, might be expected to matter in a demand analysis.

The results are in Table 9.5 (American League, AL) and Table 9.6 (National League, NL). Nearly all of the results are as expected. Ticket price effects are negative

Table 9.4
Attendance Regression Data

Variables	Description	NL Mean (S.D.) 1989	1990	AL Mean (S.D.) 1989	1990
Dependent Variable Base[a]					
ATTEND	Game Attendance.	26,510 (11,804)	26,036 (11,673)	27,677 (18,615)	27,333 (11,575)
Price					
PRICE	Lowest non-specialty price.	$4.46 ($0.69)	$4.46 ($0.69)	$4.14 ($0.79)	$4.15 ($0.79)
FRI	1 if Friday game, 0 else.	0.159 (0.366)	0.150 (0.357)	0.161 (0.368)	0.163 (0.369)
WKEND	1 if weekend game, 0 else.	0.319 (0.466)	0.315 (0.465)	0.322 (0.467)	0.310 (0.463)
Substitutes					
POP	SMSA population (millions reported here).	6.04 (4.98)	6.00 (4.94)	5.44 (4.74)	5.49 (4.79)
Income					
INCOME	SMSA Mean Per-Capita Income.	$19,913 ($2,782)	$19,904 ($2,779)	$20,615 ($1,815)	$20,626 (1,804)
Tastes					
DIVISION	1 if divisional opponent, 0 else.	0.495 (0.500)	0.561 (0.497)	0.473 (0.499)	0.472 (0.499)
HWIN	Home team's current win streak (0 if losing streak).	1.02 (1.32)	1.16 (1.59)	1.07 (1.40)	1.07 (1.46)

Variable	Description				
HLOSE	Home team's current losing streak (0 if winning streak).	0.975 (1.57)	0.930 (1.41)	0.916 (1.45)	0.959 (1.42)
HWIN%	Home team Winning Percent.	0.498 (0.095)	0.497 (0.114)	0.492 (0.112)	0.505 (0.108)
VWIN	Visiting team's current win streak (0 if losing streak).	0.908 (1.34)	0.936 (1.40)	0.948 (1.44)	0.916 (1.28)
VLOSE	Visiting team's current losing streak (0 if winning streak).	1.08 (1.43)	1.08 (1.39)	1.16 (1.60)	1.04 (1.45)
VWIN%	Visiting team Winning Percent.	0.494 (0.093)	0.501 (0.114)	0.497 (0.113)	0.498 (0.107)
CLOSE	$(HWIN\% - VWIN\%)^2$.	0.020 (0.093)	0.028 (0.096)	0.028 (0.098)	0.027 (0.101)
AGE	Stadium Age in years.	19.0 (7.11)	19.0 (7.04)	23.5 (19.7)	23.4 (19.6)
Other Controls					
HEAST	1 if Home team is in the Eastern Division, 0 else.	0.502 (.500)	0.502 (0.500)	0.502 (0.500)	0.498 (0.500)
CAPACITY	Stadium Capacity.	53,944 (6,412)	54,013 (6,421)	52,082 (9,783)	52,050 (9,731)
"MONTH"	1 if game is in MONTH (e.g., APR, MAY), 0 else.	b	b	b	b
DBH	1 if double header, 0 else.	0.020 (0.140)	0.027 (0.163)	0.022 (0.146)	0.037 (0.188)
"TEAM"	1 if opponent is TEAM (e.g., SF, LA), 0 else.	c	c	c	c

[a] The dependent variable in the regressions is transformed to a logit, as described in the text.
[b] About 14.7% in April to 17.5% in August.
[c] On average, each team plays each other team between 8% and 9% of the time.

(but in an interesting way in the AL). As the opportunity cost of time falls, chances of attendance increase (Friday and weekends). Chances of attendance rise with population; apparently, scale effects outweigh the larger substitution variety in larger cities. Baseball attendance is an inferior good in the AL (Noll, 1974, found this, as well) but not in the NL. In fact, for the NL attendance is a normal good in 1990. Whether or not play against a division opponent effects attendance chances appears to depend on the season. People usually like to see home teams that are winners and visiting teams that are less successful. The evidence on games between evenly matched teams is mixed, but a game against a more evenly matched division opponent decreases the chances of attendance (an unexpected outcome). Fans do not like old stadiums. Playing at home in the east increases chances of attendance. Attendance chances are inelastic with respect to stadium capacity. Attendance usually picks up as the season progresses. There is evidence for one year that double-headers increase the chance of attendance. Finally, some teams definitely are a visiting draw (Boston and Oakland, compared to Toronto, in the AL, and Chicago, Cincinnati, Los Angeles, New York, Pittsburgh, and San Francisco, relative to Atlanta, in the NL).

The punch-line for this chapter concerns the impacts that streaks have upon attendance chances. Winning streaks for both the home and visiting teams, when they matter, almost always increase the chance of attendance. The only exception is in the NL, 1989, where home winning streaks do not matter but visiting team win streaks lower attendance. Losing streaks do not matter as often as winning streaks, but there is evidence that they decrease the chance of attendance regardless of whether the home or visiting team has hit the skids.

These results imply that streak management is valuable. Fans are more (less) likely to attend when their team is on a roll (has hit the skids) and gate revenues can be increased through effective streak management. The goal is clear. Win in streaks at home. If losing streaks occur, see to it that they occur while your team is on the road and try to end any losing streak at home.

In addition to the resource misallocation that follows when streaks are too long for streak managers of poor teams (found in the previous section), we speculate that the misallocation during the season may be even worse. The setting seems ripe for a lemons problem. First, it is difficult to determine whether or not a manager is a streak manager just by observing their behavior. Second, especially since even some streak managers run streaks too long for poor teams, it is easy for any other manager to claim responsibility for streaks that do occur and blame the cruel world of "bad breaks" for any unhappy outcomes. This seems especially problematic in pro sports, where every contest is "a game of inches" and wins and losses can turn on twists of fate. To the extent that streaks pay and no market mechanism protects owners, we suspect that any manager can claim to be a streak manager and misallocate talent on their team during the season.

CONCLUSIONS

In MLB, by and large, streaks are random, but some managers appear to be "streak managers." While we have not established how or why a given manager is a streak

Table 9.5
Attendance Estimation (American League)
Dependent Variable: ln (ATTEND/CAPACITY)

Variable	1989	1990	Variable	1989	1990
Price	8.958* (1.815)	14.135* (1.826)	*Tastes continued*		
PRICE	-1.874* (0.596)	-2.997* (0.611)	DIVISION x HWIN%	-0.300 (0.535)	2.077* (0.658)
PRICE²	0.239* (0.070)	0.368* (0.073)	VWIN	0.055* (0.026)	0.012 (0.027)
FRI	0.669* (0.079)	0.578* (0.082)	VLOSE	-0.032 (0.023)	-0.044 (0.024)
WKEND	0.852* (0.062)	0.829* (0.065)	VWIN%	-0.604 (0.044)	-2.846* (0.467)
Substitutes			CLOSE	-1.371* (0.527)	2.052* (0.895)
POP	1.920E-8* (1.000E-8)	4.987E-8* (1.00E-8)	DIVISION x CLOSE	0.404 (0.692)	-3.436* (1.183)
Income			AGE	-0.028* (0.002)	-0.022* (0.002)
INCOME	-1.380E-4* (0.374E-4)	-1.910E-4 (0.379E-4)	*Other Controls*		
Tastes			HEAST	0.791* (0.077)	0.777* (0.077)
DIVISION	0.491 (0.412)	-2.016* (0.459)	CAPACITY	-6.224E-5* (0.372E-5)	-7.709E-5* (0.434E-5)
HWIN	0.055* (0.026)	0.016 (0.026)	APR	-0.162 (0.370)	-0.009 (0.243)
HLOSE	-0.016 (0.024)	-0.007 (0.025)	MAY	-0.213 (0.366)	0.267 (0.234)
HWIN%	1.578* (0.379)	1.097* (0.440)	JUNE	0.248 (0.366)	0.616* (0.234)

Table 9.5 continued

Variable	1989	1990	Variable	1989	1990
Other Controls continued			*Other Controls continued*		
JULY	0.474 (0.365)	0.835* (0.234)	Kansas City	0.150 (0.149)	-0.125 (0.158)
AUG	0.523 (0.366)	0.639* (0.233)	Milwaukee	0.196 (0.143)	0.063 (0.148)
SEPT	-0.217 (0.366)	0.166 (0.233)	Minnesota	-0.045 (0.146)	-0.075 (0.157)
DBH	0.147 (0.179)	0.231 (0.162)	New York	0.564* (0.143)	0.129 (0.167)
Baltimore	0.036 (0.148)	-0.101 (0.156)	Oakland	0.559* (0.155)	1.027* (0.159)
Boston	0.461* (0.141)	0.494* (0.145)	Seattle	-0.069 (0.148)	0.059 (0.156)
California	0.108 (0.161)	-0.063 (0.161)	Texas	0.136 (0.150)	-0.187 (0.153)
Chicago	-0.076 (0.148)	0.224 (0.152)	R^2	0.628	0.592
Cleveland	-0.045 (0.148)	-0.281 (0.155)	Adj. R^2	0.614	0.576
Detroit	-0.027 (0.150)	0.001 (0.159)	#Obs.	1068	1089

Standard errors are in parentheses.
*Significant at the 5% level.

Table 9.6
Attendance Estimation (National League)
Dependent Variable: ln (ATTEND/CAPACITY)

Variable	1989	1990	Variable	1989	1990
Constant	-0.236	4.687*	_Tastes continued_		
	(1.122)	(0.619)			
Price			VLOSE	-0.051*	-0.015
				(0.023)	(0.022)
PRICE	-0.389*	-1.301*	VWIN%	2.406*	-1.388*
	(0.170)	(0.111)		(0.799)	(0.514)
FRI	0.477*	0.419*	DIVISION	-3.329*	1.600*
	(0.067)	(0.070)	x VWIN%	(0.853)	(0.493)
WKEND	0.946*	0.781*	CLOSE	1.242	-2.544
	(0.055)	(0.054)		(1.328)	(1.410)
Substitutes			DIVISION	-3.912*	0.712
			x CLOSE	(1.785)	(1.416)
POP	1.530E-7*	2.140E-7*	AGE	-0.062*	-0.026*
	(0.200E-7)	(0.100E-7)		(0.007)	(0.005)
Income			_Other Controls_		
INCOME	-1.720E-5	9.667E-5*	HEAST	-0.133	0.521*
	(2.148E-5)	(1.542E-5)		(0.086)	(0.066)
Tastes			CAPACITY	-3.629E-5*	-5.712E-5*
				(1.184E-5)	(0.673E-5)
DIVISION	3.242*	-1.362*	APR	0.433	0.674*
	(0.592)	(0.341)		(0.384)	(0.192)
HWIN	-0.021	0.046*	MAY	0.685	0.697*
	(0.026)	(0.018)		(0.378)	(0.192)
HLOSE	0.009	-0.044*	JUNE	0.796*	0.910*
	(0.021)	(0.021)		(0.383)	(0.182)
HWIN%	4.630*	0.708*	JULY	1.046*	1.100*
	(0.786)	(0.368)		(0.381)	(0.186)
DIVISION	-3.340*	1.639*	AUG	0.872*	0.995*
x HWIN%	(0.897)	(0.448)		(0.381)	(0.185)

Table 9.6 continued

Variable	1989	1990	Variable	1989	1990
Other Controls continued			*Other Controls continued*		
SEPT	0.246	0.233	Philadelphia	0.003	0.159
	(0.379)	(0.184)		(0.147)	(0.126)
DBH	0.010	0.316*	Pittsburgh	-0.078	0.383*
	(0.170)	(0.151)		(0.129)	(0.145)
Chicago	0.361*	0.355*	San Diego	0.686*	0.100
	(0.135)	(0.123)		(0.141)	(0.121)
Cincinnati	0.504*	0.765*	San	-0.015	0.456*
	(0.138)	(0.162)	Francisco	(0.123)	(0.124)
Houston	0.422*	0.041	St. Louis	0.091	0.089
	(0.138)	(0.119)		(0.141)	(0.119)
Los	0.518*	0.464*	R^2	0.604	0.573
Angeles	(0.117)	(0.134)			
Montreal	0.102	0.142	Adj. R^2	0.586	0.556
	(0.151)	(0.134)			
New York	0.739*	0.747*	#Obs.	854	953
	(0.152)	(0.138)			

Standard errors are in parentheses.
*Significant at the 5% level.

manager, such managers are above average in terms of managerial efficiency. But, sometimes, streak managers for poor teams allow streaks that are too long. Thus, it appears that streak managers can misallocate a team's talent during a season.

But there is reason to believe that talent misallocation can be even worse than the mistakes of streak managers would generate. Incentives for a manager to behave like a streak manager, even though he is not one, also will be detrimental to the use of a team's talent during the season. We find that fans respond to streaks in statistically significant, predictable ways. Revenues can be expected to rise during winning streaks and fall during losing streaks so that streak managers can raise the value of play on the field. But the usual lemons logic may lead those who are not streak managers to portray themselves as such to the detriment of efficient talent allocation within a season.

There may even be another complicating factor. Especially in sports, individuals often over-rate their chances in the face of overwhelming odds. If those without the knack for streak management convince themselves otherwise, then resources may be wasted in the vain pursuit of the returns to streak management for which only a very few managers have demonstrated talent.

NOTES

The work here is better than it would have been thanks to comments by Andrew Gill, Elizabeth Gustafson, Wayne Joerding, Tong Li, and James Quirk. We acknowledge the able research assistance of Jennifer Schultz.

1. Finding that streaks are random in professional basketball and football, past works seek to determine whether participants in sports betting markets treat streaks as random. The empirical evidence is mixed. Camerer (1989) finds no evidence of betting market belief in the so-called "hot hand" phenomenon in professional basketball. However, Brown and Sauer (1993) disagree and Badarinathi and Kochman (1994) find that betting against the hot hand in professional football is profitable. Essentially, streaks effect betting markets but it remains to be seen whether steals effect score differences.

2. If there had been managerial changes during a given year, an argument could be made that wins and losses should be observed across managers, rather than teams. However, there only were four changes in each of 1989 and 1990. None of the changes in 1989 involved teams where non-random streaks were detected at the 5% level. In 1990, the Yankees had a change of managers and non-random streaks. But Stump Merrill managed 113 of their games (70%) to Bucky Dent's 49 (30%); we attribute the outcome to Merrill.

3. It is entirely possible that we are understating the ability to manage streaks. Suppose that a team with a +3 streak meets a team with a +4 streak. The +3 team wins, but the other team (after its loss) proceeds to win two more games. Isn't this really a +6 streak, interrupted by having run into a better streak manager? The time required in order to define streaks in this way proved prohibitive, especially since evidence of non-randomness seems so apparent.

4. Camerer (1989) includes the longest of the streaks in a given game as the observation; if team i is +6 while team j is -3, the observation is a win streak of +6. "To use the same observation as evidence for streaks of +6 and -3 would cause statistical dependence across streak categories" (p. 1258). The dependence claim is obvious (one team's win is another team's loss) if looking across all teams at streaks. However, we examine a given team's streak history, so that such dependence is beside the point. Brown and Sauer (1993) define a streak as a run of games where the team beat the spread or a run where the team failed to beat the spread. Their streak variable measures whether the home team is on a short (2-3) or long (4+) streak and, similarly, for the visitor.

10

Trading Players in the National Basketball Association: For Better or Worse?

David J. Berri and Stacey L. Brook

INTRODUCTION

Neoclassical theory assumes that a firm's personnel decisions are made on the basis of maximizing behavior. Firms decide to add or subtract a worker by comparing the worker's wage with the worker's marginal revenue product (MRP). However, for most industries, empirical tests of this hypothesis are difficult because data on worker productivity are scarce.

In contrast, economists have demonstrated that MRP estimates can be made in professional sports industries, where extensive data are tabulated to measure worker productivity. For example, the National Basketball Association (NBA) allocates considerable resources to compile a variety of statistics that can be employed in player evaluation. This chapter proposes that such statistics can be utilized to measure a player's value, and therefore the Pareto optimality of player(s)-for-player(s) trade in the NBA can be objectively tested.

Neoclassical theory would predict that when a team trades a player(s), the new player(s) should contribute a greater or equal value, in terms of wins and/or rents,[1] to the team than the player(s) lost. If this is true for both teams, then the trade is Pareto optimal. At the onset of this study, however, it is suspected that neoclassical theory will not adequately explain the empirical evidence. In essence, we believe that general managers (GMs) have perfect information about a player's performance from statistics such as points, rebounds, and turnovers. However, we hypothesize that the mapping of the input vectors (individual performance statistics) to the output vector (number of team wins) is uncertain. Therefore, given a player's statistical production, GMs can arrive at erroneous valuations regarding the impact these inputs have on wins.

The purpose of this chapter is as follows: 1) present a game-theoretic model of the NBA decision-making process with respect to player(s)-for-player(s) trades, 2) employ the methodology first proposed by Gerald Scully (1974) to arrive at a valuation of player-for-player trades in the NBA, and 3) examine several player transactions in light of the research results presented herein.

THE GAME-THEORETICAL MODEL

The first step in examining personnel decisions in the NBA involves constructing a game-theoretic model to describe the decision-making process. This objective is accomplished with the following simple game for player(s)-for-player(s) trades.

The game begins with GM_i offering to trade player(s) to GM_j for player(s), where, $I \neq j$. Let π^j be the marginal payoff in wins to team j. When no trade takes place, or a trade is rejected, $\pi^j = 0$. Let λ^j denote the marginal value of player performance gained to team j for each player acquired. Similarly ρ^j is the marginal value of player performance lost to team j for each player traded away. The payoff function for trading talent is

$$\pi^j = \Sigma \ \lambda^j - \Sigma \ \rho^j. \tag{1}$$

The empirical model presented below will specify λ^j and ρ^j.

The contention at the heart of this chapter is that GMs do not know λ^j and ρ^j. Rather, each GM attempts to approximate the marginal value of each player as follows: Let Θ_j be the value function for GM_j. Then

$$\theta \ (\pi^j) = \Sigma\Theta(\lambda^j) - \Sigma\Theta(\rho^j). \tag{2}$$

In general, π^j is the marginal payoff to team j when trading player(s) for player(s). GMs will *ex ante* trade if and only if $\theta \ (\pi^j) > 0$; but *ex post,* the actual trade may reveal that $\pi^j < 0$.

In sum, given the game theoretic model, why do suboptimal trades take place? The basic hypothesis is that GMs reach incorrect conclusions regarding the true value of each player's production. It is proposed that GMs have access to complete information regarding a player's past performance. However, the value of this past performance in terms of future wins and revenue is not certain. Hence, GMs can consummate transactions that reduce the probability that their teams will be successful in the future.

MEASURING THE VALUE OF A PLAYER'S PRODUCTION

According to economic theory, the value of a worker is his marginal revenue product (MRP). To understand the value of a professional basketball player, then, each player's MRP must be estimated.

Following Gerald Scully's basic methodology, a player's MRP can be indirectly estimated by two relationships. First, a team's performance is hypothesized to be a function of the players' production. Second, team revenue is posited to be a function of wins, team history, and other team characteristic variables. This two-step method assigns a dollar value to a player's production. This dollar value is an estimate of a player's MRP (Scully, 1974 b).

CONNECTING PLAYER PERFORMANCE VARIABLES TO TEAM WINS

The estimation of a player's contribution to wins and revenue can be accomplished with the factors listed in Table 10.1. To ascertain the relationship between wins and a player's performance, our objective is to isolate the impact that each performance statistic has on the number of team victories, and then connect team victories to team revenue.

Table 10.1
The List of Variables
Team Performance Variables*

PTS = Points scored	FTM = Free throws made
DPTS = Points surrendered	AST = Assists
PPS = [PTS-FTM] / FGA = Points per shot**	TO = Turnovers
ASTO = AST / TO = Assist to turnover ratio	ORB = Offensive rebounds
FT = FTM / FTA = Free throw percentage	DRB = Defensive rebounds
FGA = Field goal attempts	STL = Steals
FTA = Free throw attempts	PF = Personal fouls

Team Revenue Variables*

REV = Team revenue	LAGWINS = Games won during the previous season
WCHM20 = Championship won in the past twenty season, weighted****	OLD = Age of the stadium
SCAP = Stadium capacity	POP = population

*The source of the data for each of the player and team statistics utilized in this study was the *The Official NBA Guide,* Carter and Sachare (eds.) 1996.

**Employing points per shot (Neyer, 1996, 322–323), rather than field goal percentage, allowed for the impact of three point shooting to be captured more efficiently.

***The data utilized to construct the team revenue variables came from a variety of sources. Revenue data came from various issues of *Financial World.* The age of the stadiums and the stadium capacity was found in *The Official NBA Guide* (Carter and Sachare (eds.) 1996). Population data came from the *Population Estimates Program, Population Division, U.S. Bureau of the Census.* For Los Angeles and New York, where more than one team reside, population was divided by two for each team examined.

****The calculation WCHM20 involved assigning a value to a team for each championship won in the past twenty years. This value was twenty if the team captured a championship during the prior season, nineteen if the championship was won seasons past, etc. The choice of twenty years was made after testing WCHM for five, ten, fifteen, and twenty-five years. The twenty-year time period was more significant than each of these, though a theoretical reason for this result is not apparent.

The construction of a model[2] that describes team victories begins with the primary determinants of wins: points scored and points surrendered. Not surprisingly, the total points a team scores and surrenders in a season explains 93% of the variation in team wins.[3]

However, employing this information in the evaluation of playing talent is difficult. Although data on how many points each player scores are easy to uncover, determining how many points each player surrenders is not as simple. Furthermore, even if such data were available, would the value of a player be correctly estimated by how many points each player scored and surrendered? If the answer to this query is yes, then the policy prescription for each player is to ignore his teammates and simply focus on outscoring his individual opponent. In this case the objective of accumulating rebounds, steals, and assists would be ignored, since these factors would not be considered in the evaluation of a player's productivity.

Such an approach fails to capture the essence of professional basketball. To evaluate a player solely on his ability to score and play defense fails to account for other factors crucial to the success of a basketball team. An alternative approach is to recognize that the number of points a team scores or surrenders is determined by various quantifiable factors. A team's scoring should be a function of how often the team has the ball, the efficiency of its ball handling, and its ability to convert its possessions into points. Likewise, the opposing team's scoring should be a function of how frequently its has the ball and its ability to use possessions efficiently. Therefore the following fixed effects[4] model should relate the player's statistical production to team wins.[5] The unit of observation is the team's aggregate performance in a season.
where

$$Y_{1n} = A_{1m} + \sum_{k=1}^{6} \alpha_{1k} X_{1kn} + \alpha_7 Y_{2n} + \epsilon_{1n} \tag{3}$$

$$Y_{2n} = A_{2m} + \sum_{k=1}^{} \alpha_{2k} X_{2kn} + \epsilon_{2n}, \tag{4}$$

where

Y_1 = WINS	X_{11} = PPS (+)	X_{21} = ORB (-)
Y_2 = DPTS (-)	X_{12} = FT (+)	X_{22} = DRB (-)
	X_{13} = ASTO (+)	X_{23} = STL (-)
	X_{14} = ORB (+)	X_{24} = TO (+)
	X_{15} = DRB (+)	X_{25} = FGA (+)
	X_{16} = STL (+)	X_{26} = FTA (+)
		X_{27} = PF (+ or -)

$m = 1, \ldots, 5$ with $1 = 1991-92$ season
$n = 1, \ldots, z$ with $z = 137$ team seasons

Theorized impact of each factor is listed in parentheses.

Equation (3) relates wins to points scored and points surrendered. Points scored[6] are theorized to be a positive function of shooting efficiency (PPS, FT), ball handling (ASTO), and possessions (DRB, ORB, STL, DPTS). Except for DPTS, each factor should have a positive impact on points scored and wins. DPTS is expected to have a net negative impact on wins. The positive impact DPTS has on points scored can be explained if one notes that every time an opponent scores, a team acquires possession of the ball, and thus also has an opportunity to score.

Equation (4) is utilized to explain the number of points a team surrenders on defense. It cannot be precisely known how many points each player surrenders, so it is necessary to estimate an additional equation to measure a player's defensive contribution accurately. Following is an interpretation of the impact that each statistic has on points surrendered.[7] A team's rebounding (ORB and DRB), represents not only a gain of possession, but also, in the case of defensive rebounds, indicates the frequency the opponent is failing to convert on opportunities. Steals are a measure of the opponent's ball handling, and like turnovers, represent a change of possession.

The impact of field goal and free throw attempts is more difficult to explain. Equation (4) accounts for the impact of offensive rebounds. In general, each additional shot attempt represents a change in possession.[8] Therefore, the more one team shoots, the more the other team will score. In essence, shot attempts represent the tempo at which a team plays. Some teams attempt to push the pace of the game, and hence take more shots. As a result, their opponents will also take more shots, and thus these opponents will score more points. Other teams prefer a more defensive approach. By playing at a slower tempo, these teams' opponents will have fewer shot attempts, and thus score fewer points.

The final factor listed in equation (4) is personal fouls. As noted by Robert Bellotti (1993), personal fouls can have both a positive and negative impact on team defense. For example, a personal foul can be an indication of aggressive defense. A personal foul can also send a poor free throw shooter to the free throw line as an alternative to the likely conversion of a two-point field goal attempt (Bellotti 1993: 270). Each of these factors will improve the likelihood that a team will be successful defensively. Whether the positive or negative impact of personal fouls dominates, however, is an empirical question.

As with each model utilized by this study, these two equations[9] were estimated with five seasons of data, beginning in 1991–1992 and concluding with the 1995–1996 campaign. Given that these equations are simultaneously determined, the estimation method was two-stage least squares. The results are reported in Tables 10.2 and 10.3. These results indicate that the above system of equations explains much of the variation in wins and DPTS. Furthermore, each of the variables utilized to explain wins and DPTS is statistically significant. Such findings are evidence that the statistics the NBA tabulates are potentially very useful in measuring the productivity of a player. However, the determination of a player's production of wins only begins with the estimation of this model.

To employ these results in the evaluation of playing talent, the next step is to derive the reduced form equation. This single equation will relate wins to each of the variables included within this system. The derivation of the single equation model involved substituting equation (4), which estimates the number of points a team surrenders, into equation (3). The estimates for the reduced form equation are reported in Table 10.4

Table 10.2
Estimated Coefficients from Equation (3)
Dependent Variable Is Wins

Independent Variables	Estimated Coefficients	t-Statistics
PPS	199.446	13.695
FT	46.549	2.937
ORB	0.030	7.660
DRB	0.031	8.935
ASTO	11.074	4.809
STL	0.027	5.512
DPTS	-0.014	-12.774

Adjusted R-Squared = 0.902.
Observations = 137.

Table 10.3
Estimated Coefficients from Equation (4)
Dependent Variable Is DPTS

Independent Variables	Estimated Coefficients	t-Statistics
ORB	-1.823	-16.085
DRB	-1.432	-15.453
TO	1.826	14.707
STL	-1.533	-11.662
FGA	1.689	28.432
FTA	0.708	10.870
PF	-0.212	-2.658

Adjusted R-Squared = 0.920.
Observations = 137.

Table 10.4
The Reduced Form Coefficients
Dependent Variable Is Wins

Independent Variables	Estimated Coefficients
PPS	199.446
FT	46.549
ASTO	11.074
ORB	0.056
DRB	0.051
STL	0.049
TO	-0.026
FGA	-0.024
FTA	-0.010
PF	0.003

The reduced-form equation includes three ratios: PPS, FT, and ASTO. The interpretation and utilization of each would be eased if the components were examined individually. For example, Table 10.4 shows that an increase in ASTO by one leads to approximately eleven additional wins. When one considers that the range of this variable is from a maximum of 2.18 to a minimum of 1.11 over the time period examined, one can conclude that significant changes in ASTO do not generally have a correspondingly significant impact on team wins. Although the impact of a change in ASTO on wins may be interesting, a more useful issue in evaluating the productivity of a player is the impact of an additional assist on wins. To estimate this, the derivative of wins with respect to assists was determined. Such a calculation was also done for each of the performance statistics. With this information in hand, the impact of three-point field goals made,[10] two-point field goals made, missed field goals, assists, turnovers, free throws made, and missed free throws could be ascertained. The statistics are ranked in Table 10.5, in descending order from highest absolute marginal value to the lowest.

An examination of these marginal values reveals that there is a substantial difference in the impact of each statistic. With the exception of three-point field goals made, the factors representing the greatest impact on wins are rebounds, steals, and turnovers. With respect to scoring, a player must convert 50% of his field goals from two-point range to break even, while a 33% conversion rate from beyond the three-point arc produces the same result. Such a result indicates that it is not total scoring that is relevant in evaluating a player. Rather it is the efficiency by which the player utilizes his respective shot attempts. In sum, a player's productivity is primarily a function of his ability to acquire and maintain possession of the ball, and his ability to convert his field goal attempts efficiently.

Table 10.5
The Marginal Values

Statistic	Marginal Values
Three-point field goals made	0.058
Offensive rebounds	0.056
Defensive rebounds	0.051
Steals	0.049
Turnovers	-0.040
Missed field goals	-0.029
Two-point field goals made	0.029
Missed free throws	-0.016
Assists	0.009
Free throws made	0.005
Personal fouls	0.003

Tempo statistics	Marginal Values
Field goal attempts	-0.024
Free throw attempts	-0.010

DETERMINING A PLAYER'S PRODUCTION OF WINS

The determination of a player's production of wins begins by simply multiplying the player's accumulation of each statistic by the corresponding marginal value. To determine wins, however, three adjustments to this initial calculation need to be made. The first centers on the differences between the tempos each team attempts to impose during the games played.

The latter factors noted in Table 10.5 are entitled tempo statistics.[11] Once offensive rebounds are accounted for, each shot a team takes generally results in the other team gaining possession of the ball. To a large extent, the average number of shots a team takes per game is determined by the pace the coaching staff wishes to play. Teams that play at a relatively slow tempo will on average take fewer shots, and hence surrender fewer points. Conversely, teams that play at a faster tempo shoot a great deal more, and therefore appear to be poorer on defensive in absolute terms. To simply multiply the number of shots a player takes by the value of a shot attempt penalizes shooters and rewards those who shoot infrequently. Such a calculation biases the measurement of player productivity downward for players who take a large percentage of their teams' shots. But these players probably are greater offensive threats.

To solve this problem, each team's per-minute-tempo-bias[12] was calculated. The per-minute tempo-bias is then added to each player's per-minute production.[13] In doing this, each player's production is weighted according to the tempo imposed by his team. Such an adjustment is reasonable when one considers that a faster tempo translates into more opportunities for a player, and therefore an average player from an up-tempo team will have a greater statistical production than a player with comparable skills from a slower-paced team. By considering each team's tempo in calculating a player's value, this bias is minimized.

After calculating a player's per-minute production, and adjusting this production by the tempo factor, two additional adjustments still need to be made. These final steps follow from the work of Andrew Zimbalist (1992). According to Zimbalist, a player's value is determined by examining the difference between the production the team received with the player and the production the team would have with a replacement player that Zimbalist calls the counter factual. Zimbalist proposed a counter factual equivalent to the average player. His hypothesis is that if a player performs below an average player, then he is subtracting from his team's ability to win (Zimbalist 1992, p. 188).

Following the methodology introduced by Zimbalist, a player's contribution is determined by the following method. As illustrated in equation (5), each player's production is adjusted by the tempo his team imposed, the average performance at his respective position,[14] and the average performance in the league.[15] The adjusted per-minute performance is then multiplied by the total minutes played to determine the player's production of wins.

Production of Wins = [(PM + TB) - (PA) + TA] X Total Minutes Played,   (5)

where
  PM = Production per-minute
  TB = Team per-minute tempo-bias
  PA = Average per-minute production at position[16]
  TA = Average player's per-minute production

DETERMINING THE VALUE OF A WIN

With each player's production valued in terms of the number of wins he produces; the next step is to determine the dollar value of team wins. This is done with the following fixed effects equation[17]:

$$Y_{3n} = A_{3m} + \sum_{k=1}^{6} \alpha_{3k} X_{3kn} + \epsilon_{3n},$$ (6)

where Y_3 = REV $\qquad$ X_1 = WINS (+)
$\qquad\qquad\qquad X_2$ = LAGWINS (+)
$\qquad\qquad\qquad X_3$ = WCHM20 (+)
$\qquad\qquad\qquad X_4$ = OLD (+)
$\qquad\qquad\qquad X_5$ = SCAP (+)
$\qquad\qquad\qquad X_6$ = SMSA (+)
m = 1, ..., 5 with 1 = 1991-1992 season

$n = 1, \ldots, z$ with $z = 135$ team seasons.

Theorized impact of each factor is listed in parentheses.

As with the analysis of player productivity, the revenue model was inspired by the work of Scully (1974 b). Team revenue is hypothesized to be a function of team performance (WINS, LAGWINS, WCHM20), stadium attributes (OLD, SCAP), and market characteristics (SMSA). Each of these variables, with the exception of OLD, is expected to have a positive impact on team revenue. The estimation of equation (6) produced the results reported in Table10.6.

Table 10.6
Estimated Coefficients from Equation (5)
Dependent Variable Is Team Revenue

Independent Variables	Estimated Coefficients	T-Statistic
WINS	0.196	2.465
LAGWINS	0.282	3.485
WCHM20	0.425	8.431
OLD	-0.213	-3.268
SCAP	0.001	3.266
SMSA	1.009E-06	3.094

Adjusted R-Squared = 0.720.
Observations = 135.

Each of the above-cited variables had a statistically significant impact on revenue, and the explanatory power of the equation is consistent with the results reported in similar studies.[18] For the purpose of this study, the most important variables are WINS and LAGWINS. The estimation of equation (6) revealed that each additional win was worth an estimated $196,000. A win from the previous campaign was estimated to add an additional $282,000 to team revenue. Following the lead of Zimbalist (1992, p. 190), if the impact of LAGWINS is discounted by the average short-term treasury bill rate,[19] the total value of a win can be determined by adding the value of a current victory to the value of a win the previous season. Hence, a win is estimated to be worth an additional $467,000 in revenue over the time period examined.

EXAMINING PLAYER(S)-FOR-PLAYER(S) TRADES

With the player's production of wins and the value of a win estimated, it is now possible to ascertain the value of a player in terms of both wins and rents. This information can in turn be utilized to evaluate the outcome of player(s)-for-player(s) trades. The hypothesis advanced by the game-theoretic model was that general

Table 10.7
The Trades to Be Examined

Team One	Player(s) Acquired	Team Two	Player(s) Acquired
Denver, 1995	Don MacLean Doug Overton	Washington, 1995	Robert Pack
Chicago, 1995	Dennis Rodman	San Antonio, 1995	Will Perdue
Atlanta, 1994	Tyrone Corbin	Utah, 1994	Adam Keefe
Indiana, 1993	Derrick McKey Gerald Paddio	Seattle, 1993	Detlef Schrempf
Detroit, 1993	Sean Elliott David Wood	San Antonio, 1993	Dennis Rodman
Minnesota, 1993	Mike Brown	Utah, 1993	Felton Spencer
Portland, 1993	Harvey Grant	Washington, 1993	Kevin Duckworth
L.A. Lakers, 1993	Sam Bowie	New Jersey, 1993	Benoit Benjamin
Atlanta, 1992	Mookie Blaylock Roy Hinson	New Jersey, 1992	Rumeal Robinson
Indiana, 1992	Sam Mitchell Pooh Richardson	Minnesota, 1992	Chuck Person Michael Williams
Philadelphia, 1992	Jeff Hornacek Tim Perry Andrew Lang	Phoenix, 1992	Charles Barkley

managers employ information suboptimally. To test this proposition, several player transactions will be examined in an effort to determine how frequently general managers conclude player(s)-for-player(s) trades that are inconsistent with either the objective of maximizing profits or maximizing wins.

To determine if and how often teams conclude transactions that leave them worse off, eleven trades that occurred during the summers of 1992, 1993, 1994, and 1995 were examined. Each of these trades was strictly player(s)-for-player(s) trades, with no exchanges of first-round draft choices, draft rights, or cash incorporated into any transaction. Table 10.7 lists the participants in these transactions.

Table 10.8
Net Benefits from Player Transactions

Teams	Net Rents	Net Wins
Denver, 1995	$-1,485,933	-2.18
Washington, 1995	$607,667	1.33
Chicago, 1995	$6,343,193	16.68
San Antonio, 1995	$-6,668,779	-16.76
Atlanta, 1994	$1,554,811	4.19
Utah, 1994	$381,010	1.03
Indiana, 1993	$-2,218,473	-5.03
Seattle, 1993	$2,715,358	5.38
Detroit, 1993	$-17,092,451	-36.71
San Antonio, 1993	$1,992,082	43.23
Minnesota, 1993	$493,021	0.55
Utah, 1993	$3,422,113	7.98
Portland, 1993	$1,667,209	4.03
Washington, 1993	$-4,065,141	-7.23
L.A. Lakers, 1993	$-810,433	-1.68
New Jersey, 1993	$-349,076	1.34
Atlanta, 1992	$3,271,314	8.90
New Jersey, 1992	$-2,141,539	-5.87
Indiana, 1992	$-2,238,053	-7.53
Minnesota, 1992	$-1,016,784	3.26
Philadelphia, 1992	$-3,680,838	-7.05
Phoenix, 1992	$-2,863,287	-6.74

Each of these trades occurred during the off-season, so it was possible to determine how productive each player was for his original team and new employer. Following the methodology outlined above, the number of wins produced was estimated for each player involved in these transactions. This information, along with data on player salary,[20] was utilized to determine the rents accrued by the teams. Hence we were able to determine how much production each team was losing (ρ^j), in terms of rents and wins; and how much production the team acquired (λ^j). These findings were in turn utilized to determine the net rents or net wins (π^j) that accrued to each team. The results of these calculations are reported in Table 10.8.

An examination of the results detailed in Table 10.8 reveals that within this sample, NBA teams concluded transactions that left the team worse off, in terms of net rents, in twelve cases that are 54.6% of the trades examined. In terms of wins, the above transactions resulted in a net loss for 45% of the teams evaluated. Of the trades analyzed, only two transactions, the 1994 trade involving Atlanta and Utah and the 1993 trade involving Minnesota and Utah, left both participants better off in terms of rents and wins. In other words, only two of the eleven trades were Pareto optimal. In sum, whether we assume that teams are maximizing wins or maximizing profits, their personnel decisions were inconsistent with either objective in 50% of the transactions examined. Furthermore, the hypothesis that teams would only conclude Pareto optimal trades were rejected in 82% of the trades examined.

Could such results be predicted prior to the consummation of the transaction? To test this, the expected number of wins each player produced was determined. Such a calculation involved assuming a player's per-minute wins production would be identical to the previous season, and that the team knew how many minutes they would allocate to the player and the position he would play. Given this information, then, what value should the team have expected to receive from each player in terms of rents and wins? The results of this calculation are reported in Table 10.9.

The findings reported in Table 10.9 reveal that many of the teams that experience negative rents by the above transactions could have correctly forecast this result. In terms of net rents, eighteen of the twenty-two participants could have estimated correctly prior to the transaction whether the trade would have a positive or negative impact. Of the twelve teams that were worse off in terms of rents, ten could have predicted by these methods that losses would occur. With respect to wins, ten teams surrendered more wins then they acquired. Of these ten, nine could have forecast correctly this result.

How can this result be explained? Milton Friedman argues that, like the general absence of advanced physics degrees among professional pool players, economic actors do not need to conduct extensive cost-benefit analysis to arrive at a correct decision. Rather, through trial and error people will mimic the conclusion derived from sophisticated economic models (Frank, 1997, pp. 6-7). Although it is not proposed herein that GMs deliberately conclude trades that lessen the probability of success, the evidence offered does suggest GMs do not evaluate players correctly. Certainly the most obvious explanation is that they are not evaluating professional team sports. Team sports are a classic example of a zero-sum game. Even if every team utilized information suboptimally, the number of wins and losses in the league would still be equal. Furthermore, since the NBA restricts entry into this industry, an individual or group of individuals with superior methods could not enter and dominate the competition. The market discipline necessary for Friedman's analogy to ring true simply does not exist in the NBA.

Table 10.9
Expected Net Benefits from Player Transactions

Teams	Expected Net Rents	Expected Net Wins
Denver, 1995	$-1,658,553	-2.55
Washington, 1995	$52,523	0.14
Chicago, 1995	$10,386,365	25.34
San Antonio, 1995	$-7,268,342	-18.04
Atlanta, 1994	$1,784,023	4.68
Utah, 1994	$-1,580,129	-3.17
Indiana, 1993	$-2,941,753	-6.58
Seattle, 1993	$7,873,024	16.42
Detroit, 1993	$-16,982,662	-36.47
San Antonio, 1993	$19,405,208	42.13
Minnesota, 1993	$-437,110	-1.44
Utah, 1993	$942,251	2.67
Portland, 1993	$2,042,458	4.83
Washington, 1993	$-4,066,472	-7.23
L.A. Lakers, 1993	$-161,082	-0.29
New Jersey, 1993	$389,748	2.92
Atlanta, 1992	$1,866,404	5.89
New Jersey, 1992	$-2,231,126	-6.06
Indiana, 1992	$-1,404,227	-5.74
Minnesota, 1992	$1,404,901	8.45
Philadelphia, 1992	$3,915,197	9.21
Phoenix, 1992	$-5,329,980	-12.02

CONCLUDING REMARKS

At the onset of this exposition a game theoretic model was proposed that posited NBA GMs have access to information regarding a player's productivity, yet the valuation of this information is suboptimal. Utilizing Scully's methods, the value of NBA players was ascertained in terms of wins and rents. This information was then employed to assess how frequently player(s)-for-player(s) trades in the NBA are Pareto optimal. The evaluation of these trades demonstrated that less than 20% of these player transactions were Pareto optimal, indicating that NBA GMs do not generally employ information optimally. In other words, there exists a multibillion-dollar industry, where decisions are made beneath the intense scrutiny of millions of interested observers, where motives are clear and consequences for failure severe, and yet information that could effect better decisions is employed incorrectly. Such a finding begs an important question. If an industry, where information is abundant and motives clear, does not utilize information correctly, does any industry make decisions strictly according to the dictates of economic theory?

NOTES

In addition to the tremendous support of the editors, we wish to also acknowledge the comments of Alexandra Bernasek, Dennis Black, Nancy Jianakopolos, and Lynn Watson. Any errors are, of course, our own.

1. The value of a player depends upon the motivation of the decision maker. If one assumes the objective is to maximize profits, then the value of a player is the rents a team accrues from his employment, where rents are the difference between the marginal revenue product of the player and his salary. In contrast, if one assumes the objective is to maximize wins, then the value of a player is simply the number of wins he produces. Because it is not known for certain whether teams primarily seek to maximize profits or maximize wins, both values will be estimated herein.

2. The model utilized herein was also employed in "Do Coaches Coach to Win? Rationality, Resource Allocation, and Professional Basketball." (Berri, 1997, working paper).

3. The relationship between teams wins and the team's accumulation of points scored and points surrendered was examined utilizing data from the 1991–1992 season through the 1995–1996 campaign. The estimation of this relationship, utilizing a fixed effects model, produced the following result:

Independent Variables	Estimated Coefficients	t-Statistics
PTS	0.031	33.967
DPTS	-0.031	-34.952

Adjusted R^2 = .930.
Observation = 137.

4. To capture only the variation within each season, each model estimated within this discourse will follow the fixed effects methodology. Hence, the constant term in this regression is A_{lm}, where m runs from one to five, representing the five seasons examined in this study.

5. The article authored by Zak, et al. (1979, pp. 379–392) presents a model that has inspired both the works of Scott, et al. (1985, pp. 50–59) and Hofler and Payne (1997, pp. 293–299). Each of these studies included the opponent's accumulation of each statistic. However, by including the opponent's statistics, it is not possible to precisely determine the impact each player has on team wins. The model employed in this chapter, through the utilization of two equations, proposes to connect factors tabulated for each individual player to team wins. A comparison of the explanatory power of the Zak, et al. double log model and the linear system of equations presented herein demonstrates that the methods utilized here are able to explain wins as well, if not better, than the model previously offered in the literature.

6. A player's offensive contribution cannot be simply measured by a player's scoring. Such an approach would fail to acknowledge the impact the player's teammates have on his accumulation of points. After all, it is rare that one player rebounds the basketball, traverses the entire court, and takes the shot without another member of his team handling the ball. In fact, if a player attempts to play in such a fashion on a consistent basis, it is likely that he will quickly fall out of favor with both his teammates and his coach. Therefore, a player's offensive contribution must not only consider the player's efficient utilization of shot attempts, but also his ball handling and rebounding production.

7. Unlike the model presented by Zak et al. (1979, pp. 379–392) and Hofler and Payne (1997, pp. 291–299), blocked shots are not included as an explanatory variable. Both the work of Zak et al. and Hofler and Payne demonstrated that blocked shots were not a statistically significant determinant of wins. Zak et al. explained such a result by noting the infrequency that shots are blocked in the NBA. According to Zak et al., about ten shots are blocked per game, an amount those authors considered too small to impact the outcome of a game (1979, p. 386). Like the previously cited works, blocked shots were originally included in this model. However, blocked shots were not a statistically significant determinant of wins or DPTS; thus this factor was not included in our final model.

8. The lone exception to this statement occurs when an opponent coverts the first of two free throws.

9. The model presented is slightly more efficient than the structural, three-equation model. A single equation would offer further efficiency gains, but such an equation would suffer from significant multicollinearity. Furthermore, as explained later, the impact shot attempts have on the opponent's scoring needs to be calculated separately if a player's production of wins is to be accurately determined.

10. By taking the derivative of wins with respect to the numerator of PPS, one can determine the value of a point from a field goal attempt. The derivative of wins with respect to the denominator of PPS yields the value of a field goat attempt. The impact of a made three-point field goal is then ascertained by multiplying the value of a point from a field goal attempt by three, and then adjusting this total by the value of a field goal attempt. The value of a two-point field goal made is determined in a similar fashion, while the value of a missed field goal is simply the value of a field goal attempt.

11. The value of the tempo statistics is determined by examining the impact shot attempts have on DPTS, and the impact DPTS has on wins. In other words, field goal and free throw attempts are explanatory variables in both equation (3) and equation (4). The impact shot attempts have on wins is utilized to determine the value of three-point field goals made, two-point field goals made, missed field goals, etc. The impact shot attempts have on DPTS are utilized to estimate the impact of tempo and to determine the per-minute tempo bias, as explained below.

12. Per-minute-tempo-bias (for the team) =

$$\frac{[(\text{Team Field Goal Attempts})\,(-0.024) + (\text{Team Field Throw Attempts})\,(-0.10)]}{\text{Total Minutes Played}}$$

13. Per-minute production =

$$\frac{\Sigma \left[(\text{Marginal Value of Statistic}) \, (\text{Accumulation of Statistic}) \right]}{\text{Total Minutes Played}}$$

By calculating a player's per-minute production it is possible to make the adjustments necessary to calculate a player's total production of wins.

14. An examination of the player's production reveals that the position a player played dictated the player's production of wins. Given that rebounds are one of the most significant positive factors, and turnovers the most significant negative statistic, it is not surprising that forwards and centers produce the most wins in absolute terms. Guards generally rebound very little and turn the ball over more frequently, and therefore produce fewer wins in absolute terms. However, the nature of basketball is such that teams generally employ two guards, two forwards, and a center. Therefore, players are most accurately evaluated when their production is compared relative to others who play their position.

15. If a player's production is only evaluated relative to the average performance at each position, the summation of all player's production would be zero. By also considering the average performance of all players, the summation of the player's production equals the total wins of the teams. Average per-minute production is determined by dividing the total number of wins in the league by the total number of minutes played.

16. To determine the positions of each player the following sources were consulted: *The Pro Basketball Bible* (Cohn and Barry, various years), *The Complete Handbook of Pro Basketball* (Hollander (ed.), various years); and *The Official NBA Register* (Bonavita et al., 1996). The average positional values are calculated after each player's production is adjusted according to the tempo of his respective team. The average per-minute production at the center position, for example, is determined by summing each centers' tempo adjusted production, and dividing by the summation of the centers' minutes played. If a player played more than one position, then his minutes were examined to estimate how much time was spent at each position. His production was then evaluated at each of the positions he played.

17. The number of observations utilized in estimating this equation is two fewer than those employed in estimating equations (3) and (4). The difference lies in the inclusion of lagged wins. For the final season considered by this study, 1995–1996, franchises began playing in both Toronto and Vancouver. Because neither had played the previous season, and thus neither had any lagged wins, these two teams were not examined by this model.

18. In addition to Scully (1974), models designed to explain professional team revenue have been offered by Medoff (1976), Scott, et al. (1985), and Zimbalist (1992), among others.

19. The source for this rate was the St. Louis Federal Reserve.

20. Unlike professional baseball, player salaries are not generally released by the NBA. However, both *The Complete Handbook of Pro Basketball* (Hollander (ed.), various years) and the *Basketball Digest* did uncover salary data for the listed players. The exceptions were Chuck Person and Roy Hinson for the 1991–1992 season, and Gerald Paddio during the 1993–1994 campaign. For both Person and Hinson, the salary utilized to determine rents for the 1991–1992 campaign was determined by averaging the salary each player was paid during the 1990–1991 and 1992–1993 seasons. Paddio, however, was released by Indiana soon after the start of the 1993–1994 season and was nearly an NBA minimum wage player for Seattle the previous season. Hence the rents accrued to Indiana from this trade are overestimated by the minimum salary Indiana paid Paddio for the fifty-five minutes he played.

11

The Benefit of the Designated Hitter in Professional Baseball

Craig A. Depken II

INTRODUCTION

Which is the better league: the National League (NL) or the American League (AL)? The debate is perennial. Coupled with this is the debate over the designated hitter (DH) rule and its effect on the playing of baseball. This chapter investigates both questions by utilizing interleague baseball games from the 1997 regular season to estimate the benefit to AL teams when using the DH rule and the relative strengths of the two leagues in head-to-head competition.

In the debate over which league is better, some point to the greater number of World Series championships won by the AL to support their claim that the AL is stronger. Fans of the NL could point out that their league has won more All Star games. While this comparison is a bit more appropriate than the World Series comparison, it is still not clear that All Star game victories prove the relative strength of one league against another.

Moreover, the comparison of World Series championships is faulty for two reasons. First, comparing World Series titles is no more than a comparison between the best team in each league rather than a comparison of all the teams in each league. Second, since 1973 the AL has played under a fundamentally different set of rules with the inclusion of the DH. It was implemented to provide more offense and thus stimulate interest and attendance on the part of fans.

It is not clear that this strategy has been successful in raising offensive output. The average runs per game in the AL is only marginally higher than in the NL (Butler and Moore, 1996). Moreover, contradictory evidence has been found concerning the effect of the designated hitter on attendance. Domazlicky and Kerr (1990) found that attendance was enhanced with the designated hitter, but Butler and Moore (1996) did not. Still, it is clear that the DH fundamentally alters the strategies most often employed by AL managers vis-à-vis their NL counterparts. Furthermore, AL and NL teams typically employ different types of labor so as to maximize their output under different rules.

In 1997, Major League Baseball (MLB) introduced regular season games between teams in the two leagues for the first time. Interleague games count as regular season games, all statistics count for all players, and the DH is used only when the game is played in an AL ballpark. In the first year, interleague play was restricted to the corresponding divisions in each league. Teams in the AL Eastern division played teams in the NL Eastern division, and so on.

The introduction of interleague regular-season games offers the chance of a more complete view of the strengths of the AL and the NL because all teams are involved in interleague play and several series are played by each team. The temptation is to look strictly at the number of games won by each league and declare the league that wins the most games the strongest. However, this comparison would overlook the issue of the DH and its effects on the outcomes of games. A straight comparison of wins in either league implicitly assumes that the DH rule has no bearing on either the constitution of a team or the typical strategic behavior employed by the manager of the team.

The DH is important in this discussion because it fundamentally alters the rules of the game and thus the strategies most often employed by the managers of each league. When pitchers must hit for themselves, more strategic maneuvering may be required on the part of the manager. These additional strategies include the pinch hitter, pinch runner, the double-switch, and sacrifice bunts. All are less common in the AL.[1]

These interleague games provide useful evidence to measure the relative strength of the AL versus the NL. Using data from 211 interleague games from the 1997 baseball season, I employ a probit analysis to investigate first, what advantage, if any, the DH gives an AL team over an NL team, and second, the relative strengths of the two leagues as reflected in the outcomes of the games played.

A SIMPLE MODEL OF BASEBALL LABOR AND AN EMPIRICAL TEST

While many are tempted to look only at the number of games won by the AL (46% of all interleague games), such a comparison is misleading because it does not account for the DH and its possible effects on team hiring practices and labor productivity under the different rules of each league. Typically, AL teams hire an extra power hitter who bats in the place of the pitcher, thus increasing potential run production and ostensibly the ability to win. However, most AL teams employ these extra power hitters, and thus within that league, the DH probably has little to do with the actual outcome of any one particular game. On the other hand, NL teams typically do not hire an extra power hitter. Because the rules and the strategies are different, NL teams are more likely to hire an extra defensive player (typically an infielder) or an extra pitcher. This facilitates strategies such as double-switches, pinch runners and late-inning defensive replacements. Much like the DH, these extra defensive players (be they pitchers or field players) probably have very little to do with the outcome of a particular game.[2]

Assume that teams hire players such that marginal revenue product under their respective league rules equals the given wage rate. There are two sets of rules, R_N in the NL and R_A in the AL. These sets of rules suggest different sets of strategies to be employed at varying levels, σ_N and σ_A. Therefore, teams hire labor best fitted to the rules and strategies employed in their league. If labor is hired in such a manner, and team-roster changes are not possible or feasible when the rules change temporarily (which is most likely in regular season interleague play and definitely true in post-season interleague play), then the marginal product of labor hired by a team may differ when the rules are changed.

Therefore, NL and AL teams should be fundamentally different in the composition of their players because of the different rules. Assuming that prices are held constant within a given season, neoclassical profit-maximizing firms then seek to maximize output. Most studies assume that a relatively good measure of output is the number of wins of a team (e.g., Depken, 1997; Scully, 1989; and Quirk and Fort, 1992). Therefore, teams should hire players such that wins are maximized under the prevailing rules in their own league. It is difficult to isolate the influence of these different types of players on intraleague games. However, interleague play provides the opportunity to identify any advantage teams may have against opponents from the other league who most often compete under the other league's rules. It also provides an opportunity for testing the relative strength of the two leagues after controlling for the difference in the rules.

To investigate the issues of the impacts of the DH on interleague competition and the relative strengths of the two leagues, I estimate the following probit model[3]

$$ALWIN = \beta_0 + \beta_1 DH + \beta_2 ALWINS + \beta_3 NLWINS + \beta_4 AL500 + \beta_5 NL500 +$$
$$\beta_6 ALERA + \beta_7 NLERA + \beta_8 DAY + \beta_9 ALATTPER + \beta_{10} NLATTPER + \epsilon, \qquad (1)$$

where the β_i are parameters to be estimated and ϵ is a stochastic error term. The dependent variable (ALWIN) is a dummy variable that equals one if the AL team won the game and zero otherwise.

The independent variables control for differentiation between the two teams playing in an interleague game and specific game-day variable inputs. The variable DH is a dummy variable that equals one if the DH rule is in effect and zero otherwise. Because the DH variable may also capture some "home-field" advantage enjoyed by the AL team, I also include the attendance at interleague games played in an AL (NL) park as a percentage of overall stadium capacity, ALATTPER (NLATTPER) (see Table 11.1).

Overall team characteristics include the total number of wins by the AL team (ALWINS) and the NL team (NLWINS). Because the relative ranking of the teams within their own league may be important in determining which team wins a particular game, I also include the number of games above (or below) a 500 record for both the AL team (AL500) and the NL team (NL500). These two variables control for the relative strengths of the two teams within their own league.

There are many game-day specific factors that influence the winner of an interleague game. In particular, I include a dummy variable, DAY, which equals one if the game is played during the day and zero otherwise. The quality of the starting pitcher is the most variable input for a particular game. To control for variable quality of the starting pitcher, I include the earned-run-averages of both starters (ALERA and NLERA).

If the DH rule affords AL teams an added advantage, then the DH dummy variable should have a positive estimated coefficient. If the AL is relatively stronger than the NL, one would expect that a win attributed to the AL team to outweigh the influence of a win for the NL team. In other words, one would expect that the difference between β_2 and β_3 to be positive. However, if the NL is stronger, relative to the AL, the reverse would hold true.

Table 11.1
Descriptive Statistics of the Data

Variable	Definition	Mean	Std. Deviation
ALWIN	AL Team Wins Game	0.469	0.500
DH	DH Rule Used	0.516	0.500
AMWINS	AL Team Total Wins	47.638	17.196
NAWINS	NL Team Total Wins	48.042	17.611
ALERA	AL Starting Pitcher ERA	4.581	1.506
NLERA	NL Starting Pitcher ERA	4.135	1.567
DAY	Game Played During Day	0.314	0.465
AL500	AL Team Games Above Average	0.700	13.424
NL500	NL Team Games Above Average	-0.826	13.856
ALATTPER	AL Stadium Attendance	0.723	0.239
NLATTPER	NL Stadium Attendance	0.645	0.233

Unfortunately, the relationship may be more complex. Looking at wins alone may not completely reveal the relative strengths of the two leagues. The reason is that interleague play is restricted to like-divisions. Therefore, if one league's division is substantially more competitive than the corresponding division in the other league, looking only at wins may be misleading. Therefore, the NL500 and AL500 variables provide an additional control in the model for the relative strengths of the teams within each league. If their coefficients (β_4 and β_5) sum to zero, then it indicates that two teams that are at the same relative position within their respective divisions will be equally competitive in interleague games.

Table 11.2
Probit Analysis Results
(Dependent Variable Is ALWIN)

Parameter	Estimate	dP/dX (ALWIN = 1)
Intercept	0.121 (.198)	0.043
DH	1.327* (2.334)	0.479
ALWINS	-0.154** (-1.551)	-0.055
NLWINS	0.142 (1.418)	0.051
ALERA	-0.097** (-1.584)	-0.035
NLERA	-0.000 (-.011)	-0.000
AL500	0.0747** (1.509)	0.027
NL500	-0.077** (-1.529)	-0.027
DAY	0.161 (.816)	0.058
ALATTPER	-0.486 (-.871)	-0.175
NLATTPER	0.577 (.969)	0.208
N	211	

One-Tailed t-Statistics are reported in parentheses. *Note*: * (**), indicates 0.05 (0.10) significance level in a one-tailed test.

Of the game-specific characteristics, one would expect the estimated coefficients on ALATTPER to be positive and on NLATTPER to be negative if there is a home-field advantage from the fans in attendance. Further, one would expect the estimated coefficient on NLERA to be positive, and the coefficient of ALERA to be negative. The expected sign of the coefficient on DAY is ambiguous.

The results of the estimation are reported in Table 11.2 and confirm expectations. Many of the estimated coefficients are statistically significant at the 0.10 level, and the model accurately predicts the outcome of an interleague game 62% of the time.

The estimated coefficient of DH is positive and statistically significant. As mentioned, the DH variable not only captures rules changes but also any possible home-field advantage enjoyed by AL teams when playing in their own ballparks. However, the estimated coefficient on ALATTPER is not statistically significant. This indicates that there is no tremendous home-field advantage associated with the fans that attend the game, on average. Admittedly, though, the home-field advantage may be reflected in some other hard-to-measure metric.

The estimated parameters on the team quality variables indicate that the NL teams are stronger, on average, than AL teams. The difference between β_2 and β_3 is negative and statistically different from zero at the 0.10 level. This implies that an advantage lies with the NL team if the two teams have an equal number of wins. To see if this difference extends to the measure of relative strengths of teams within their respective leagues, the linear restriction that β_4 is equal to β_5 is tested. This null hypothesis has a P-value of 0.99, and thus cannot be rejected. Overall, these results imply that the NL is stronger than the AL when it comes to head-to-head competition.

The estimated effects of the game-day variable inputs show that the time of the game has no influence on the outcome of a particular interleague game. Starting pitchers, on the other hand, do influence the outcome of the game. The higher the AL starting pitcher's ERA, the lower the chances of the AL team winning the game. This follows intuition. However, the ERA of the NL starting pitcher has no influence on the outcome of the game. A linear test that the two estimated parameters on starting pitchers' ERA's are equal is rejected at the 0.10 level.

Table 11.2 also lists the actual effects of each independent variable on the probability of an AL team winning a particular game. If two teams play a night game with the DH rule, and those two team have equal team wins, and the starting pitchers have the same ERAs, the DH rule gives the AL team a 47.9% greater probability of winning.

In light of these results, a few conclusions can be drawn. First, the average NL team is stronger than the average AL team as represented in head-to-head competition. Second, as the same number of games are played in AL parks and NL parks, the AL has an inherent advantage, and on average, can be expected to win more games than the NL if the same interleague format is used in the future. But the greater number of expected wins by AL teams is not a direct indication that the AL is stronger than the NL. It is the result of the advantage of the DH rule. This study offers partial explanation as to why the AL has won more world series championships since the inception of the designated hitter. Since the DH rule was introduced in 1973, the average world series has lasted 6 games, and 53 percent of all World Series games have been played in AL ballparks (*Total Baseball,* 1996). This puts the NL pennant-winning teams at a disadvantage because their players have not been hired to maximize production under the DH rule. But they play more World Series games under the DH rule.

Finally, major league baseball should consider uniform rules for the sport. The removal of the DH rule in the AL or the extension of the rule to the NL would allow teams to hire players in the same operating environment. This, in turn, would remove the bias toward the AL with respect to the designated hitter and make interleague play (both regular and post-season) neutral with respect to the rules of the game. It is clear that the difference in the rules affects the relative productivity of the players hired by teams in each league.

NOTES

1. One complaint levied against Tony LaRussa, who became the manager of the NL St. Louis Cardinals after managing the AL Oakland Athletics for a number of years, was that he was untrained in NL tactics and strategies. This became more pronounced in the Cardinals 1996 NL championship series that they lost to the Atlanta Braves. The Braves were managed by an experienced NL manager.

2. One possible exception may be the hiring of a closing pitcher who specializes in maintaining late-inning leads of three runs or less (typical requirements for a save opportunity). However, the popularity of these specialists is not limited to one particular league.

3. Alternative specifications of equation (1) were estimated including an interaction term between DAY and DH (i.e., whether the game was played in an AL ballpark) and home-game attendance as a percentage of stadium capacity. Neither variables were statistically significant and neither altered the qualitative nor the quantitative results substantially.

12

Participation in Collegiate Athletics and Academic Performance

John Fizel and Timothy Smaby

INTRODUCTION

The stereotype of the "dumb jock" seems to have coincided with the advent of collegiate sports. Similarly, so began the tales of the unethical means by which many varsity athletes are recruited and kept eligible. Revelations such as falsified transcripts, credit for phantom courses, surrogates for tests, phony test scores, and illiterate athletes have continually tarnished the reputation of college sports (Bergmann, 1991; Sperber, 1990; Telander, 1989). These violations appear to have been exacerbated by the financial climate of contemporary sports. Winning programs attract lucrative television money, bowl and tourney bids, alumni donations, and high attendance figures. While coaches may publicly espouse that their athletes are students first and athletes second, they and their institutions have a strong financial interest in recruiting good players and keeping them eligible by whatever means (Knight Foundation Commission 1991; Lederman 1991).

Historically, the organization responsible for policing collegiate athletic programs, the National Collegiate Athletic Association (NCAA), had focused on violations of amateurism—such as athletes receiving financial inducements to play —and neglected the investigation of charges that athletes may be receiving an inferior education. Recently, however, the NCAA has enacted reforms designed to put the "student" back into "student athlete." Propositions 48 and 42 define specific academic eligibility criteria for freshmen athletes. These criteria consist of a sliding scale that focuses on the grade point average earned in thirteen core high school subjects and a score on either the SAT or ACT. Those who fall short of the standards are not able to participate but can earn eligibility if a 1.8 GPA (out of 4.0) is maintained over twenty-four credits during their freshmen year of college.

The NCAA has also limited athlete practice and conditioning time so that more attention could be devoted to academics. Student athletes are limited to twenty hours of practice per week, four hours per day, and a maximum of six days of practice per week. Out-of-season conditioning activities are limited to eight hours per week.

Finally, graduation rates for athletes in all sports must be publicly available. As a result, incoming athletes can be aware of the typical educational outcomes of the institution.

What effect have these reforms had on the relationship(s) between athletics and academics? Research to date typically suggests that athletic participation complements rather than undermines academic performance. Successful athletic programs have been shown to increase student interest in a given institution. The increased interest is reflected in increased applications, which permits admission personnel to be more selective in setting entrance standards. Thus, freshmen classes at universities with successful athletic programs have higher average SAT scores than freshmen classes at universities with less successful programs (Bremmer and Kesselring, 1993; McCormick and Tinsley, 1987). This effect is more pronounced for big time football programs than for big time basketball programs (Tucker and Amato, 1994). Participation in successful athletic programs also tends to increase graduation rates (Tucker 1992; Lederman 1991). Again, basketball participation may be an exception (Lederman 1991). However, faculty academic performance, when measured by research output, is reduced as football success increases (Shugart, Tollison, and Goff, 1986).

Although previous studies provide important insights into the relationships between athletics and academics, they focus on the college in aggregate. They largely ignore the individual student athlete and the time allocation decisions that these individuals must make in attempting to perform admirably on the field and in the classroom. The purpose of this study is to focus on the individual athlete. Rather than examining the effects of a successful sports program on the academic performance of an entire collegiate class, we examine the effects of athletic participation on the *individual* student's grade point average.

MODEL OF ACADEMIC ACHIEVEMENT

Ascertaining the effect of athletic participation on a student's grade point average requires a model of academic achievement. It must capture the characteristics of the student and his/her environment. We specify the following:

$$GPA = a_0 + a_1 \text{Human Capital} + a_2 \text{Environment} + a_3 \text{Support} + a_4 \text{Activities} + \epsilon,$$

where GPA is cumulative grade point average for each student.

Human Capital

Human capital variables include student SAT score, age, and gender. SAT score measures a student's academic capabilities upon entering college. Age is a proxy for the maturity of the student. Both are expected to be positively related to GPA. Gender, which takes a value of 1 for males and 0 for females, attempts to capture any inherent differences, should any exist, in male and female academic achievement.

Environment

The academic environment of the student includes the university environment and the home/community environment. Student GPAs may be expected to differ depending on the student's choice of major/college. While unable to make *a priori* judgments as to how a particular college choice may affect GPA after accounting for the many other factors in our achievement model, we do acknowledge that different colleges have different average GPAs, and that students often claim that certain curricula are easier than others. Student semester standing should also affect GPA, with an increase in semester standing increasing GPA. As students continue in a university they become more comfortable with their environment, have the opportunity to improve study habits, and become more focused in their educational studies and goals.

Two variables are used to describe characteristics of a student's home/community environment.[1] An increase in the median household income (MedInc) for a student's hometown suggests more educational opportunities available to the student and/or more tax revenue available to support the student's secondary education. Each would imply a higher expected university GPA. The expectations for the percent of the hometown population that is urban (PopUrb) are less clear. Anecdotally, urban environments are often associated with larger class sizes, higher crime, and harsher learning milieus, but are also associated with faster maturation by its inhabitants.

Support

Student support is the percent of full cost (as defined by the university) covered by athletic scholarships (AthlSchol), academic scholarships (AcadSchol), loans, grants, and work study. All but work study should allow students more time to pursue their studies and enhance academic performance. Work study represents time spent on jobs in lieu of studying and therefore may limit scholastic achievement.

Activities

Data were limited concerning student activities. Variables indicating whether a student was an initiate or pledge is used to indicate extracurricular participation in fraternities or sororities. Other extracurricular activities include participation in club sports. Women club sports (WClub) include bowling, cycling, equestrian, racquetball, rifle, rugby, alpine skiing and soccer, whereas men club sports (MClub) include bowling, boxing, cycling, ice hockey, rifle, racquetball, rugby, alpine skiing, and volleyball. Participation in varsity sports is the key activity identified in our model. Varsity participation is the basis for defining two variables: participation in revenue-producing sports (RevAthl) and participation in nonrevenue producing sports (NoRevAthl). The revenue producing sports are men's football, men's basketball and women's basketball. Varsity participation is also desegregated into thirteen different female and thirteen different male sports programs.[2] MultiVar is used to identify individuals who participate in multiple varsity sports.

THE DATA

Data were compiled for all spring 1995, full-time baccalaureate students at Penn State University at University Park (PSU). PSU's Offices of Administrative Systems,

Table 12.1
SAT Averages by Group

Student Group	N	Avg. SAT	Std. Dev. SAT	Student Group	N	Avg. SAT	Std. Dev. SAT
All Students	19566	1030	172	WSoccer	18	949	132
All Athletes	583	989	146	WinTrack	41	977	127
Male Athletes	369	996	150	WCross Cntry	18	967	136
Female Athletes	214	977	138	MBaseball	26	955	138
RevAthl	119	927	143	MBaskball	18	1021	143
NoRevAthl	466	1005	143	MFence	12	1012	176
WBaskball	9	877	78	MFootball	92	914	140
WFence	11	1104	180	MGolf	14	1039	91
WFldHockey	17	924	124	MGymnast	7	1076	185
WGolf	14	979	139	MLacross	39	1042	117
WGymnast	16	994	135	MSwim	23	1027	161
WLacross	22	970	113	MTennis	11	965	115
WSwim	27	995	132	MOutTrack	58	1058	136
WTennis	9	952	173	MVllyBall	15	1057	130
WOutTrack	42	981	127	MSoccer	20	1020	164
WVllyBall	12	1021	120	MWrestle	34	988	166

Financial Aid, Registrar, and Student Information Systems are the sources of these data. A total of 19,566 students, including 583 varsity athletes, were identified for our sample after deleting records with missing information.

ACADEMICS AND ATHLETICS: PRELIMINARY ANALYSIS

Key concerns of the academic community are preferential treatment in admissions (or recruitment) for athletes and academic subsidies for athletes to enhance retention and eligibility. The data in Table 12.1 addresses the first of these concerns. It reports average SAT scores for all students and various varsity athlete subgroups. The average SAT score of 989 for athletes is less than the overall student average of 1,030. This difference is more pronounced for women athletes (977) than for male athletes (996), and is more pronounced for athletes in revenue-producing sports (927) than for those in nonrevenue sports (989). Participants in twenty of the twenty-six reported sports have SAT averages below the average for all students. The two lowest SAT averages are for participants in women's basketball (877) and men's football (914), both revenue-producing sports. Therefore, athletes are at a disadvantage relative to other students in terms of expected academic achievement. As a result, retention and eligibility may be a concern.

Table 12.2
College GPA and Enrollment

COLLEGE	% ATHLETE	% STUDENT
Education (3.18)	9.09	6.83
Health, Human Dev. (2.97)	23.16	13.91
Arts and Architecture (2.93)	1.37	4.76
Business Admin. (2.92)	12.69	14.33
Sciences (2.92)	4.46	9.22
Liberal Arts (2.91)	16.30	14.67
Communications (2.89)	3.60	5.30
Engineering (2.83)	10.12	16.32
Earth, Mineral Sci. (2.78)	1.72	2.64
Agriculture (2.72)	2.57	6.56
Undergrad Studies (2.58)	14.92	5.44

Note: GPA is estimated holding constant SAT. This is done through calculating the fitted value for GPA (at the mean SAT) by estimating the following regression equation: GPA = $b_0 + c_i$SAT + d_i College$_i$, (i = 1, 2, 3. . ., 11). Using actual GPA gave similar qualitative results.

Do athletes then major in easier curricular programs to offset their SAT disadvantage? Table 12.2 provides data necessary to address this question, including the average student GPA for each college, and the percentage of athletes and total students enrolled in that college. Easy curricula, or "grade-inflated" curricula, should be associated with higher average student GPAs. In the two colleges with highest estimated GPAs, athletes enroll at a disproportionately higher rate than other students. Athletes do appear to take "easier" courses to enhance their level of "academic achievement." The clear exception is the 14.92% of athletes who enroll in the Division of Undergraduate Studies, which has the lowest average GPA. However, this college is only for freshmen and sophomores who have yet to declare a major, so the data suggest that a larger proportion of athletes are not making significant progress toward their degrees. For the athletes that have declared a major, many attempt to offset their SAT disadvantage with an easier curriculum.

ESTIMATING THE MODEL OF ACADEMIC ACHIEVEMENT

The data in the previous section provide evidence that the academic potential for athletes is lower than other students (i.e., SAT scores), and that athletes may enroll in less rigorous curricula to help retain eligibility. But, these data do not tell whether the act of participating in athletics helps or hinders a student's academic achievement. Coaches and athletic competition may help structure the student athlete's life, enhance self-esteem, and lead to improved athletic and academic performance. On the other hand, student athletes may be forced to commit so much time and effort to their sports that there is a negative impact on their grades. To address this relationship between athletic participation and academic performance we estimate our model of academic achievement.

The results of the estimation identifying varsity participation in revenue-generating and non revenue-generating sports are reported in Table 12.3, and the results of estimation identifying all individual varsity sports are reported in Table 12.4. The results on the variables unrelated to sports participation are similar across models. As expected, higher SAT scores and higher semester standing are associated with higher GPAs. In contrast, older students and male students have lower grades than their counterparts. The former result suggests that the increase in the population of nontraditional students may be a harbinger of lower overall GPAs at the university.

Curricular choice is important in determining GPA. For the sake of brevity, we will not interpret each coefficient. But as a group, the college variables have significant explanatory power, and within the group there is significant variation. Students from higher income and more urban hometowns have lower academic achievement, although the effect is marginal. Student support has mixed effects on academic performance. Counter to our expectations, grant and loan recipients have reduced performance while work study recipients perform better. Perhaps, in the face of multiple demands on their time, the work study students learn to be more organized and develop better time management skills. Membership in fraternities and sororities is associated with lower academic performance.

Finally, we see that, as a group, sports club participants and nonrevenue sports participants have grades comparable to other students. However, revenue sports participants as a group have significantly lower grades than other students. The impact on the expected GPA of participants in revenue sports is -0.148. The magnitude of this effect seems small, but with an average GPA for all students equal to 2.916 and a standard deviation of 0.53, this result implies that the average revenue sport athlete has a GPA equivalent to approximately the thirty-ninth percentile of the entire student body. Moreover, this effect occurs even after controlling for SAT disadvantages and curricular choices made by the athletes.

The impact of athletic participation on GPA, however, is not uniform between particular sports groups. Although participants in nonrevenue sports as a group exhibited no significant differences in GPA, we find that grades are significantly different in three individual nonrevenue sports. Women's field hockey and men's fencing participants face dramatic declines in GPA. On the other hand, the women's swim team participants have above average academic performance. Participants in all other nonrevenue sports perform equivalently to their nonathletic peers.

Regarding revenue sports, the athletes exhibit no significant differences in GPAs except for men's football. Participants in men's football perform worse than their peers with comparable backgrounds. Because men's football is the only revenue sport with a significant effect on GPA, the quantitative remarks concerning revenue sports participants made in the above paragraph should apply only to those in men's football. Interestingly, men's football is the primary source of sports revenue to the university. Also, there are more athletes competing in men's football than other sports. The ninety-two participants in men's football is almost twice the number of athletes competing in any other sport. It is also interesting to see that multiple varsity athletes have grades that are no worse (or better) than their peers.

CONCLUSION

We compiled data on all full-time baccalaureate students at Penn State University for spring 1995. Using these data, we examined the effects of athletic participation on classroom achievement. In the process we uncovered a number of interesting findings.

First, athletes have average SAT scores that are below those of other students. Two of the three revenue-producing sports for the university show the lowest SAT averages. This occurs despite the SAT and high school core course requirements of Propositions 42 and 48. While the initiation of these propositions may have reduced the differences between the scholastic backgrounds of athletes and nonathletes, measurable differences continue to exist. These data are consistent with admission policies that pave the way to recruit an excellent athlete who is a marginal student, but they also create a situation where the student athlete will continually be at a disadvantage in competing with peers in the classroom.

If the student athlete begins with a competitive disadvantage in the classroom, maintaining eligibility may become a problem. Perhaps in an attempt to offset this academic disadvantage, athletes will opt for less rigorous curricula as suggested by our results. If this is the primary reason for curricula choices, athletes have had their academic opportunities compromised. Our results also imply that athletes may be

Table 12.3

Academic Achievement Model (RevAthl and NoRevAthl)

Variable	Coefficient	|t-stat|	Variable	Coefficient	|t-stat|
Constant	2.199	41.82***	Semester	0.047	24.99***
SAT	0.001	51.03***	Medinc	-0.00004	1.74*
Age	-0.026	11.33***	PopUrb	-0.0005	4.30***
Gender	-0.176	24.86***	AthlSchol	0.0006	1.04
Agriculture	-0.193	9.76***	AcadSchol	0.007	22.42***
Business Admin.	0.025	1.47	Loans	-0.002	11.70***
Communications	-0.024	1.18	Grants	-0.0006	2.73***
Undergrad. Studies	-0.237	11.36***	Work Study	0.004	2.27**
Education	0.206	10.50***	Initiate	-0.057	6.07***
Earth, Mineral Sci.	-0.132	5.23***	Pledge	-0.074	2.99***
Engineering	-0.063	3.65***	WClub	-0.094	1.303
Health, Human	0.017	1.02	MClub	0.029	0.63
Liberal Arts	-0.024	1.04	RevAthl	-0.148	2.74***
Science	-0.012	0.62	NoRevAthl	-0.007	0.24
Other Colleges	0.025	0.11	MultiVar	0.089	1.74*

Adjusted R^2 = 0.2664   F statistic = 237.84

Notes: Using two-tailed t-tests, *** indicates statistical significance at the .01 level of significance; ** at the .05 level; and * at the .10 level. The College of Arts and Architecture is used as the benchmark in assessing the effect of college on GPA.

Table 12.4
Academic Achievement Model (All Varsity Sports)

Variable	Coefficient	|t-stat|	Variable	Coefficient	|t-stat|
Constant	2.201	41.85***	MClub	0.029	0.63
SAT	0.001	50.98***	WBaskball	-0.163	1.02
Age	-0.026	11.34***	WFence	0.042	0.30
Gender	-0.176	24.47***	WFldHockey	-0.204	1.79*
Agriculture	-0.193	9.78***	WGolf	0.182	1.47
Business Admin.	0.025	1.41	WGymnast	0.035	0.29
Communications	-0.024	1.18	WLacross	-0.033	0.33
Undergrad. Studies	-0.238	11.41***	WSwim	0.102	1.72*
Education	0.207	10.52***	WTennis	-0.012	0.81
Earth, Mineral Sci.	-0.134	5.31***	WTrack	-0.234	0.79
Engineering	-0.064	3.71***	WVllyBall	-0.100	0.72
Health, Human Dev.	0.018	1.03	WSoccer	-0.008	0.07
Liberal Arts	-0.025	1.46	MBaseball	-0.146	1.60
Science	-0.012	0.64	MBaskball	-0.033	0.30
Other Colleges	0.024	0.11	MFence	-0.252	1.91*
Semester	0.047	25.01***	MFootball	-0.151	2.45**
Medinc.	-0.00004	1.79*	MGolf	-0.06	0.49

169

Table 12.4 continued

PopUrb	-0.0006	4.36***	MGymnast	0.236	1.35
AthlSchol	0.0004	0.55	MLacross	-0.082	1.12
AcadSchol	0.006	22.40***	MSwim	0.155	1.59
Loans	-0.002	11.71***	MTennis	0.223	1.60
Grants	-0.0006	2.67***	MTrack	-0.181	0.62
Work Study	0.004	2.26**	MVllvBall	-0.021	0.17
Initiate	-0.056	6.05***	MSoccer	0.09	0.90
Pledge	-0.073	2.97***	MWrestle	-0.073	0.92
WClub	-0.094	1.29	MultiVar	0.288	1.01
Adjusted R^2 = 0.2666			F statistic = 135.21		

Notes: Using two-tailed t-tests, ***indicates statistical significance at the .01 level of significance; ** at the .05 level; and * at the .10 level. The College of Arts and Architecture is used as the benchmark in assessing the effect of college GPA.

significantly slower in advancing toward an academic degree. If the university is willing to bring in athletes as "disadvantaged" students, then the university should consider allocating more resources to help the athletes overcome their disadvantage.

Even after holding constant SAT scores and curricular choices, participants in a few sports still exhibited significantly different GPAs than their student peers. Men's football, which represents the largest number of athletes, had average GPAs consistent with only the thirty-ninth percentile of the student body. The NCAA prohibits these athletes from being paid for their athletic services, despite the fact that football is the largest source of sports revenue to the university. Now it appears that the exploitation of these athletes, the big money sports athlete, has been extended to the classroom. Post-season football playoffs would exacerbate exploitation in both the athletic and academic arenas.

NOTES

1. Personal data on students could not be released for use in this study so hometown characteristics were used as proxies. The percentage of people with baccalaureate degrees in the home town of the student was initially used in addition to the variables described in this section. However, this variable was omitted because of high collinearity with MedInc.

2. Women's indoor track, outdoor track, and cross-country were combined into one variable, WTrack, and men's indoor track, outdoor track, and cross-country were combined into one variable, MTrack, due to the high collinearity between these sports variables.

Section V

LABOR MARKET ISSUES IN TEAM SPORTS

13

Did Collusion Adversely Affect Outcomes in the Baseball Player's Labor Market?: A Panel Study of Salary Determination from 1986 to 1992

Timothy R. Hylan, Maureen J. Lage, and Michael Treglia

INTRODUCTION

> Does anyone who thinks about it for one minute believe that ballplayers voluntarily played for less than they were worth, or that owners fought for one hundred years to keep the reserve rule because of idealism and not because of a profit motive?— Marvin Miller, *A Whole Different Ballgame*

One of the most notable characteristics of the employment relationship in professional baseball has been continuing conflict between the players and team owners. Although there have been numerous points of contention between labor and management in this industry, the main issue separating the two sides has been the distribution of the rents that are generated by selling viewing rights to the contests. In an early effort to restrain labor's share of these rents, the owners imposed a contract provision known as the reserve clause to "protect" certain players on each team, that is, beginning in 1879, other teams were prevented from enticing the protected players away from the original team through higher salary offers. By establishing monopsony power over players, the reserve clause enabled team owners to keep labor costs relatively low.

Two of the important institutional innovations that weakened the reserve clause were the 1973 implementation of final offer salary arbitration for players with at least three years of Major League Baseball (MLB) experience, and the 1976 advent of free agency for players with at least six years of service. Given the behavior of the arbitrator, final offer salary arbitration is expected to reduce the monopsonistic power of the team owner and, thus, increase baseball players' bargaining power and their salaries.[1] In fact, these expectations were borne out.[2]

Burgess and Marburger (1992) found that starting pitchers who were eligible for final offer salary arbitration were paid 89% more than arbitration ineligible starting pitchers. Similar results were obtained for relief pitchers and hitters. On average, arbitration eligible relief pitchers were paid 58% more than ineligible relief pitchers, and arbitration eligible hitters received salaries that were 86% higher than arbitration ineligible hitters. However, since arbitration eligibles are still bound to a specific team, on average the salaries of these players might be expected to remain below the level of free agent salaries. Hirschberg, Scully, and Slottje (1992) conclude that salary arbitration does not equate player pay with player marginal revenue products. In a contrasting view, Marburger (1996) suggests that the salary determination process is similar for free agents and arbitration eligible players although arbitrators do incorporate an experience factor that, relative to the free agent salary level, adjusts downward the arbitration eligible player's salary.[3]

The 1976 introduction of free agency removed the monopsonistic power that team owners held over players who met the service requirement of six years or more in MLB. As expected, the competitive bidding for players who declared themselves free agents led to increased salaries. Cassing and Douglas (1980), Fort and Quirk (1995), Quirk and Fort (1992), Raimondo (1983), and Scully (1989), among others, document the rise in salaries for eligible players after the introduction of free agency. Furthermore, higher salaries also extended to nonfree agent eligible players; see Hill (1985), Hill and Spellman (1983), and Sommers and Quinton (1982). The increase in player salaries during the free agent era was accompanied by a decline in reported team profits. In 1980, the owners of MLB teams attempted to obtain restrictions on the freedom of players in the free agent market through negotiation with the players' union. However, the players went on strike during the last week of the exhibition season and threatened to go back on strike after playing for six weeks of the regular season. The owners capitulated.[4] Having failed to negotiate restrictions on the mobility of free agents, the owners' next step was to exercise restraint in their bidding for free agents. The owners colluded to restrain their bids on each other's free agents in an effort to reduce player costs and increase team profitability. Lower salaries for free agents would directly achieve this purpose. Indirect effects may also contribute to this goal through the arbitration-eligible players if the salaries of these players are linked to the (now lower) salaries of free agents. Scully (1989) describes the incidents that led to the filing of a grievance by the MLB Players Association (the fifth and current organization of professional ballplayers) and the subsequent findings by two independent arbitrators that the owners had acted to suppress free agency in violation of MLB's Basic Agreement after the 1985 and 1986 seasons. Zimbalist (1992b) also discusses these incidents and updates the story to include the finding that owners again colluded to restrain salaries in the free agent market after the 1987 season.[5]

In contrast to the number of studies on the effects associated with alterations in the rules governing negotiations between players and team owners, relatively little work has assessed the economic impact of owner conduct on player salaries during the 1980s. Bruggink and Rose (1990) provide a systematic analysis of the "financial restraint" hypothesis that owners paid free agents lower salaries during the first two collusion years. Their study employs the Scully (1974b) two-equation model of marginal revenue determination. It compares the ratio of actual salary to estimated marginal revenue product (MRP) for free agents in 1984 (the last year before collusion) to that ratio during the years 1985–1986.[6] The unweighted salary/MRP ratio for free agents in the first two years of the collusion period was 28% below the 1984 ratio.[7] Ferguson, Jones, and Stewart (1996) estimate a parametric model of league conduct to examine the collusive behavior of team owners. They show a reduction in the power of the league as a cartel in the 1989–1991 seasons relative to the 1986–1988 period. Both studies yield results that are consistent with the financial restraint hypothesis and charges of collusion.

Bruggink and Rose (1990) further hypothesize that by restraining bids for free agents, the owners also saved salary expenditures for nonfree agent eligible players. This spillover effect could arise if the nonfree agent players based their salary demands upon comparisons with the free agents. Similarly, Burgess and Marburger (1992) suggest that their results, which show that arbitration eligible players receive higher salaries than noneligible players, may actually be underestimates of the effect of gaining the right to salary arbitration. The reason is that their sample of players was drawn after the 1987–1988 seasons when salaries of arbitration eligible players may have been artificially depressed. One last piece of evidence consistent with salaries being suppressed during the collusion years is that the spread between the amount requested by arbitration eligible players and the amount offered by the team was reduced by approximately 9% during the collusion years.[8]

This chapter examines the labor market for MLB players during the 1986–1992 seasons to assess the impact of team owners' collusive behavior from 1986 to 1988 on the salary structure. The wealth of data on both player and team performance and other characteristics makes MLB an industry that is especially suited for an analysis of conduct on market outcomes. In contrast to previous analyses of the collusion era, this study employs a direct salary equation that relates a player's compensation to his productivity statistics as well as to characteristics of the player's team and his home market.[9] In addition, although many participants in MLB and observers of this industry emphasize the importance of "intangibles" as determinants of productivity and, presumably, compensation, few of the previous studies have controlled for the presence of individual effects.[10] We employ panel data techniques to control for unobservable individual effects such as those due to a player's "heart," personality, and/or fan appeal. The period of owner collusion is flagged with an indicator variable to measure the effects of this behavior on player salaries. Since the panel data contains observations on players at different points in their career, an important contribution of this chapter is that it provides an examination of differential effects on salaries due to the regime change. In contrast, Bruggink and Rose (1990) consider the effect of collusion on only those players who are eligible for free agency.

The next section describes the econometric methodology in greater detail. "Data and Description Statistics" presents the data and gives descriptive statistics. The results are discussed in "Results" and the last section concludes the chapter.

ECONOMETRIC METHODOLOGY
This section details the empirical model employed to examine the conduct of

teamowners in the market for baseball players as a determinant of the wealth distribution in MLB. Consider the following salary equation:

$$\ln W_{i,t} = f_i + \beta X_{i,t-1} + \gamma Z_{i,t-1} + \eta J_{i,t} + e_{i,t} \tag{1}$$

where:

$W_{i,t} \equiv$ real, total compensation of player i in period t;

$f_i \equiv$ individual specific fixed effect;

$X_{i,t-1} \equiv$ productivity characteristics of player i during period t-1;

$Z_{i,t-1} \equiv$ characteristics of the team for which player i played during period t-1;

$J_{i,t} \equiv$ an indicator variable identifying the period of owner collusion;

$e_{i,t} \equiv$ error term that is assumed to be *i.i.d.*; and

β, γ, and η are parameters to be estimated.

Equation (1) is a classic model of salary determination incorporating a rich set of explanatory variables. Salaries of the players are directly linked to their on-field performance, experience, and star-attraction, as well as to characteristics relevant to their team, and other structural variables.

For the most part, the variables employed in the analysis and their expected effects are described in the following section. At this point, we wish to emphasize that in the labor literature in general, and for observers of MLB in particular, there is recognition of the importance of unobserved individual effects as determinants of both productivity and earnings. Abraham and Farber (1987), Altonji and Shakotko (1987), Topel (1991), and *Total Baseball* (1996) are examples of such individual effects. Not controlling for individual effects can bias the estimated returns to the other variables. More precisely, if the unobserved individual specific term (f_i in equation (1)) is uncorrelated with the **X**, **Z**, and **J** variables, then it is appropriate to aggregate f_i into the error term and apply OLS. However, if the fixed effects are correlated with the other regressors, then this procedure will result in biased estimates. The specification employed in this chapter controls for this possibility by estimating a fixed-effects model of salary determination and is one characteristic that distinguishes our work from that of Fort (1992), Quirk and Fort (1992), and all of the studies employing the two-equation approach in the estimation of MRP.[11]

The $J_{i,t}$ indicator variable and its interactions with the individual performance variables, $X_{i,t}$, are the measures that assess the extent to which the owners' attempt to regain market power after the introduction of free agency altered the distribution of wealth in MLB. Collusion in MLB is taken to be the coordinated actions of input purchasers in an attempt to establish monopsony power. If baseball team owners are successful in this endeavor, it would be expected that they would pay lower salaries for players in the free agent market. Thus, the test for the general impact of collusion is a negative η, the coefficient on the variable indicating the collusion era. Further, statistically significant interactions of the collusion era indicator with the individual performance variables and team characteristics could capture the differential influences of collusion on salaries.

DATA AND DESCRIPTIVE STATISTICS

The analysis distinguishes between pitchers and hitters since the former are generally thought of as "defensive" players and the latter are "offensive" players. There are 1,353 observations on 441 pitchers and 1,929 observations on 558 hitters. Table 13.1 presents descriptive statistics on the annual salaries for pitchers and hitters. The mean salary for pitchers rose from approximately $389,640 in 1986 to $1,088,781 in 1992. The average salary for hitters in our sample increased from $448,270 to $1,077,150 during the same period. Average salaries for pitchers declined 1.9% between 1986 and 1987 while average hitter salaries declined approximately 3% in 1987.[12] However, between 1990 and 1991, mean pitcher salaries soared 88% while mean hitter salaries rose almost 64%.

Equation (1) posits that a player's salary will be related to his playing performance. In general, it is expected that "better" players will help teams win more games; that winning will increase attendance and fan support; and, in turn, higher attendance and fan support will lead to higher revenues and profits for ball clubs. It is further anticipated that those players who generate more wins and/or fan support for their

Table 13.1
Descriptive Statistics of Salaries for Pitchers and Hitters—By Year

Hitters' Salaries

Year	Mean	Std. Dev.	Minimum	Maximum
1986	44.827	43.667	6	337.75
1987	43.474	44.743	6	212.733
1988	47.081	48.023	6.25	234
1989	51.182	53.232	6.8	246.667
1990	55.495	58.052	10	320
1991	90.877	92.987	10	380
1992	107.715	119.006	10.9	610

Pitchers' Salaries

Year	Mean	Std. Dev.	Minimum	Maximum
1986	38.964	36.458	6	182.5
1987	38.211	37.680	6.25	185
1988	44.391	40.662	6.25	207
1989	48.160	51.383	6.8	276.667
1990	49.340	52.850	10	260
1991	93.211	95.298	10	362.5
1992	108.878	119.416	10.9	491.667

Figures are in 10,000s nominal dollars.

teams will receive higher salaries, *ceteris paribus*. The performance variables for hitters and pitchers are defined in Table 13.2. The data on the performance of MLB players are taken from *Total Baseball*.

Hitter performance is measured by the player's slugging average, strikeout to base-on-balls ratio, the number of stolen bases, and two indicator variables identifying players winning the Golden Glove or Most Valuable Player awards. The strikeout to base-on-balls ratio is expected to be negatively related to salary while the others are anticipated to have a positive association. The statistics from the previous year are included in the salary regression to measure the impact of recent past performance while cumulative values of player performance capture the effect of lifetime performance on salary. In the salary regression for pitchers, individual performance is measured by winning percentage, the ratio of games started to games in which the pitcher appeared, the ratio of games saved to games in which the pitcher appeared, the ratio of strikeouts to bases-on-balls allowed, and indicator variables for whether the pitcher won twenty games in the previous season, won the Cy Young award, or won the Golden Glove award.[13] All these variables are expected to be positively related to the pitcher's salary. Again, all performance variables are lagged one year in the regression equation determining the player's salary in a given year, and cumulative measures are included to distinguish between the impact on salaries for players who are consistent performers and those who had a "good year."

At least since Rottenberg (1956), it has been recognized in the literature that characteristics of the team or the home market may also influence a player's MRP. For instance, teams gain revenue from both fan attendance and selling media rights to broadcast games. Hence, a player's value to a team is expected to be greater in a large market area than a small market area, *ceteris paribus*.[14] Further, fan interest is greater for those teams that are winning during a particular season. The owners of baseball teams have long contended that these drivers of marginal revenue product will also be determinants of the level of baseball players' salaries. Thus, for each player, we include his team's winning percentage from the preceding season to measure the effect on salary of a team being a "winner" or a "loser." Another control for a team's winning record and fan interest is an indicator variable that identifies whether the player was on a team that won the League Championship Series during the previous season. Likewise, a measure of the size of the population of the home city is included in the salary equation as well as the annual media revenues for each team.[15] Finally, as a control for institutional differences between leagues, an indicator for teams in the National League is included.

MLB delineates classes of players by ownership of the property rights to the player's services. In general, the number of years of experience in MLB that a player has accrued determines the player's property rights. Players with less than two years of experience are subject to the full power of baseball's reserve clause. This section of a player's contract gives a particular team owner the exclusive right to a given player's services. Players with three to five years of experience are eligible for final offer salary arbitration if disputes over compensation arise. An indicator variable, *YRSLG0*,

Table 13.2
Definitions of Variables

Variable	Description
LGSAL	Log of real, annual salary
SLG	Hitter's slugging percentage for the previous season
CUMSLG	Hitter's cumulative slugging percentage
SB	Hitter's stolen bases for the previous season
CUMSB	Hitter's cumulative stolen bases
MVP	Dummy variable equal to 1 if hitter won Most Valuable Player award in previous season
PCT	Pitcher's winning percentage for the previous season
CUMPCT	Pitcher's cumulative winning percentage
GSG	Pitcher's ratio of games started to games appeared in during previous season
CUMSGS	Pitcher's cumulative ratio of games started to games appeared in
SVG	Pitcher's ratio of games saved to games appeared in during previous season
CUMSVG	Pitcher's cumulative average ratio of games saved to games appeared in
TWENT	Dummy variable equal to 1 for pitchers who won twenty games
CYYOUNG	Dummy variable equal to 1 for Cy Young award winners
SOBB	Hitter or pitcher's strikeouts to base-on-balls ratio for the previous season
CUMSOBB	Hitters or pitcher's cumulative strikeouts to base-on-balls ratio
GGLOVE	Dummy variable equal to 1 if pitcher or hitter won Golden Glove award
CUMGLOVE	Cumulative number of Golden Glove awards for the pitcher or hitter
TPCT	Winning percentage for the team
POP	Population of the SMSA where the team is located
LCS	Dummy variable coded 1 if team won the league championship series

Table 13.2 continued

RREV	Real media revenues
NATL	Dummy variable equal to 1 if played in National League in previous season
YRSLG0	Dummy variable coded 1 for hitters with 3 to 5 years of experience
YRSLG1	Dummy variable coded 1 for hitters with 6 years of experience
YRSLG2	Dummy variable coded 1 for hitters with 7 TO 10 years of experience
YRSLG3	Dummy variable coded 1 for hitters with greater than 10 years of experience
AGENT	Dummy variable coded 1 for players who were declared free agents
COLLUSION	Dummy variable coded 1 from 1986 to 1988
COLAGENT	Interaction of *Collusion* and *Agent*

denotes this class of ballplayer. Players who have at least six years of service in MLB are eligible to negotiate with any team as a free agent. By identifying those players with six years of service, the *YRSLG1* variable allows measurement of the effect on salary of attaining the longevity required to attain free agent status. *YRSLG2* and *YRSLG3* denote the most experienced classes of ballplayers, in other words, those with seven to ten years, and eleven or more years of experience, respectively.

While the *YRSLG** (* = 0, 1, 2, 3) controls can identify longevity requirements for the ownership of property rights, these are still coarse measures since not all players eligible for free agency actually declare themselves to be a free agent. Thus, we collected data identifying each player who actually declared himself a free agent during the 1986–1992 period. *Agent* is coded "1" for a player who declares himself to be a free agent in a given year.[16] Someone who engages in this action is signaling a desire to improve the terms on which he is employed. Since free agents may have a number of teams bidding for their services, it is expected that *Agent* will have a positive impact on a player's compensation.

As indicated earlier, the owners were found by independent arbitrators to have colluded in the market for free agents after the 1985, 1986, and 1987 seasons. We define the *Collusion* variable to be coded "1" for all players during the 1986 through 1988 seasons. This variable captures any general effect on salaries during these years. Since the arbitrators found the owners to be in collusion in the market for free agents, *Collusion* was interacted with *Agent* to assess the impact of the collusion era on the players who declared as free agents. It is expected that the coefficient on the interaction between *Collusion* and *Agent* will be negative since this is the direct group targeted by the owner's collusion. Tables 13.3 and 13.4 present the descriptive statistics on the above variables as they pertain to hitters and pitchers, respectively.

RESULTS

This section presents the estimates of the MLB players salary equation and, in particular, examines the effect on player salaries due to the alleged collusive behavior of team owners during the 1986–1988 seasons. Separate results are presented for "offensive" and "defensive" players. Tables 13.5 and 13.6 contain the estimates of equation (1) using the fixed effects technique and, for comparison, an OLS regression.

Table 13.3
Descriptive Statistics—Hitters

Variable	Mean	Std. Dev.	Minimum	Maximum
LSGSAL	13.212	0.999	10.931	15.583
SLG	0.387	0.078	0	0.9
CUMSLG	0.394	0.059	0.211	0.597
SOBB	2.065	1.617	0	26
CUMSOBB	1.997	1.085	0.429	11
SB	8.825	11.764	0	109
CUMSB	66.748	88.212	0	632
GGLOVE	0.049	0.216	0	1
CUMGLOVE	0.441	1.436	0	12
MVP	0.003	0.054	0	1
AGENT	0.104	0.306	0	1
YRSLG0	0.330	0.470	0	1
YRSLG1	0.095	0.293	0	1
YRSLG2	0.274	0.446	0	1
YRSLG3	0.220	0.415	0	1
NATL	0.522	0.500	0	1
TPCT	0.506	0.064	0.338	0.667
LCS	0.087	0.281	0	1
POP	3267.776	1644.744	1122.886	6402.145
RREV	17.772	10.245	0	59.342
COLLUSION	0.434	0.496	0	1
COLAGENT	0.043	0.203	0	1

n = 1735.

Table 13.5 reports the results of the estimation for hitters over the 1986–1992 period. As expected, better individual performance statistics were associated, on average, with higher salaries. The lagged and cumulative measures of both slugging average and the number of stolen bases are positive determinants of salary while the ratio of strikeouts to bases-on-balls has the expected negative impact on hitter salaries. Winning a Golden Glove award is indicative of superior defensive ability and is associated with an approximate 27% higher salary.[17] However, winning a MVP award

Table 13.4
Descriptive Statistics—Pitchers

Variable	Mean	Std. Dev	Minimum	Maximum
LGSAL	13.019	1.043	10.704	15.349
PTC	0.491	0.197	0	1
CUMPCT	0.227	0.131	0	0.589
GSG	0.496	0.449	0	1
CUMGSG	0.491	0.386	0	1
SVG	0.074	0.146	0	0.762
CUMSVG	0.070	0.107	0	0.534
SOBB	1.996	1.090	0	18.333
CUMSOBB	1.849	0.534	0	0.464
GGLOVE	0.009	0.094	0	1
CUMGLOVE	0.044	0.334	0	5
TWENT	0.021	0.145	0	1
CYYOUNG	0.010	0.098	0	1
AGENT	0.114	0.318	0	1
YRSLG0	0.339	0.473	0	1
YRSLG1	0.093	0.291	0	1
YRSLG2	0.267	0.443	0	1
YRSLG3	0.184	0.388	0	1
NATL	0.541	0.499	0	1
TPCT	0.507	0.063	0.338	0.667
LCS	0.087	0.282	0	1
POP	3273.687	1659.801	1122.886	6402.145
RREV	20.621	8.735	10.710	59.342
COLLUSION	0.338	0.488	0	1
COLAGENT	0.041	0.198	0	1

n = 1353.

did not significantly raise salary for hitters.

Perhaps somewhat surprisingly, hitters who were declared free agents did not receive significantly higher salaries. However, after controlling for other attributes of the player, *Agent* may be reflecting other differences between a player and a team that lead to difficulties in negotiations rather than a difference between the team's assessment of the player's worth and the market's assessment of the player. Alternatively, this result may reflect the arbitration process and the suggestion that arbitrators replicate the free market salaries of comparable free agents (Marburger, 1996; and Hadley and Gustafson, 1991).

In contrast, the *YRSLG** variables that control for a player's experience in MLB and, thus, proxy for the property rights held by the player, do have the expected positive effect on hitter's salaries. Hitters who have three to five years of experience and,

Table 13.5
Regression Results—Hitters, 1986–1992

Variable	OLS Coefficient	OLS t-statistic	Fixed Effects Coefficient	Fixed Effects t-statistic
Constant	9.959***	50.053	---	---
SLG	1.415***	4.368	1.409***	3.546
CUMSLG	4.747***	11.127	3.534***	2.449
SOBB	-0.038***	-2.51	-0.039**	-2.103
CUMSOBB	-0.054***	-2.363	-0.139*	-1.884
SB	0.010***	4.945	0.008***	2.846
CUMSB	0.001***	4.504	0.004***	4.119
GGLOVE	0.351***	3.804	0.268***	2.429
CUMGLOVE	0.051***	3.417	0.001	0.020
MVP	0.484	1.554	0.120	0.393
AGENT	-0.074	-1.002	0.008	0.102
YRSLG0	0.749***	11.545	0.821***	10.753
YRSLG1	1.280***	15.954	1.273***	12.435
YRSLG2	1.390***	19.718	1.324***	11.065
YRSLG3	1.228***	14.972	1.020***	6.215
NATL	0.014	0.419	0.055	0.806
TPCT	-0.258	-0.881	-0.543	-1.605
LCS	0.198***	2.989	0.151**	2.089
POP	0.000	-0.156	0.000**	2.030
RREV	0.003	1.365	0.004	1.52
COLLUSION	-0.302***	-7.006	-0.236***	-4.434
COLAGENT	-0.147	-1.338	0.049	0.403
N	1735		1735	
Adj. R^2	0.529		0.625	

Note: *, **, and *** represent significance at the ten, five, and one percent levels, respectively.

hence, have attained the right to final offer salary arbitration, receive salaries that are approximately 82% higher than arbitration ineligible players. Those players with six years of service in MLB and, thus, have attained the right to become a free agent, receive salaries that are approximately 127% above those of the base salary. The more experienced hitters with seven to ten years of experience, that is, those who have earned free agency and established themselves as proven performers, have over a 130% salary differential. Finally, players who have been proven performers in the past but may now be in the twilight of their careers, those with eleven or more years of experience, earn a salary approximately double that of an inexperienced player. The concavity of this earnings-service profile is consistent with results reported by Blass (1992) who finds that salaries for hitters peak at twelve years of experience.

Table 13.6
Regression Results—Pitchers, 1986–1992

Variable	OLS Coefficient	t-statistic	Fixed Effects Coefficient	t-statistic
Constant	10.884***	56.659	---	---
PCT	0.141	1.398	0.153	1.274
CUMPCT	4.653***	10.772	6.097***	5.229
GSG	0.594***	6.404	0.432***	3.486
CUMGSG	-1.179***	-7.092	-0.987**	-1.983
SVG	1.920***	7.531	1.113***	3.579
CUMSVG	0.340	0.906	3.788***	4.138
SOBB	-0.011	-0.502	-0.021	-0.729
CUMSOBB	0.099**	2.115	0.308**	2.069
GGLOVE	0.421*	1.738	0.124	0.457
CUMGLOVE	-0.016	-0.241	0.064	0.379
TWENT	0.239*	1.817	-0.055	-0.387
CYYOUNG	0.428**	2.267	0.168	0.891
AGENT	-0.198***	-2.660	-0.118	-1.533
YRSLG0	0.813***	13.278	0.739***	9.864
YRSLG1	1.462***	18.236	1.368***	12.964
YRSLG2	1.597***	24.069	1.526***	13.204
YRSLG3	1.510***	20.569	1.547***	9.744
NATL	0.057	1.540	-0.016	-0.233
TPCT	-0.210	-0.630	-0.404	-1.057
LCS	0.033	0.458	0.010	0.125
POP	0.000	0.143	0.000	0.662
RREV	0.006***	2.428	0.009***	2.877
COLLUS	-0.382***	-8.593	-0.293***	-4.681
COLAGENT	-0.023	-0.195	0.146	1.072
N	1353		1353	
Adj. R^2	0.600		0.686	

Note: *, **, and *** represent significance at the ten, five, and one percent levels, respectively.

The National League indicator variable was not significant, which indicates that the salary setting process does not differ systematically between the two leagues.[18] Also, the population of the home city, media revenues, and team winning percentage were not significant determinants of salary for hitters. However, playing on a team that won a league championship series during the previous year did have a positive impact on hitter's salary.

The main result for hitters shows the effect of the owners' collusion on player salaries. The fixed effects model shows that owners were able to reduce salaries of hitters by approximately 24%, on average, during the 1986–1988 seasons.[19] However, the interaction of *Collusion* and *Agent* was not significantly different from zero. This implies the coordinated actions by the owners to restrain player costs had a general depressing effect on salaries and was not restricted to the market for free agents. The 24% reduction in hitter compensation while controlling for fixed effects is slightly less than the 28% decline in salaries (assuming MRPs remained the same) reported by Bruggink and Rose (1990).

Table 13.6 shows the estimates of equation (1) for salaries of pitchers over the 1986–1992 period. The estimates on the performance measures are in broad agreement with expectations. For instance, although a pitcher's lagged winning percentage was not a significant determinant of salary, cumulative winning percentage did have a positive impact. The lagged ratio of games started to number of games appeared-in was positively related to salary, as expected, but the cumulative measure of this variable was negatively related to salary. Both the lagged and cumulative measures of games saved to games appeared-in had the expected positive impact on salary. Only the cumulative measure of strikeouts to bases-on-balls was significant in the expected direction. Golden Glove award winners, twenty-game winners, and Cy Young award winners did not, on average, receive additional salary along with these accolades.

The OLS specification yielded the surprising result that pitchers who declared themselves to be free agents saw their salary decline approximately 20%. However, this result disappeared when controlling for the fixed effects; as with hitters, declaring free agency had no statistically significant effect on a player's salary. The controls for a pitcher's years of service in MLB (*YRSLG**) have the expected positive effect on salaries. For pitchers, attaining the right to final offer salary arbitration raises salaries approximately 74%. Pitchers who have six years of service in MLB generally earn salaries 137% above those of the least experienced pitchers. Finally, pitchers with the most years of experience in MLB (*YRSLG2* and *YRSLG3*) earn salaries over 150% above those pitchers who are subject to the full power of the reserve clause. In contrast to the hitters, pitchers with the greatest number of years of experience (*YRSLG3*) did not see a decline in salaries.

As above, the salary determination process for pitchers does not appear to differ between leagues; the National League indicator variable was statistically insignificant. Also, the winning percentage of the team and the population of the home city were not related to salaries. However, unlike the case of hitters, playing for a team that won a League Championship Series did not lead to higher salaries for pitchers, *ceteris paribus*, and media revenues were positively related to a pitcher's salary, albeit only modestly.

We now turn to the main result for the pitchers. In the fixed effects model, collusion by team owners during the 1986–1988 seasons lowered average salaries for pitchers by approximately 29%. This result is significant at the 1% level. As with hitters, this shows a general decline in salaries suffered by all pitchers. There was not an additional impact on players in the free agent market since the interaction of *Collusion* and *Agent* shows an insignificant effect.

The above results have established that the salary determination process during the 1986–1988 collusion period was different from the process during the 1989–1992 era. The 24% decline in hitter salaries and the 29% decline for pitchers roughly agree with the Bruggink and Rose (1990) estimate of a 28% decline in the unweighted salary to MRP ratio for players in their sample. The general decline in player salaries during the collusion era also supports the suggestion that spillover effects from the free agent market to both the arbitration eligible and arbitration ineligible players were important in salary determination (see Burgess and Marburger, 1992; and Frederick, Kaempfer, and Wobbekind, 1992).

Given the above results showing differences in the salary determination process between the collusion era and the latter years in the sample, further analysis was conducted by splitting the sample.[20] Specifically, the salary equations for both pitchers and hitters were estimated separately for the 1986–1988 and the 1989–1992 periods. For hitters, there are widespread differences in the coefficients on almost all explanatory variables in both the OLS and fixed effects models. The hypothesis that the coefficients are the same in both models is rejected by an F-test at the 1% confidence level. For pitchers, while the coefficients show apparent dissimilarities between the two periods, an F-test failed to reject the hypothesis of equal coefficients in the two models at the 5% significance level.

CONCLUSION

In contrast to the large number of studies of the economic effects of final offer salary arbitration and free agency in the market for professional baseball players, there has been relatively little analysis of the impact of owner conduct during the 1980s on player salaries. This chapter employs a direct model of salary determination that exploits panel data techniques to control for unobservable individual effects such as those due to a player's "heart," personality, or fan appeal. Further, a rich set of human capital and experience variables makes it possible to assess the differential impacts on player salaries that stem from collusion by the team owners.

The fixed effects model shows that, on average, collusion among the owners during the 1986–1988 period lowered salaries for hitters by approximately 24%. Similarly, pitcher salaries were reduced by about 29% during the collusion years. This effect was not limited to declared free agents nor was there an additional impact on salaries for this class of player.

NOTES

1. In all cases, the self-interest of the arbitrator leads to behavior that can be interpreted as "fair." However, fairness can manifest itself in a variety of ways. Frederick, Kaempfer, and Wobbekind (1992) summarize three different types of decision behaviors that have been employed in analysis of arbitrator behavior in MLB.

2. Chelius and Dworkin (1980) and Dworkin (1981).

3. See also Hadley and Gustafson (1991).

4. DeBrock and Roth (1981) analyze a variable-threat model of bargaining between owners and players that explains the unusual discontinuous strike behavior threatened by the players

association.

5. Scully (1989) suggests that collusion may have occurred through 1989.

6. Salary negotiations in MLB occur after the season ends. The dates in Bruggink and Rose (1990) refer to the season that was just completed. In contrast, this chapter dates the negotiations as applying to the upcoming season.

7. Bruggink and Rose (1990) also report that the salary/MRP ratio was 38% smaller in the collusion period when calculated using weighted means.

8. The collusion period in Frederick, Kaempfer, and Wobbekind (1992) corresponds to the arbitration cases heard during 1986–1988.

9. Fort (1992) and Fort and Quirk (1992) also employ a direct model of salary determination.

10. Blass (1992) and Kahn (1993a) control for fixed effects although those studies were not concerned with the effect of owner collusion.

11. A Hausman test rejected the hypothesis that the individual effects are uncorrelated with the regressor and, hence, a random effects specification was inappropriate.

12. Hirschberg, Scully, and Slottje (1992, Table 1) show that MLB average player salaries declined 2.1% between 1986 and 1987.

13. Due to increasing specialization in the use of pitchers, the ratios of games started to games appeared and games saved to games appeared are included to differentiate between starting pitchers and relievers.

14. See Rottenberg (1956), Cymrot (1983), and Fort and Quick (1995), among others.

15. The population measure is adjusted for the number of baseball teams in the home city. See Coffin (1996).

16. The source for data on Agent is the *Official Baseball Guide*, various issues.

17. The cumulative number of Golden Glove awards is statistically insignificant in the fixed effects model.

18. Zimbalist (1992a) found a positive and significant coefficient for NL teams in a regression determining team revenues. This was attributed to differential sharing from the MLB's media revenue package. The disproportionate sharing was eliminated after the 1988 season.

19. The OLS results yielded a 30% reduction in hitter salaries during the collusion years.

20. These results are available from the authors upon request.

14

Baseball's New Collective Bargaining Agreement: How Will It Affect the National Pastime?

Daniel R. Marburger

INTRODUCTION

Perhaps only the 1919 Black Sox scandal rivaled the cancellation of the 1994 World Series in damaging the image of the national pastime. To add insult to injury, the strike that caused the abrupt end to the 1994 season also delayed the start of the 1995 season. Fan reaction to the two-season strike was severe. Attendance plummeted once the game resumed, and baseball has yet to post attendance figures that rival its pre-strike level (Major League Baseball, MLB@archives, WWW.majorleaguebaseball .com).

Yet strikes and lockouts are hardly new to Major League Baseball (MLB). Indeed, since 1972, no new agreement has been signed and ratified without the accompaniment of a work stoppage. Of baseball's six stoppages, however, none was as contentious as the 1994–1995 strike.

The 1994 negotiations were stalemated by management's call for a salary cap. The salary cap would fix league payrolls to an agreed-on percentage of baseball revenues. Eventually, the clubs succeeded in placing a substitute version of a salary cap, the luxury tax, into the bargaining agreement. Clubs whose payrolls exceeded an established threshold will have to pay a tax. The proceeds from the tax will be largely used to promote the game.

The 1996 agreement contains some other conspicuous changes. For the first time, revenue-sharing appears in the collective bargaining agreement, and the new scheme radically departs from its predecessor. The new agreement also calls for a temporary payroll tax to be assessed on players and a joint request by Congress to amend baseball's antitrust exemption.

The purpose of this chapter is to examine the 1996 collective bargaining agreement and to predict its effects on the game of baseball. Relying on the economics of sports literature, this study will concentrate on the impact that the new revenue-sharing plan, luxury tax, salary arbitration, and antitrust agenda will have on MLB.

BACKGROUND ON THE 1996 AGREEMENT

Although the cancellation of the 1994 season resulted from a player strike, the skirmish began in the executive suite. Gate and media revenues soared during the 1980s and early 1990s, but not all clubs were equal benefactors. Teams located in the largest cities saw their revenues skyrocket whereas clubs in smaller markets witnessed more modest growth (Zimbalist, 1992a; Quirk and Fort, 1992). As the revenue potentials of the large- and small-market clubs diverged, the teams in larger cities routinely swallowed up the games' choicest free agents while smaller market clubs were left developing the talent and later giving it away. To the clubs in smaller cities, baseball's revenue-sharing scheme seemed old, antiquated, and the source of their problems. They demanded that the revenue-sharing plan be amended such that large-market teams would share more of their surplus with the smaller market clubs (Helyar, 1994).

Not surprisingly, the large-market owners balked at the proposed welfare system. When the owner/owner negotiations reached a stalemate, the two sides joined forces and directed their efforts toward the players. MLB would adopt a more aggressive revenue-sharing plan, but only if the players replaced the lost revenue by agreeing to a salary cap.

Salary caps, which seek to stem salary growth by pegging team payrolls to league revenues, are not new to professional sports. The National Basketball Association (NBA) was the first professional league to agree to a cap and the National Football League (NFL) adopted its own version in recent years. League experience with the cap showed mixed results. Some veteran football players with high salaries found themselves unemployed. Franchise owners repeatedly found loopholes in the cap rules and exploited them to the fullest.

In the spring of 1995, management demands for a salary cap were replaced by a call for a luxury tax. The luxury tax would require teams whose payrolls exceeded a set limit to pay a tax on the excess. The intent of the tax was conceived not so much as a means for redistributing revenues as it was a device aimed at suppressing salaries. By levying a hefty penalty on big spenders like New York Yankees' owner George Steinbrenner, the tax could conceivably slow down the bidding wars that accompanied November's free agent market. As they had done with the salary cap, the players' union resisted the luxury tax proposal.

During the spring of 1995, a court ruling ended the player strike. However, with the turnstiles spinning and money flowing, the incentive to bargain intensively was gone. The 1995 season was played with no bargaining agreement in sight. Finally, on November 6, 1996, management negotiator Randy Levine presented the owners with a tentative agreement, which the owners voted not to accept.

Three weeks later, however, management dramatically reversed its stance. Chicago White Sox owner Jerry Reinsdorf announced that he had signed Cleveland Indians' star Albert Belle to a five-year contract worth a reported $55 million. The salary so greatly exceeded the norm that the owners promptly reconvened and voted to accept the deal. Fearing the specter of another round of spiraling salaries, the owners were only too happy to sign a pact that would usher in luxury taxes and an infusion of new money from league expansion and interleague play.

The 1996 agreement guarantees uninterrupted play through the year 2000. The players retain the option to extend the agreement to include the 2001 season. In the following section, I will review the most significant changes in the new agreement and predict their likely impact on the game.

THE IMPACT OF THE 1996 COLLECTIVE BARGAINING AGREEMENT

Interleague Play and Expansion

The 1996 agreement ushered in the era of interleague play. Management retains the option to extend interleague play into the 1998 season. Subsequent interleague play must be agreed on by both sides. In addition, the pact allows for the creation of four new franchises. In 1998, the Arizona Diamondbacks and the Tampa Bay Devil Rays become the newest major league franchises. Two more franchises are permitted provided that management gives notice to the players by the end of 1999.

Changes in the Minimum Salary

Beginning in 1997, baseball's minimum salary rose from $109,000 to $150,000. The minimum will rise to $170,000 in 1998, $200,000 in 1999, and $200,000 in 2000 and 2001 if the players exercise the option to extend the agreement ($200,000 plus a cost of living adjustment if they do not).

The Luxury Tax

Enforcement Problems. The 1997 season was the first to include the luxury tax. Although the purpose of the luxury tax is to hold down player salaries by making the free agent bidding wars increasingly expensive, economic literature suggests that salary control mechanisms such as salary caps and luxury taxes are destined to fail (Fort and Quirk, 1995; Quirk, 1997; Marburger, 1997b). Free agent salaries rise for one reason: an owner believes that he/she will be more profitable by upping the bid to sign a player than by allowing the individual to sign with another team. For this reason, owners have a powerful incentive to circumvent the rules that constrain their profits.

In the case of salary caps, limits on team payrolls lead owners to find creative means to bid away a player without exceeding the cap. Quirk (1997) summarized the NBA's failed attempts to control player salaries and Barra (1995) provided intriguing insight into the San Francisco 49ers' creative cap evasion schemes.

Just as owners have an incentive to exceed the salary cap, so do they wish to sign players without having to pay a tax (Marburger, 1997c). Because the players unambiguously benefit from cap/tax evasion, their agents are only too happy to oblige. Nevertheless, baseball's owners have benefited from the folly of their NBA and NFL counterparts. Consequently, much of the 1996 agreement establishes a myriad of guidelines to protect itself against tax evasion.

For example, NFL and NBA owners demonstrated the effectiveness of restructuring the players' contracts to stay within the salary cap. To guard against similar restructurings in baseball, the *average annual value* of a player's contract is to be used to tabulate team payroll rather than the actual amount paid in any given season. The average value of the contract includes signing bonuses, low-interest loans, and deferred compensation. The means for computing the latter is explicitly spelled out in the agreement. Similarly, unlike the other sports' agreements, the luxury tax is not grandfathered. This keeps owners from signing their top players to lucrative long-term contracts before the tax is officially implemented. Further, any third-party payments (i.e., tie-ins to promotional deals) that are part of the player's contract are also treated as "taxable" compensation.

Regardless of the innumerable steps taken by the owners to enforce the tax, the fact remains that they have powerful incentives to circumvent it. Having examined the agreement, here are a few means by which owners might successfully elude the tax:

Two-year contracts, payable in the years 2000 and 2001. The Players' Association successfully bargained for the removal of the tax in the final two years of the agreement. Although the "average annual salary" clause diminishes the incentive for clubs to backload multiyear contract payments into these seasons, two-year agreements that span these two seasons are officially exempt from any tax.

Long-term contracts that are really short-term contracts. If an owner wishes to up the ante on a player who has been offered a three-year, $15 million contract by another club, but stands to pay a tax if he/she does so, an attractive option is to lengthen the agreement. By signing the player to a four-year $16 million contract, the average annual salary falls from $5.3 million to $4 million. Because the owner may have only been interested in the player's services over the first three seasons, the club may either retain the player for the fourth year or it may release him and pay the $4 million salary. Keeping in mind that the agreement calls for no tax in the 2000/2001 seasons, lengthening the contract is an attractive means to minimize the tax burden.

Time constraints do not permit one to elaborate on all of the means by which management can circumvent the tax. Nonetheless, the agreement contains explicit language to protect the league against tax evasion by clubs. Article XXIII Section E(4) states that special covenants that call for a player's future salary to increase after reaching a performance goal in a previous season will not count as salary "unless it is determined by the Arbitration Panel that the special Covenant was designed to defeat or circumvent the intention of the Parties as reflected in this Article XXIII." Further, Section G(1) states that no player or club may enter into any agreement with the intent "to defeat or circumvent the intention of the [luxury tax]," and Section G(2) formally bars any "unreported understandings or agreements of any kind between the Player and the Club."

Implications for an enforceable tax. Even if the luxury tax were effectively enforced, its scope is limited. Over the life of the agreement, taxes will only be assessed to clubs with payrolls exceeding $51 million, $55 million, and $58.9 million in 1997, 1998, and 1999, respectively. If salaries rise such that more than five teams exceed these levels in any given season, the thresholds will be adjusted such that only five teams are liable for the tax. The penalties for exceeding the thresholds include a 35% tax on the excess in 1997 and 1998 and a 34% tax on the surplus payroll in 1999. Under no circumstances will the thresholds be reduced below these levels. Therefore, the rules establish that a *maximum* of five teams will be liable for tax payments in any given year.

For example, the fifth highest payroll in 1997 was $55.6 million, which exceeded the established $51 million threshold (*USA Today Major League Baseball* web page, January 6, 1998). Consequently, although thirteen teams reported payrolls in excess of $51 million, only the New York Yankees, Baltimore Orioles, Cleveland Indians, Atlanta Braves, and Florida Marlins paid a tax (the taxes ranged from the $4.4 million assessed to the Yankees to $0.14 million paid by Florida). Due to indexing, the tax threshold for 1998 rises from $55 million to $59.9 million.

Marburger (1997a) showed the impact of various means of assessing and distributing the luxury tax on salaries and competitive balance. All variations of the tax are likely to hold down player salaries. The intuition is straightforward. Prior to the tax, free agent salaries were driven by the teams' assessments of the players' marginal revenue products. Subsequent to the tax, the MRP net of tax is the relevant means for gauging a player's worth.

Marburger (1997a) and Vrooman (1995) show that the impact of a tax on league balance is hard to predict. Clearly, an enforceable tax makes the stockpiling of star players a less profitable venture, which would improve league balance. However, if the proceeds from the tax are used to subsidize low-revenue clubs, the tax could conceivably reward clubs for stocking low-quality rosters. Although the bargaining agreement calls for the redistribution of 1997 tax proceeds, most proceeds will fund the Industry Growth Fund, which will be described later.

The absence of a luxury tax in the final two years of the agreement contains other relevant implications. In 1995, the circuit court upheld the NLRB's ruling that management had failed to bargain in good faith, and it ordered baseball to resume play under the terms of the previous agreement. Upon the expiration of the 1996 agreement, another misstep by management could lead to another court-ordered enforcement of the last agreement. In other words, after two years of fighting to get a luxury tax into the pact, the owners find themselves bargaining to get it in all over again.

Revenue-sharing

Prior to 1996, gate receipts were shared between clubs. Gate revenue from American League games was split 80/20 between the home and visiting teams whereas in the National League, the visiting team received roughly $.56 for each ticket sold. With the exception of superstation revenues, 100% of local media revenues were retained by the home team. The 1996 agreement replaces the old revenue-sharing plan with a more complicated cross-subsidization scheme. The plan will be phased in gradually and will not be completely operational until 2000.

The transitional years are the most complicated. The "Straight Pool Plan" calls for each club to contribute 39% of its net local revenue (defined as local revenue minus stadium operating expenses) into a pool. The pool is then divided evenly among all clubs. In contrast, the "Split Pool Plan" requires each club to contribute 20% of its net local revenue into a pool. Seventy-five percent of that money is divided evenly among all clubs and the remaining 25% is divided as additional subsidies to the seven clubs with the lowest net local revenue. The size of the subsidy varies inversely with each team's net local revenue.

The "Hybrid Plan" was implemented during the 1996 and 1997 seasons. The Hybrid Plan assigned each club whichever plan (Straight or Split) was most favorable. Because the Hybrid Plan, by its structure, implied that the amount of revenue due to poorer clubs exceeded the amount of revenue due to be paid by wealthier teams, the shortfalls in revenue were made up by superstation payments in 1996 and superstation payments and luxury tax proceeds in 1997.

In 1998, the Hybrid Plan will be replaced by the Split Plan, which will be phased in over 1998 and 1999. Supplemental pool payments will be made for teams that would have fared better with the Hybrid Plan during these years.

Fort and Quirk (1995) showed that revenue-sharing tends to diminish player salaries. The marginal revenue product (MRP) assessments that drive free agent salaries are based on the assumption that players contribute to winning which increases revenues. However, any additional games won by one team necessitates additional games lost by opponents, which implies falling revenues for other clubs. With revenue-sharing, the team that signs a player retains a smaller share of the rising home receipts and a larger share of the declining road revenues. Therefore, with revenue-sharing, the players are worth less and accordingly, are likely to be paid less.

Hadley and Gustafson (1997) noted that some revenue sources are more variable than others. Because media revenues are fixed for several years, the increased sharing of media money will have less of an impact on salaries than increased gate revenue-sharing.

Had the revenue-sharing plan simply called for clubs to ante up a percentage to their opponents, Fort and Quirk (1995), Hadley and Gustafson (1997), and Vrooman (1995) showed that the plan would have no effect on league balance. In general, the implication derives from the landmark Coase Theorem (1960)—players will be allocated to their highest valued use regardless of how revenues are shared.

However, this assumes that each team pays and receives a fixed percentage of the revenues generated from its home and away games. In fact, whereas 75% of the pooled local net revenue is divided evenly among teams in the league, the remaining 25% is earmarked for the poorest teams.

The special subsidy for poor teams could be problematic, as it is consistent with the questions raised by Vrooman (1995) and Marburger (1997a) regarding the redistribution of luxury tax proceeds. Teams such as Pittsburgh and Montreal have a history of replacing quality players with cheaper, inexperienced players once the quality players begin to earn market-level salaries. Such practices would constitute "bad business" if gate/local broadcast revenues dropped more than proportionately as a result. However, because the subsidies specifically target teams with low revenues, the practice is encouraged. The result may be an increase in the number of mid-season cost-cutting trades as teams with losing records jockey to position themselves for post-season subsidies.

One aspect of increased revenue-sharing that has not been addressed in the literature is its potential impact on league revenues. Fort and Quirk (1995) and Vrooman (1995) assumed that each team's revenue-generating potential is the same regardless of how the receipts are distributed. However, some of the team's revenue is derived through promotional activities of the franchise. A team is willing to expend $5 million in advertising if it generates $8 million in additional gate receipts. The club would not be willing to spend the $5 million, however, if it only were permitted to retain $4 million. Because increased revenue-sharing diminishes the incentive for teams to expend money for promotional purposes, the league must pick up the slack.

In fact, the 1996 agreement allows for such a shift in responsibility. In 1997, the Industry Growth Fund (IGF) was established to promote the game of baseball through advertising, international development such as player tours and media relations, developing media technology, and community service activities. The IGF is jointly administered by the clubs and the Players' Association. The IGF will be funded by luxury tax proceeds as well as the proceeds from the payroll tax to be described below.

Payroll Tax
In the 1997 and 1998 seasons only, the players agree to pay a tax equal to 2.5% of the final actual payrolls for all clubs to the IGF. Unlike the luxury tax, which applies to each team's forty-man roster, the payroll tax only applies to players on the twenty-five-man major league roster. Further, the tax is assessed only after deductions are made for the lower-paid players (salaries of roughly $175,000 or less) and it does not include player benefits.

Salary Arbitration
Salary arbitration has been available to players since 1973. Players with between roughly three and six years of major league service may unilaterally opt to have their salaries determined by an independent arbitrator. Under baseball's arbitration system, each side submits an offer to the arbitrator. Following a hearing, the arbitrator determines which of the two offers will be the player's salary for the upcoming season.

Historically, arbitration decisions have been rendered by one arbitrator. Beginning with the 1998 season, however, baseball will phase in three-person arbitrator panels jointly selected by management and the Players' Association. Although the decisions of the panel will be revealed as each case is heard, each individual panel member's vote will not be revealed until after all the cases have been resolved.

Management has often blamed salary arbitration for the escalation of player salaries. Arbitrators were frequently accused of randomly distributing decisions to appease both management and the union (Helyar, 1994). In fact, however, arbitration literature suggests that the appearance of compromise is an illusion. Farber (1980, 1981) showed that both sides strategically tailor their final offers to suit the preferences of the arbitrators. As a result, the arbitrators are confronted with two "reasonable" offers, which makes the arbitrators' final decisions appear to be random. In fact, Burgess,

Marburger, and Scoggins (1996) showed that baseball arbitration decisions are based on the merits of the case.

Arbitration literature foresees little change resulting from the three-person panel. Ashenfelter (1987) developed the arbitrator exchangeability hypothesis. Because the two sides jointly select the arbitrators, Ashenfelter theorized that arbitrators would seek to replicate precedential decisions to avoid veto. If the hypothesis is correct, a three-person panel will view each case in much the same manner as a single arbitrator would.

The Players' Option in the Year 2000

The collective bargaining agreement officially expires on October 31, 2000. Given the historical pattern of strikes and lockouts, fans may find themselves once again cursing the players and owners in the near future. The players, however, retain the option to extend the agreement through the 2001 season. Fans should not make vacation plans to visit spring training in 2001. Beyond their desire to shed the luxury tax, the bargaining agreement is likely to penalize the players if they extend it and reward them if they terminate it.

Should the players opt to extend the agreement, they must pay the clubs a total of $2 million. Even more telling are the implications should the players choose not to extend the agreement. In contrast to past contracts, the players are due to receive only 60% of the gate receipts from the first three games of the Division Series (down from 80%). They get this money back with interest if they do not exercise the option within fifty days of the end of the 2000 World Series. In other words, by failing to extend the agreement, not only do the players avoid the $2 million payment to the clubs, they also receive a strike fund collected by management!

Service Days

The last stumbling block in finalizing the agreement concerned service days. A player is credited with one service day for each day spent on the major league roster. Service days are used to determine arbitration eligibility, free agent eligibility, and retirement pensions. Because service days were not credited during the 1994–1995 strike, many players stood to lose out on quite a substantial sum of money over the remainder of their careers.

From the owners' perspective, denying service days was an extraordinary bargaining tool. It added to the lost income during the strike and some (perhaps many) players may have lost more money from the combination of the strike and lost service days than was gained at the bargaining table. This would place the players in a far more conciliatory position during future contract negotiations. However, in the final agreement, the owners agreed to restore the players' lost service days on the condition that the Players' Association drop its unfair labor practices charges against management.

The Antitrust Exemption

During the 1994/1995 impasse, Congress wrestled with the possibility of eliminating baseball's longstanding exemption from antitrust legislation. The Players'

Association actively lobbied for its removal whereas the owners maintained that the exemption was necessary. The 1996 agreement calls for the two sides to request that the exemption not apply to labor matters.

A partial exemption would be a victory for the players, a loss for management, and its long-term implications may be bad for fans. Prior to the creation of the players' union in the late 1960s, the antitrust exemption gave management unlimited authority to impose rules to limit the salaries of players—rules that would simply be unenforceable in a competitive marketplace. The addition of the Players' Association, however, created a bilateral monopoly in which management's monopoly power is offset by the monopoly power of the union.

During the congressional hearings, the union argued that with the exemption fully intact, management was free to declare a bargaining impasse and impose a set of rules on the players. In fact, however, when management attempted to do exactly that in December 1994, the union successfully argued that management had failed to bargain in good faith. In any case, as long as the union is recognized by the National Labor Relations Board as the bargaining agent of the players, management is never really free to "impose" any set of terms. Absent an intrusion by the government, if the terms offered by management are not satisfactory, the players have no legal obligation to play without a bargaining agreement. The result is really no different than if the players were to "impose" their set of demands on the owners. Both sides lose money during work stoppages, and the purpose of strike and lockout threats is to create an incentive to find a mutually acceptable set of terms.

By removing the exemption as they pertain to labor matters, the players gain an advantage. After the 1987 NFL players' strike failed to produce free agency, the players' union officially decertified and several players sued the league in *McNeil v. NFL*. The court eventually ruled that the NFL rules violated antitrust provisions, free agency was established, and the union reappeared. In essence, the players successfully used the courts as a surrogate bargaining tool.

At the present time, MLB players have no such avenue. If the exemption were partially lifted, however, the union could threaten a similar maneuver during collective bargaining negotiations. Management has no offsetting legal power against the union because the 1914 Clayton Act essentially declared all unions to be exempt from antitrust legislation.

None of this represents either good or bad news for the fans. Although a partial exemption is likely to affect the terms of an eventual agreement, it will do little to eliminate work stoppages. The other major sports leagues are not protected from antitrust legislation, yet they all have their share of strikes and lockouts.

An amended exemption may be bad news for baseball fans in the long run simply because Congress may view itself as having completed its "good deed." By creating the exemption in 1922, MLB became free to wield its monopoly power in any manner it sees fit. Unless modified, baseball is free to erect barriers to deter the formation of competing leagues and create territorial agreements that essentially forbid teams from competing for fans.

Perhaps the most insidious abuse of monopoly power can be found through "stadium extortion." Vrooman (1997) showed that monopolized sports leagues have an incentive to restrict the number of franchises such that potentially profitable locations are left without a team. The excess demand for franchises can be used to the advantage of owners, who can threaten to relocate if the taxpayers do not provide them with a new facility. Although Shughart (1997) argued that removing the exemption could lead to an overexpansion of teams and the dilution of league quality, such concerns coexist with the potential monopolistic exploitation of fans and local municipalities.

Ironically, whereas the Players' Association argued for the removal of the antitrust exemption during the Congressional hearings, the players have at least as much to gain from baseball's monopoly status as does management. Scully (1995) noted that the monopoly profits generated by baseball represent extra cash for both owners *and* players. If the sports market contained no barriers, the number of franchises would likely rise. Competition between franchises would result in lower ticket prices and less lucrative media contracts. As a result, the players' MRPs would decrease and salaries would fall. From this perspective, the apparent compromise between players and owners is more of an implicit agreement to further empower the monopoly status of the industry.

FINAL THOUGHTS

Despite the constant bickering between players and clubs, both sides benefit only when the sport generates money. This should be a source of solace for fans. Neither side wants to see the game destroyed and the popularity of baseball is the key to prosperity.

Nevertheless, many details of the contract are an issue for concern. First and foremost, the language virtually guarantees that the players will not extend the agreement into 2001. Because the contract essentially requires management to create a strike fund, the players are once again preparing for battle. Hopefully both sides will recall the lingering effects that the 1994/1995 strike had on league revenues and salaries, however, and a new bargaining agreement will be established with the minimal threat of a work stoppage.

A new source of player/management disagreement concerns the revenue-sharing plan. Collective bargaining contracts often include a "management's rights" clause to discern bargaining issues from management prerogatives. The management rights clauses in the 1990 and 1996 agreements are identical. By its inclusion in the 1996 agreement, however, revenue-sharing is no longer a management right. Fort and Quirk (1995), Vrooman (1995), and Marburger (1997a) showed that increased revenue-sharing redistributes industry rents from the players to the owners. For this reason, it represents another source of bargaining impasse as the owners seek to increase revenue-sharing while the players resist management's demands.

A less publicized problem lies with the role of a union in an industry that enjoys monopoly power. Much criticism has been directed at management for artificially restricting the number of major league franchises (Vrooman, 1997; Zimbalist, 1997; Fort, 1997). As this chapter notes, the antitrust-exempt Players' Association *also* benefits from a restricted marketplace. Although public policy may diminish the monopoly power of management, it can do little to stem similar abuses initiated by the union. For example, Fort and Quirk (1995) imply that when revenue-sharing is inadequate, salary expenditures will be excessive. The result could be fewer franchisesthan the market would bear if external effects of free agent auctions were fully internalized. In this case, by fighting to decrease the sharing of revenues, the union, rather than management, acts to restrict the number of franchises.

NOTE

I thank the Major League Baseball Player Relations Committee for furnishing me a copy of the 1996 Collective Bargaining Agreement.

15

"These People Aren't Very Big on Player Reps"[1]: Career Length, Mobility, and Union Activism in Major League Baseball

Donald A. Coffin

INTRODUCTION

The Labor-Management Relations Act explicitly protects union members, and more specifically union activists, against differential or discriminatory treatment by employers.[2] Discharge of an employee because of that employee's union activity is prohibited, as are certain transfers or disciplinary actions. This does not, however, eliminate concerns among employees that union activities may lead to employer retaliation. Indeed, the long-time executive director (Marvin Miller) of the Major League Baseball (MLB) Players' Association has made it clear that he believes that owners of MLB clubs frequently take actions to shorten the careers of player representatives, or to rid themselves of the player reps by trading their contracts to other clubs.[3]

Although the number of cases cited by Miller may be limited, and although there may be differing interpretations of these cases, he raises an interesting and difficult issue. All players see their careers end, generally while they are still younger than forty. Almost all players move between teams during their careers. Disentangling the causes of the end of a career, or of a particular player move, is difficult. Nonetheless, the larger questions (Are player reps treated differently? Do they have shorter careers? Do they move between teams more often?) may be approach for statistically, rather than anecdotally.

This chapter examines the length of the careers of player reps and of other players and the frequency with which player reps and others move between teams. Assuming Miller is correct, the initial hypotheses are first, that player reps will have shorter careers after having controlled for other factors affecting career length, and second, that player reps will move between teams more frequently after controlling for other factors affecting mobility.

THE SAMPLE AND THE DATA

The approach to explaining career length and moves between teams in this chapter is fairly simple. A set of player performance characteristics, including fielding position, is identified. A variable (IMP for Importance) measuring the extent to which a player has been (on average) a full-time player during his career is created.[4] Players who have served and who have not served as player representatives are identified. Career length (the likelihood of moving between teams) is regressed on this set of variables, to determine the effect of serving as a player rep on career length (the likelihood of moving between teams).

Table 15.1
Descriptive Performance Statistics for Pitchers: Means with Standard Deviations in Parentheses

Variables	All Pitchers	Player Reps	Others
Years	8.85	12.60	8.33
	(4.56)	(5.02)	(4.24)
Number of	2.54	3.02	2.47
Moves	(1.88)	(2.09)	(1.84)
Moves/Years	0.29	0.24	0.30
	(0.19)	(0.19)	(0.15)
Games	267	403	248
	(137)	(194)	(182)
Games Started	104	239	89
	(137)	(197)	(115)
Innings Pitched	917	1847	788
	(910)	(1242)	(770)
Base Runners per	12.78	12.17	12.86
Nine Innings	(1.12)	(0.73)	(1.14)
Earned Run Av-	4.05	3.70	4.09
erage	(0.65)	(0.41)	(0.67)
IMP	43.82	59.71	41.63
	(20.57)	(15.73)	(20.20)
Left-Handed	0.32	0.32	0.32
Pitchers			
N	768	93	675

Doug Pappas, chair of the Business of Baseball Committee of the Society for American Baseball Research, provided a list of players serving as player reps during the 1974 through 1989 seasons.[5] Players who are still active were excluded from the analysis, since the lengths of their careers cannot yet be determined and because some of those players who have not yet served as player reps may do so in the future. Using *Total Baseball*,[6] all other players who have retired during this period were identified, and a relevant set of characteristics for all players was compiled. In order for players to be included in the sample, they had to have made a minimum number of appearances. For pitchers, the minimum cutoffs for inclusion were sixty games or 100 innings pitched. For position players, the cutoffs were 200 games or 500 at-bats. Players were divided, by position, into pitchers and position players for purposes of analysis.

The resulting sample included 768 pitchers (93 player reps and 675 non-reps) and 792 position players (85 player reps and 717 non-reps). Tables 15.1 and 15.2 present the descriptive statistics for each group of players. In general, better players (players with "better" performance statistics) and players who were more likely to play full-time would have longer careers. There may be reason to expect that such players would be less likely to move between teams, because they would, in general, be harder to replace.

It is worth noting that there are substantive differences in the (average) career statistics of players who have served as player reps and those who have not. In general, player reps have had longer and better careers than the other players. Among pitchers, player reps have had careers averaging about four years longer than non-reps. They appear on average in 60% more games, and they pitch on average 130% more innings. Player reps started 60% of the games in which they appeared; non-reps started only one-third of the games in which they appeared. Player reps allowed fewer base-runners per nine innings (BR9) and had lower ERAs. On the constructed variable (IMP), which measures how nearly a pitcher could be considered a "full-time" performer, player reps had an average seasonal score of 59.7 compared to 41.6 for non-reps. Pitchers who were player reps did tend to move between teams more often (3.02 moves each compared to 2.47), but had fewer moves per player-year in the major leagues (0.24 moves per year compared to 0.30).

For position players, a similar pattern emerges. Player reps had longer careers (14.1 years to 10.7 years), played in more games (1,472 to 960), had more at-bats (4,771 to 3,026), and hit better (higher batting averages, slugging averages, and on-base percentages). They also had a higher average IMP score (59.6 to 48.1). Catchers, first basemen, and third basemen were much more likely to serve as player reps. Positon players who served as player reps actually moved between teams less often (2.55 moves, compared to 2.80), with (obviously) fewer moves per player year (0.19 compared to 0.27).

Based solely on these on performance characteristics, player reps would be expected to have longer careers and to move less often because they tend to be better players. However, after controlling for their performance characteristics, did player reps have

Table 15.2
Descriptive Performance Statistics for Position Players:
Means with Standard Deviations in Parentheses

Variable	All-Position Pitchers	Player Reps	Others
Years	11.10	14.10	10.70
	(4.31)	(4.27)	(4.17)
Moves	2.77	2.55	2.80
	(1.77)	(1.54)	(1.79)
Moves/Year	0.26	0.19	0.27
	(0.16)	(0.12)	(0.16)
Games	1015	1472	960
	(636)	(672)	(609)
At-Bats	3213	4771	3026
	(2658)	(2633)	(2598)
Batting Average	0.253	0.259	0.253
	(0.023)	(0.030)	(0.022)
On-Base Average	0.320	0.332	0.318
	(0.030)	(0.030)	(0.030)
Slugging Average	0.371	0.388	0.369
	(0.054)	(0.050)	(0.054)
IMP	49.33	59.62	48.09
	(20.48)	(17.50)	(20.47)
CATCHER	0.15	0.25	0.14
CORNER	0.21	0.34	0.20
MIDDLE INFIELDER	0.23	0.16	0.24
OUTFIELDER/ DESIGNATED HITTER	0.41	0.25	0.45
N	792	85	717

CATCHER, CORNER, MIDDLE INFIELDER and OUTFIELDER/DESIGNATED HITTER identify
a player's primary position: Catcher, first/third base; second base/shortstop; and outfield/designated hitter,
respectively.

shorter or longer careers than expected? Given their performance characteristics, did they move between teams more or less often than expected?

CAREER LENGTH

The measure of career length used in this chapter is the number of years in which a player appears in at least one major league game. This may tend to provide a higher-than-accurate measure of career length for part-time or fringe players since they may spend several partial seasons in the major leagues. The results of regressing career length on player characteristics are reported in Tables 15.3 and 15.4.

Table 15.3
Regression Results: Career Length in Years for Pitchers

Variable	Coefficient	t-Statistic
Constant	14.11	7.10
REP	1.44	3.54
Left-Handed	0.59	2.20
STARTER	2.48	6.19
Base Runners per Nine Innings	-0.45	-2.27
Earn Run Average	-1.11	-3.20
IMP	0.084	10.89

Adjusted R^2	0.434
N of Cases	768

Of key importance is the coefficient on REP, a binary variable equal to one for union player representatives. It indicates that player reps who were pitchers had careers 1.44 years longer, on average, than can be explained using the performance characteristics identified in Table 15.1. (The generally "better" performance of player rep pitchers accounts for 2.88 years of additional major league time.) For position players, serving as a player rep extends a player's career by 1.63 years (after controlling for performance). The generally better performance of player reps accounts for 1.56 additional years of major league experience. For both categories of players, the effect of being a player rep on length of major league career is highly significant. For both categories of players, the performance characteristics are also significant determinants of career length, and the signs of the coefficients are as expected.

Both regressions explain about 40% of the variance in years played. This suggests that there are missing variables. To the extent that being a player rep is correlated with unobservable variables that positively affect career length, then the effect of being a

Table 15.4
Regression Results: Career Length in Years for Position Players

Variable	Coefficient	t-Statistic
Constant	-12.07	-4.84
REP	1.63	4.10
CATCHER	2.19	5.75
CORNER	-0.28	-0.87
MIDDLE	0.98	2.64
Batting Average	53.57	7.10
On-Base Average	2.77	3.14
EBP	10.90	3.07
IMP	0.08	10.70

Adjusted R^2 .413
N of Cases   792

player rep on career length is overstated. This is not only possible; it may be likely. Player reps may be (for example) more ambitious (willing to take on additional work and responsibilities); they may be "smarter." They may be more committed to baseball as a career, and therefore may work harder. Some evidence for this may be suggested by the large number of former player reps who now have, or have had, management positions in baseball (either as a manager or a general manager)—Dave Johnson, Bob Rodgers, Russ Nixon, Joe Torre, Darrell Chaney, Bob Boone, Sal Bando, Bob Watson, Ray Knight, Ron Schueler, Don Baylor, Larry Bowa, Phil Garner, Ted Simmons, Bruce Bochte, Mike Hargrove, Jim Beattie, Ed Lynch, Buck Martinez. A number of others have served as coaches (Rod Carew, Bill Buckner) or broadcasters (Steve Stone).

In conclusion, these regression results do not suggest that player reps have had shorter careers than warranted by their performances as players.

MOVEMENT BETWEEN TEAMS

The relevant measure of movement between teams is the likelihood that a player will change teams. This is calculated as Moves/Years. Across all players in the sample, about 28% of players move between teams in any given year (29% of the pitchers and 26% of the position players). The results of regressing this measure of mobility are reported in Tables 15.5 and 15.6.

Modeling player movement is inherently more difficult than modeling career length. Since 1976, player movement is determined by the interests of the team that gives up

Table 15.5
Regression Results: Likelihood of Moving between Teams for Pitchers

Variable	Coefficient	t-Statistic
Constant	-0.049	-0.49
REP	-0.007	-0.33
Left Handed	0.010	0.71
STARTER	-0.149	-7.33
Base Runners per Nine Innings	0.007	0.073
Earned Run Average	0.065	3.70
IMP	0.0009	2.26

Adjusted R^2 0.118
N of Cases 768

Table 15.6
Regression Results: Likelihood of Moving between Teams for Position Players

Variable	Coefficent	t-Statistic
Constant	0.701	6.17
REP	-0.038	-2.08
CATCHER	-0.043	-2.49
CORNER	-0.027	-1.85
MIDDLE INFIELDER	-0.019	-1.13
Batting Average	-0.874	-2.54
On-Base Average	-0.080	-1.99
EBP	0.074	0.46
IMP	-0.002	-5.83

Adjusted R^2 0.127
N of Cases 792

a player, the interests of the team that acquires rights to a player, and (because of free agency) the interests of the player. A team may, other things being equal, prefer to retain a player. But the player may become a free agent and choose to leave. Or the team may be offered so much (potential) talent in exchange that it makes a trade it did not initially seek. On the other hand, teams wish to acquire the rights to better players, and give up the rights to worse players. As a result, the effect of player performance on player movement is ambiguous, perhaps highly ambiguous. The results in Tables 15.5 and 15.6 do little to dispel this ambiguity.

However, the coefficients on REP are negative and statistically significantly for position players. This suggests that being a player rep reduces, rather than increases, a player's probability of moving between teams.

For reasons discussed above, we should not expect much explanatory power from these regressions, and this expectation is upheld. The R^2's are about 0.12, and performance characteristics are not consistently related to movement between teams. Nonetheless, these results provide no support for the idea that serving as a player rep increases the liklihood of a trade.

TENTATIVE CONCLUSIONS

There are other paths by which management can treat player representatives in a discriminatory manner. For example, management may be less willing to pay comparable salaries to player reps. Or, the bargaining environment may be tougher, leading player reps to file for arbitration more frequently. Or they may be more likely to end up with shorter contracts. Player reps may be forced to exercise their free agent rights more often as a result of not being offered acceptable contracts. Player reps may find it more difficult to find or to sustain non-playing careers in major league baseball after their playing days have ended (although this appears, given the number of former player reps in relatively high-level management positions, unlikely).

However, the results of this paper indicate that player reps are not disadvantaged in terms of career length, and that they do not move between teams more often than to other players. If there is discriminatory treatment of player reps by management in major league baseball, it has yet to be documented.

NOTES

All player statistics cited in this chapter come from John Thorn, Pete Palmer, Michael Gershamn, and David Pietrusza, *Total Baseball*, 5th ed. (New York: Viking Press, 1997).

1. Gene Mauch to Mike Marshall, as quoted in Marvin Miller, *A Whole Different Ballgame: The Sport and Business of Baseball* (New York: Birch Lane Press, 1991), p. 304.

2. Labor Management Relations Act, as amended, Section 8(a)(3): "Section 8. (a) It shall be an unfair labor practice for an employer (3) by discrimination in regard to hire or tenure of employment or ant term or condition of employment to encourage or discourage membership in any labor organization," [as quoted in Raymond L. Hilgert and Sterlung H. Schoen, *Cases in Collective Bargaining and Industrial Relations: A Decisional Approach*, 7th ed. (Homewood, IL: Richard D. Irwin, 1993), p. 38].

3. Miller says, for example, that he did not encourage players to attend the trial of Curt Flood's

antitrust lawsuit against Major League Baseball: "For another [reason], it was in the back of my mind that a great many marginal players might be targets of owner revenge if Flood lost: A utility infielder who was active in the union and made a public show of support for Flood might find himself losing a job to a utility infielder who wasn't active in the union. Union reps had a tough time as it was; they tended to be traded more often than players who were less active in the union." Miller, op. cit. pp. 196–197 (emphasis in original). Miller discusses at some length three cases in which he alleges discriminatory treatment of players (Jim Bunning, Milt Pappas, and Mike Marshall; pp. 63, 164–165, 303–304); for a detailed analysis of these situations, contact the author.

4. For pitchers, IMP is calculated as $(1/3)*$(games per year/6)$*$(square root of innings pitched per year); the measure is scaled to make a score of 100 represent a pitcher who makes a "full-time" contribution to his team. A pitcher appearing in 36 games and pitching 267 innings (Greg Maddux in 1993) received an IMP score of 98.0; a relief pitcher appearing in 71 games and pitching 75 innings (Lee Smith in 1993) receives and IMP rating of 101.0. The highest seasonal IMP score I have calculated was Mike Marshall's 254.8 in 1974 (106 games; 208 IP). For position players, IMP is calculated as $(1/3)*$SQRT[(games/year)$*$(at-bats/year)]; again, the measure is scaled to make a score of 100 represent a player who makes a "full-time" contribution to his team. For a player appearing in 150 games with 600 at-bats, IMP is 100. Dave Cash (1975, 699 AB, 162 games, IMP = 112.2) and Willie Wilson (1980, 705 AB, 161 games, IMP = 112.3) have the two highest seasonal IMP scores.

5. Papers compiled the list from *The Sporting News Guides* for the various years from 1974 through 1989. Subsequent guides apparently did not list player reps.

6. Thorn, Palmer, Gershamn, and Pietrusza, op. cit.

16

The Impact of the Salary Cap and Free Agency on the Structure and Distribution of Salaries in the NFL

Sandra Kowalewski and Michael A. Leeds

INTRODUCTION

On May 6, 1993 the National Football League (NFL) Management Council and the NFL Players' Association (NFLPA) entered into a new collective bargaining agreement (CBA). The new CBA, which is binding until the year 2000, has brought significant changes in the labor market for professional football. In this chapter we examine specific aspects of the new CBA, particularly the total team salary cap and free agency, and to a lesser extent the rookie salary cap, to determine their effect on the structure and distribution of salaries in the league.

While many studies examine salary determination in baseball (Scully, 1974b; Daly, 1992; Quirk and Fort, 1992; Kahn, 1993a), the only major study of the NFL is Kahn (1992). Kahn's study, however, was based on the monopsonistic market structure that prevailed prior to the new CBA. The introduction of free agency and salary caps has completely changed the way teams evaluate and assemble talent. Quirk and Fort (1992), for example, find that free agency has introduced greater inequality into the salary structure of Major League Baseball (MLB), exaggerating the superstar or winner-take-all effect noted by Frank and Cook (1995). One would thus expect that similar changes in the NFL should also lead to a new salary structure.

The remainder of the chapter is organized as follows: it begins with a brief history of free agency in the NFL and outlines the specifics of the collective bargaining agreement. The next section presents a simple empirical model of salary determination and describes our data. In "Results" we interpret and discuss our results, showing the winners and losers under the new CBA. The last section contains our conclusions.

FREE AGENCY AND THE SPECIFICS OF THE COLLECTIVE BARGAINING AGREEMENT

A Brief History of Free Agency in the NFL

In the mid-1970s the average salary in the NFL slightly exceeded that in MLB. Today, the average salary in MLB far exceeds that in the NFL. Quirk and Fort (1992, p. 198) attribute the declining relative position of football players to "the decision on the part of the NFLPA to go for short-term rather than long-term objectives."

Initially the NFL imitated MLB in establishing a reserve clause that effectively bound players to teams for their entire careers. Court decisions in the late 1940s established, however, that the NFL did not share MLB's exemption from antitrust laws. The formal reserve clause thus evolved into a one–year option clause supplemented by an informal "gentlemen's agreement" not to sign players who had played out their options with other teams. When the Baltimore Colts broke this agreement in 1963, the owners adopted a compensation system that came to be known as "the Rozelle Rule" (named for then-commissioner Pete Rozelle). The compensation set by the Rozelle Rule was so severe that very few players changed teams while it was in effect.

A series of lawsuits in the early 1970s attacked the Rozelle Rule as an unfair restraint of trade. In 1976 the "Mackey decision" (John Mackey was the player who brought the class action suit) established that the Rozelle Rule violated antitrust laws and created a brief period of free agency. The NFLPA, however, quickly bargained away free agency, accepting an even more stringent form of the Rozelle Rule in exchange for increased payments to the pension fund, a higher minimum salary, and a checkoff system for union dues. As a result, over the next three years only three players signed with new teams.

The NFLPA soon realized its mistake and sued the NFL for violation of antitrust laws. Now, however, the restrictions were part of CBA and were no longer subject to review by the courts. Frustrated in the courts, the NFLPA led two strikes (1982 and 1987) in unsuccessful attempts to reestablish free agency. The NFLPA decertified itself in 1989 in the hope that, without union representation or a collective bargaining agreement, individual players would be able to bring antitrust suits against the NFL. In response, the NFL created "Plan B" free agency, in which teams were able to reserve a limited number of star players while marginal players were free to sign with any team.

In 1993, a series of court rulings reestablished the principle of free agency. The NFL moved quickly to negotiate a new collective bargaining agreement with the reformed NFLPA. The new agreement phased in free agency and established the salary caps, leading to major changes in the market for and compensation received by NFL players.

Specifics of the New Collective Bargaining Agreement

For the first time the new CBA drew a distinction between how teams could pay veteran players and how they could pay players entering the NFL ("rookies"). The CBA defines the "Entering Player Pool" as a "league wide limit on the total amount of salary to which all of the NFL clubs may contract for in signing drafted rookies."[1]

(NFLPA, 1993, p. 44) It is essentially a league-wide rookie salary cap. The total rookie cap each year is the greater of:
1. $2 million multiplied by the number of teams at the time of the draft, or
2. 3.5% of Projected Defined Gross Revenue (DGR).[2]

Each team's monetary allocation for rookies is proportional to its share of the entering player pool, which is calculated from the quantity, round, and position of the team's draft picks. For the 1993 season the total rookie cap was $56 million or about $2 million per club, depending upon the above criteria. To the extent that any club spends more than its rookie cap in that year, the club must pay an equivalent amount to its veteran players in accordance with reasonable instructions given by the NFLPA. Further limiting rookie salaries is a stipulation that no rookie contract may provide for an annual increase in salary of more than 25% of the first year base salary (NFLPA, 1993, pp. 44–46).

The new CBA also established a total team salary cap for every team in the league. The salary cap in 1994 limited total team salaries to 63% of the Projected DGR minus league-wide projected benefits divided by the number of teams (NFLPA, 1993, p. 73), leaving each team about $35 million to spend on player salaries.

The new CBA established three minimum salaries, which depended on a player's number of credited seasons.[3] The minimum salaries for the 1993 season were: $100,000 for players with less than one year of credited service; $125,000 for players with one season of credited service, and $150,000 for players with two or more seasons of credited service. The CBA stipulates that minimum salaries increase at the same percentage rate as the Projected DGR for each year through 1998.[4] In 1994, the Projected DGR increased by 8% increasing the minimum salaries to $108,000, $135,000, and $162,000.

The most dramatic change implemented by the new CBA, however, was the introduction of free agency and other negotiating rights for nonfree agents. The CBA stipulates that any veteran player with less than three accrued seasons, whose contract has expired, is permitted to negotiate or sign a contract only with his prior team, as long as this team offers him a one-year contract on or before March 1.[5] If the team does not meet this requirement, the player is completely free to negotiate and sign with any team (NFLPA, 1993, p. 47).

Any player who is not designated a "franchise" or "transition" player and who has five or more accrued seasons or who has four or more accrued seasons in any capped year, becomes an unrestricted free agent upon the expiration of his contract.[6] As an unrestricted free agent, he is completely free to negotiate and sign with any team. Any player with between three and five accrued seasons becomes a restricted free agent upon the expiration of his contract. He is "completely free" to negotiate and sign with any team subject to the restrictions outlined in Article XIX of the CBA (NFLPA, 1993, pp. 49–52).

THE MODEL AND DATA
McLaughlin (1994) presents a model of labor markets in which the heterogeneity of

workers and firms place a premium on matching the needs of the firm with the skills of the worker. His model nicely describes the labor market in the NFL since both players and teams benefit from a particularly good match (for example, one would be hard-pressed to separate the success of the "West Coast Offense" introduced by the San Francisco 49ers from the successful careers of their quarterbacks, Joe Montana and Steve Young). Teams and players bargain over the premium—or "rent"— generated by such matches. Bargaining power can differ across players and teams. For example, quarterbacks are likely to have greater bargaining power than offensive linemen because the impact and drawing power of an outstanding quarterback are far greater than those of an outstanding offensive lineman. Similarly, teams that view themselves as "only a player away" from great success would have less bargaining power for a given player.

Prior to the new CBA, players had little bargaining power due to their lack of mobility within the NFL. Since players could not bargain freely with other teams, their only alternative was outside of professional football, and the labor market closely resembled a monopsony. With a few notable exceptions (e.g., Deon Sanders and John Elway), skills on the football field are likely to be uncorrelated with earning power outside of football (Reiss, 1991, suggests that the alternative pay of players in the NFL has fallen relative to nonathletes over time). Thus salaries should be relatively low and tightly grouped prior to the new CBA. Only a few "superstars" who were very popular with the public would have enough of an impact on revenues to have significant bargaining power.

Under the new CBA, free agents could bargain freely with other teams, raising their bargaining power with all NFL teams. Thus, a player could go to the team for which his value was greatest and would thus be willing to pay him the most. As a result, pay should rise and pay differences for players of different ability should become much more pronounced. Following the model used by Kahn and Sherer (1988) we estimate salaries under the two different regimes as

$$\ln (PAY_{OLD}) = X\beta_{OLD} + \varepsilon_{OLD} \tag{1}$$

for players under the old CBA and

$$\ln (PAY_{NEW}) = X\beta_{NEW} + \varepsilon_{NEW} \tag{2}$$

for players under the new CBA. If the new CBA has changed the bargaining framework, we would expect to see differences between PAY_{OLD} and PAY_{NEW} and between β_{OLD} and β_{NEW}. Estimates of equation (2) showed signs of heteroskedasticity, which we corrected by using White's estimation procedure (Greene, 1990).

The salary data are for the 1992 and 1994 seasons, and they come from *USA Today* (2-12-93, 1-18-95). This newspaper gathers much of its information from NFLPA reports and from players' agents. We used data for all the players who were on each team's roster at the start of the season. We excluded players who were traded during the regular season or preseason because of the difficulty in gathering data.

The data for 1992 did not include "practice squad" players while the data for 1994 did. Since practice squad players earn substantially less than players on the team's regular roster, including them could seriously bias our results. We deleted practice squad players from our 1994 data by selecting only those players who made more than $100,000 per year. This is below the minimum salary for players on the "regular" roster but well above the maximum salary of practice squad players.

The data for 1992 showed yearly pay per player. Pay was computed as base salary plus most bonus money including signing, reporting, and roster bonuses for the 1992 season. The data did not distinguish between base salary and bonuses but reported only the sum.

The 1994 salary data were compiled using the same method the NFL uses to determine team salary caps. The 1994 salary data showed yearly pay per player computed as base salary plus most bonuses with the exception of signing bonuses. The exception was based on the fact that signing bonuses are prorated over the life of multiyear contracts and thus should not be included as a lump sum. Suppose, for example, a player signs a four-year contract with an $8 million signing bonus. Under the salary cap system, that player's total yearly salary would be his base salary plus $2 million in bonuses (one-quarter of the signing bonus).

Because we use data for all players, we cannot use statistics that are position-specific (e.g., quarterback rating). We can thus use relatively few standardized performance variables in our salary equations. We take all data other than the salaries from *The Sporting News Pro Football Guide* for the 1992 and 1994 seasons (Carter, 1992, 1994).

Since we estimate the effect of free agency and the cap on player salary, the dependent variable in our equation is the natural logarithm of total salary.[7] We compute total salary as a player's base salary plus his bonuses for a single season. We regress the natural logarithm of salary on a vector of explanatory variables that we believe reflect the player's performance and hence determine his salary.

We expect players at certain "more skilled" positions, such as quarterback, to receive higher pay than those at "less skilled" positions. In order to account for these positional effects we used eight dummy variables, representing the positions: quarterback, running back, defensive lineman, offensive lineman, linebacker, wide receiver, defensive back and tight end. We combined defensive ends and defensive tackles into a single position, defensive linemen, because in some cases the performance information from Carter (1992, 1994) and the salary data from *USA Today* reported different positions for the same player. We combined safeties and cornerbacks into defensive backs for the same reason. If a player played a particular position, the dummy variable had a value of one; otherwise it was zero. Kicker and/or punter was the default; if a player was a kicker the value for all eight positional dummy variables was zero.

We also felt that starters would be paid more and that starting would have a greater impact for players at "more skilled" positions. Since it is not always clear who is a starter at a given position, we accounted for these effects by multiplying the positional dummy variables by the number of games the player started in the previous season. Thus, if a quarterback started eight games, the product of the quarterback dummy and number of starts is eight while the value of the seven other "interaction" variables is zero.

Standard models of wage determination all stress the importance of human capital acquired on the job. We include three variables in our equation to capture effects of experience and on-the-job training. "NFL experience," measured as a player's years of experience playing in the league, captures the positive effect of experience on salary. "NFL experience squared" captures nonlinearities in the returns to experience. We expect experience to have a positive but declining impact on pay. Finally, we account for the impact of having no experience at all by creating the dummy variable "rookie," which equaled zero for veteran players and one for players with no prior NFL experience. This variable captures salary inversion as well as the direct effects of the new CBA on the compensation received by rookies.

We expect the number of games played and started by a player to have positive impacts on his salary. To account for these effects, we include the number of regular season games played and started in the previous season. Our measure of games played includes games in which the player started and those games in which he did not start but saw some playing time. We also include the square of the number of games a player started to account for possible nonlinear returns to starting.

We include dummy variables accounting for participation in the Pro Bowl and the Super Bowl the previous season. Players who participate in the Pro Bowl (a post-season all-star game) are the best players at their position. Thus, we expect a strong positive coefficient for this variable. We also expect participating in the previous year's Super Bowl to have a positive effect on salary. Super Bowl players have frequently had "career years" in their Super Bowl season and have also gained important playoff and Super Bowl experience.

RESULTS

In order to analyze the effect of the salary caps and free agency on the degree of income inequality within the league, we plotted Lorenz curves and estimated Gini coefficients before and after their implementation. Figure 16.1 presents the Lorenz curves.

If income was distributed equally (meaning that every player received the same salary), the Lorenz curve would be a 45-degree line from the origin to the upper-right corner of the diagram, showing that the proportion of the population and the proportion of income received rise equally. In reality, income is not distributed evenly. This inequality shows up in the Lorenz curve as a "bulge" or "downward sag" (Quirk and Fort, 1992). Figure 16.1 shows that the 1994 Lorenz curve (under the new system) has a larger "bulge" than for 1992. This indicates that income was less equally distributed under the new system.

We can describe the degree of inequality more accurately by estimating the Gini coefficient. This measure of inequality equals the area of the "bulge" of the Lorenz curve divided by the total area under the equal income distribution line. This coefficient is bounded between zero and one, where a value of zero represents complete equality and a value of one implies complete inequality (i.e., one person has all the income). Our estimated Gini coefficient for 1992 is 0.393, and for 1994, it is 0.479. This is an increase of almost 22%. These coefficients indicate that the collective bargaining agreement led to more unequally distributed income in the NFL. Our finding for the new CBA is similar to the average Gini coefficient of 0.510 during

Figure 16.1
Lorenz Curves for NFL Salaries in 1992 and 1994

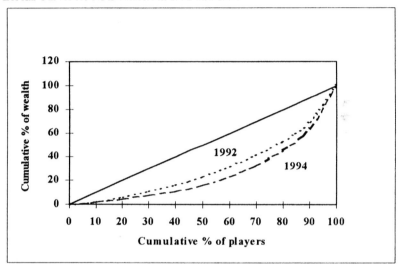

the free agency period in baseball (Quirk and Fort, 1992).

One can see the impact of the new CBA even more clearly by looking at specific quintiles of the overall distribution. Players in the three lowest quintiles received higher salaries on average under the old CBA in 1992 than under the new CBA in 1994. Those in the second and third quintiles were hardest hit, losing 3.9% and 3.4%, respectively. This amounted to average losses of $108,902 for a player in the second quintile and $95,539 for a player in the middle quintile.

At about the sixty-fifth percentile of the salary distribution players began to earn higher salaries under the new CBA. Those in the fourth quintile averaged moderate salary increases, averaging about 1.1%, or $31,205. Salaries exploded for those in the highest quintile, increasing 7.6%, or $215,598. The new CBA thus brought great gains for players already at the top of the salary distribution while bringing substantial losses for those players in the middle. The new CBA is pushing the NFL toward a two-class system with a small group of very wealthy players and a much larger group of (relatively) poor players.

In order to show how the new CBA has changed the determinants of salaries in the

NFL, we use multiple regression analysis. Table 16.1 presents descriptive statistics for the relevant variables and Table 16.2 presents the results for the OLS estimation.

Our results show that the new CBA led teams to reward players for performance on the field rather than the position they played. The premium teams pay to starters are much larger under the new CBA. Holding position constant, starters generate more victories and revenue for a team and thus receive higher salaries than "less skilled" or marginal players. Thus, while free agency has increased the bargaining power of the most–desired players, the salary cap ensures that less money remains available for lesser players.

Rows 13–20 of Table 16.2 describe the positional effects on salary. In 1992, before the new CBA, there were strong positional effects. Four positions, quarterback, defensive lineman, defensive back, and running back earn more than kickers at the 5% level of significance. Offensive lineman and linebacker are significant at the 10% level. The two other positions, wide receiver and tight end, were not statistically different from kickers at either level. After the new CBA, all the positional effects are negative (and generally significant) for all positions except quarterback. Even the return to being a quarterback drops sharply, from 44% before the new CBA to 6.5% (and statistically insignificant) after the new CBA. Before the new CBA, a defensive back earned returns of almost 22%. Afterward, he realized a loss (relative to kickers) of almost 30%.

While pay differentials by position generally disappear under the new CBA, differences arise on a new margin. Column 3, rows 5–12 of Table 16.2 reveal that starters gain significantly from the new regime. The returns to starting at all positions except quarterback almost doubled. For defensive and offensive lineman the returns more than tripled. All eight interaction variables are significant at the 1% level. Both skilled and unskilled starters fare very well under the cap. Thus, we conclude that starting at a particular position, whether skilled or unskilled, was more important under the new contract. Starters gain a disproportionate amount under the new system.

Combining the effects of the interaction and dummy variables for each position in rows 5–20 and the "Games Started Squared" variable in row 22 yields the total effect of starting at a particular position. In both years the returns to a starting quarterbacks far outstrip the returns to starters at any other position. However, the total returns do change in a number of ways. First, the rankings by position other than quarterback changed dramatically. In 1992, starters in the so-called "skill" positions (running back and receiver) generally earned more than players in the "nonskill" positions. In 1994, however, defensive and offensive linemen who consistently started earned more than any position except quarterback. They had ranked only fifth and seventh in 1992. Moreover, the position differentials for starters were generally far smaller in 1994 than in 1992. Thus the position one played mattered far less than being a starter in the new bargaining agreement.

Rows 2–4 of Table 16.2, show that all three experience variables were statistically significant before and after the cap was implemented. "NFL Experience" was positive and highly significant in both years, while "NFL Experience Squared" was negative and highly significant in both years. For 1992, we found that when one combines the two effects the positive impact of experience on salary dominated the negative

Table 16.1
Descriptives of the Variables

	1992		1994	
VARIABLE	Mean	Std. Dev.	Mean	Std. Dev.
1. NFL Experience	4.48	3.37	4.34	3.53
2. Rookie	0.14	0.34	0.17	0.37
3. NFL Experience Squared	31.42	40.09	31.26	44.59
4. Starting Quarterback	0.27	1.83	0.29	1.86
5. Starting Running Back	0.40	2.13	0.45	2.22
6. Starting Defensive Lineman	0.76	3.11	0.93	3.41
7. Starting Offensive Lineman	1.31	4.01	1.33	4.16
8. Starting Linebacker	0.84	3.29	0.82	3.25
9. Starting Wide Receiver	0.54	2.65	0.56	2.64
10. Starting Defensive Back	1.02	3.61	1.07	3.62
11. Starting Tight End	0.29	1.85	0.31	1.95
12. Quarterback	0.05	0.23	0.06	0.23
13. Defensive Lineman	0.12	0.33	0.15	0.36
14. Defensive Back	0.16	0.37	0.17	0.38
15. Running Back	0.09	0.28	0.10	0.30
16. Offensive Lineman	0.16	0.37	0.18	0.38
17. Linebacker	0.13	0.34	0.14	0.35
18. Wide Receiver	0.10	0.30	0.11	0.31
19. Tight End	0.05	0.22	0.06	0.24
20. Games Played (previous year)	10.74	6.57	10.44	6.58
21. Games Started Squared (previous year)	80.58	105.06	76.78	102.76
22. Dprobowl	0.05	0.22	0.05	0.23
23. Dsuperbowl	0.07	0.26	0.07	0.26
24. Salary + Bonus	505,742	473, 532	567,725	608, 317
(Median)	(380,000)		(325,000)	

impact of experience-squared for the first eleven years of players' careers. After eleven years of experience, additional years of experience cause salary to decline. However, only 3.4% of the players had over eleven years experience in 1992, so the returns to experience remained positive for almost all players prior to the new CBA. For 1994, the negative impact of experience-squared begins to dominate at about nine years. As a result, negative returns set in for many more players in 1994, as 8.4% of them had played more than 9 years. Thus just being on a team and gaining experience had a longer and stronger positive effect over most players' careers before the new CBA.

The coefficients for "Rookie" were positive and significant in both years. However, the coefficient in 1992 (0.751) was far larger than the coefficient in 1994 (0.522), indicating that the degree of salary inversion was much larger before the new CBA. In 1992, many teams' highest-paid player was a rookie. With the new CBA in place, this was no longer the case. As described above, the new CBA was particularly harsh to rookies. Teams were faced with a rookie salary cap of about $2 million per team with which they had to sign all of their draft picks. This rookie cap in conjunction with the total team cap led to an erosion of rookie salaries. Teams were paying experienced starters significantly more than they had paid them before the cap. Thus, they could no longer afford to pay inexperienced and unproved rookies at the pre-cap level.

The variable "games played," (row 21) was negative and significant in 1992 but positive and significant (only at the 10% level) in 1994. Again, the new CBA seems to reward players who see more action over players who see less action.

The variable "games started squared" was negative in both years but was close to being statistically significant only in 1994. This indicates that, while the returns to starting were greater in 1994, diminishing marginal returns to starting were more of a factor as well. Thus, while starting every game brings a higher return than starting only occasionally, starting occasionally brings an even larger bonus compared to not starting at all.

The variable "games started" does not appear in Table 16.2, being highly insiginficant in both years. We had expected it to have a positive impact, much the same way that measures of experience increase pay in more traditional human capital models. Once we interacted the number of games started with each position, however, games started failed to affect salary. This is probably due to the fact that most teams do not have starting and nonstarting kickers (our default position).

The dummy variable for participating in the Pro Bowl was positive and significant at the 1% level in both years. However, as predicted by our model the returns to being a Pro Bowl player were over 25% larger under the new regime. Pro Bowlers are considered superstars. They have higher-rent sharing parameters and higher reservation salaries, and hence they were able to gain disproportionately under the new CBA. The coefficient of the variable meauring participation in the Super Bowl changed from positive in 1992 to negative in 1994, but neither coefficient was statistically significant.

The regression results thus support our prediction that—in addition to changing the distribution of income—the new CBA changed the reward system in the NFL. Starters, especially superstars, received large pay increases under the new system, while the salaries of rookies and "marginal" players (i.e., those who never started) eroded.

Table 16.2
Results of the OLS Estimation

	1992		1994	
VARIABLE	Mean	Std. Dev.	Mean	Std. Dev.
1. Constant	11.708	(112.5)**	11.915	(109.7)**
2. NFL Experience	0.238	(11.99)**	0.240	(12.24)**
3. Rookie	0.751	(10.60)**	0.522	(7.10)**
4. NFL Experience Squared	-0.011	(-7.51)**	-0.013	(-10.0)**
5. Starting Quarterback	0.080	(5.49)**	0.119	(7.91)**
6. Starting Running Back	0.045	(3.35)**	0.074	(5.66)**
7. Starting Defensive Lineman	0.026	(1.98)*	0.081	(6.56)**
8. Starting Offensive Lineman	0.028	(2.24)*	0.080	(6.52)**
9. Starting Linebacker	0.040	(3.18)**	0.085	(5.91)**
10. Starting Wide Receiver	0.052	(4.06)**	0.080	(5.35)**
11. Starting Defensive Back	0.026	(2.14)*	0.078	(5.38)**
12. Starting Tight End	0.031	(2.05)*	0.085	(5.22)**
13. Quarterback	0.440	(3.91)**	0.065	(0.48)
14. Defensive Lineman	0.299	(3.11)**	-0.121	(-1.35)
15. Defensive Back	0.218	(2.41)*	-0.290	(-3.63)**
16. Running Back	0.238	(2.42)*	-0.162	(-1.81)
17. Offensive Lineman	0.181	(1.91)	-0.186	(-2.18)*
18. Linebacker	0.163	(1.75)	-0.339	-3.47**
19. Wide Receiver	0.123	(1.28)	-0.210	(-2.06)*
20. Tight End	0.028	(0.25)	-0.486	(-4.26)**
21. Games Played	-0.008	(-2.15)*	0.008	(1.84)
22. Games Started Squared	-0.0002	(-0.42)	-0.001	(-1.71)
23. Dprobowl	0.409	(6.28)**	0.498	(6.74)**
24. Dsuperbowl	0.004	(0.08)	-0.053	(-0.88)
Number of Observations	1391		1372	
Adjusted R^2	0.443		0.597[8]	

** Represents significance at 1% level, * represents significance at 5% level. Adjusted R–squared was before results were corrected for heteroskedasticity. Breusch–Pagan Chi–Squared is 85.76** (df = 23) after correcting for heteroskedasticity.

CONCLUSION

The advent of free agency with the new CBA in the NFL has not been a blessing for all players. Instead, free agency, coupled with two different salary caps, has created distinct winners and losers. Our results are very similar to those obtained by Quirk and Fort (1992) for baseball in that we find that salaries have become less equally distributed. Superstars have gained dramatically from free agency. However, the pay of the bottom two-thirds of the income distribution has fallen. In particular, the pay of mid-level players has declined dramatically. The creation of a caste system is highly ironic for a union that prided itself on emphasizing the interests of "the guards and tackles" over those of the highly paid quarterbacks (Helyar, 1995).

In addition to changing the size of the rewards, the new CBA has changed the criteria on which players' pay is evaluated. As one might expect of a union to which rookies do not yet belong, the NFLPA negotiated a salary cap for rookies that significantly depressed their pay. Even veterans, however, were affected. Prior to the new CBA, pay was heavily determined by the position one played. Thus, one was slotted at a quarterback's or a linebacker's level of pay regardless of whether one started. Under the new regime, starters experienced sharp increases in their pay while players who did not start received sharply lower pay than before. The reward structure in the NFL has thus moved markedly from "who one is" to "what one has done lately."

NOTES

We thank Andrew Buck, Elizabeth Gustafson, Lawrence Hadley, Daniel Rascher, and David Schaffer for their many helpful comments and suggestions. Jennifer Gordon and Yelena Suris provided expert research assistance.

1. The salary of any undrafted rookie shall count toward the club's rookie cap only to the extent that it exceeds the then applicable minimum salary for that player (NFLPA, 1993, p. 44).

2. DGR is "the aggregate revenues received or to be received on an accrual basis, for or with respect to a league year during the term of this agreement, by the NFL and all NFL teams, from all sources, whether known or unknown, derived from, relating to or arising out of the performance of players in NFL football games, with only the specific exceptions set forth below. The NFL and each NFL team should in good faith act and use their best efforts, consistent with sound business judgement, so as to maximize DGR for each playing season during the term of this agreement." DGR includes pre-season, regular season and post-season gate receipts (net of admission taxes and surcharges paid to municipal authorities) and any proceeds from the broadcast or rights to broadcast any NFL game (NFLPA, 1993, p. 74).

3. A player earns one credited season for each season in which he received, or should have received full pay status for a total of three or more regular season games, not including games for which the player was on: (i) the Except Commissioner Permission List, (ii) the Reserve PUP List as a result of a non-football injury, (iii) a team's practice or development squad, or (iv) the Injured Reserve List (NFLPA, 1993, p. 116).

4. The minimum salaries cannot increase by more than 10% per season and cannot decrease, regardless of the change in Projected DGR (NFLPA, 1993, p. 116).

5. The definition of accrued season is the same as that of credited season (in note 3), except that games on the injured reserve list are included and that the number of regular season games required increases from three to six (NFLPA, 1993, p. 48).

6. Each season during the term of the agreement, each club can designate one of its players

who is about to become an unrestricted free agent as a franchise player. This player cannot negotiate with any other team. On the day after his contract expires, his team must automatically offer him a new one-year contract "for the average of the five largest prior year salaries for players at the position at which he played the most games during the prior league year or 120% of his prior year salary, whichever is greater" (p. 60). Each team can designate two unrestricted free agents as transition players by February 25, 1993; one transition player between February 1 and February 15, 1994; and one between February 1 and February 15, 1999. Upon the expiration of his contract, a transition player can negotiate with any team. If he received an offer that he would like to accept, he must allow his prior team to match this offer. If the team refuses to exercise its "Right of First Refusal" then it must let the player sign with the new team. A transition player is paid the same as a franchise player except that a transition player is paid the average of the ten highest paid. (NFLPA, 1993, pp. 60–63).

7. Results of regression were similar with total salary as our dependent variable but did not fit the data as well.

Bibliography

A.C. Nielson Company. 1991. "DMA Market Rank and Demographic Rank Report." *Nielson Station Index,* September.

Abraham, Katharine, and Henry Farber. 1987. "Job Duration, Seniority and Earnings." *American Economic Review,* 278–297.

Altonji, Joseph G., and Robert A. Shakotko. 1987. "Do Wages Rise with Job Seniority?" *Review of Economic Studies,* 437–459.

Ashenfelter, Orley. 1987. "Arbitrator Behavior." *American Economic Review Papers and Proceedings,* May, 77, 342–346.

Associated Press. 1996. "Mexico Getting Taste of Major Leagues." *The Express-Times,* Easton, Pennsylvania, August 16, C4.

Atre, Tushar, Kristine Auns, Kurt Badenhausen, Kevin McAuliffe, Christopher Nikolov, and Michael K. Ozanian. 1996. "The High Stakes Game of Team Ownership." *Financial World,* May 20, 165, 8, 49–64.

Baade, Robert A., and Richard F. Dye. 1990. "The Impact of Stadiums and Professional Sports on Metropolitan Area Development." *Growth and Change,* 21, 2.

Baade, Robert A., and Richard F. Dye. 1988. "Sports Stadiums and Area Development: A Critical Review." *Economic Development Quarterly,* 2, 3, August.

Badarinathi, R., and L. Kochman. 1994. "Does the Football Market Believe in the 'Hot Hand'?" *Atlantic Economic Journal,* December 22, 76.

Badenhausen, Kurt, Christopher Nikolov, Michael Alkin, and Michael K. Ozanian. 1997. "Sports Values: More Than a Game." *Financial World,* June 17, 166, 6, 40–50.

Barra, Allen. 1995. "How the 49ers Beat the Salary Cap." *New York Times Magazine,* January 5, 34–35.

Barro, Robert J. 1996. *Getting It Right.* Cambridge, Mass.: The MIT Press.

Barro, Robert J. 1991. "Let's Play Monopoly." *Wall Street Journal,* August 27, A12.

Barry, Rick, and Jordan Cohn. 1996. *Rick Barry's Pro Basketball Bible: 1996–97 Edition.* Marina Del Rey: Basketball Books Ltd.

Barry, Rick, and Jordan Cohn. 1995. *Rick Barry's Pro Basketball Bible: 1995–96 Edition.*

Marina Del Rey: Basketball Books Ltd.

Barry, Rick, and Jordan Cohn. 1994. *Rick Barry's Pro Basketball Bible: 1994–95 Edition.* Marina Del Rey: Basketball Books Ltd.

Basketball Digest. 1996 "NBA Rosters and Salaries." May, 23, 7, 88–93.

Basketball Digest. 1993. "NBA Team Rosters and Salaries." June/July, 20, 8, 90–96.

Becker, Gary. 1987. "The NCAA: A Cartel in Sheepskin Clothing." *Business Week*, September 14, 24.

Becker, Gary. 1985. "College Athletes Should Get Paid What They Are Worth." *Business Week*, September 30, 18.

Becker, M., and Suls J., 1983. "Take Me Out to the Ballgame: The Effects of Objective, Social, and Temporal Performance Information on Attendance at Major League Baseball Games." *Journal of Sport Psychology*, 5, 3, 302–313.

Bellotti, Robert. 1993. *The Points Created Basketball Book, 1992–93.* New Brunswick, NJ: Night Work Publishing Co.

Bennett, Randall W., and John L. Fizel. 1995. "Telecast Deregulation and Competitive Balance: Regarding NCAA Division I Football." *American Journal of Economics and Sociology*, April, 54, 183–198.

Bergmann, Barbara R. 1991. "Do Sports Really Make More Money for the University?" *Academe*, January–February, 77, 28–30.

Berri, David J. 1997. "Do Coaches Coach to Win? Rationality, Resource Allocation, and Professional Basketball." Working paper.

Bernstein, Aaron. 1995. "Let's See the Owners Pitch Their Way Out of This One." *Business Week*, April 17, 32–33.

Blass, Asher A. 1992 "Does the Baseball Labor Market Contradict the Human Capital Model of Investment?" *Review of Economics and Statistics*, 261–268.

Bonavita, Mark, Mark Broussard, and Sean Stewart (eds.). 1996. *The Official NBA Register, 1996–97.* St. Louis: The Sporting News Publishing Co.

Borland, Jeff, and Jenny Lye. 1992. "Attendance at Australian Rules Football: A Panel Study." *Applied Economics*, 24, 1053–1058.

Bremmer, Dale S., and Randall G. Kesselring. 1993. "The Advertising Effect of University Athletic Success." *The Quarterly Review of Economics and Finance*, 33, 4, 409–421.

Brooker, George, and T. D. Klastorin. 1981. "To the Victors Belong the Spoils? College Athletics and Alumni Giving." *Social Science Quarterly*, December, 62, 744–750.

Brown, Robert W. 1994. "Measuring Cartel Rents in the College Basketball Player Recruitment Market." *Applied Economics*, January, 26, 27–34.

Brown, Robert W. 1993. "An Estimate of the Rent Generated by a Premium College Football Player." *Economic Inquiry*, October, 31, 671–684.

Brown, W., and R. Sauer. 1993. "Does the Basketball Market Believe in the Hot Hand? Comment." *American Economic Review*, December, 83, 1377–1386.

Bruggink, Thomas H., and David Rose. 1990. "Financial Restraint in the Free Agent Labor Market in Major League Baseball: Players Look at Strike Three." *Southern Economic Journal*, 4, 56, April, 1029–1043.

Burgess, Paul L., and Daniel R. Marburger. 1992. "Bargaining Power and Major League Baseball." In Paul M. Sommers (ed.), *Diamonds Are Forever: The Business of Baseball.* Washington, D.C.: The Brookings Institution.

Burgess, Paul L., Daniel R. Marburger, and John F. Scoggins. 1996. "Do Baseball Arbitrators Simply Flip a Coin?" In John Fizel, Elizabeth Gustafson, and Lawrence Hadley (eds.). *Baseball Economics: Current Research.* Westport, CT: Praeger Publishers.

Butler, Michael R., and Myron L. Moore. 1960. "Rules Changes and Attendance at Major League Baseball Games." Unpublished working paper, Texas Christian University.

Cairns, J., N. Jennett, and P. J. Sloane. 1986. "The Economics of Professional Team Sports: A Survey of Theory and Evidence." *Journal of Economic Studies*, 13, 1–80.

Camerer, C. 1989. "Does the Basketball Market Believe in the Hot Hand?" *American Economic Review*, December, 79, 1257–1261.

Canes, Michael E. 1974. "The Social Benefits of Restrictions on Team Quality." In Roger G. Noll (ed.), *Government and The Sports Business*. Washington, DC: The Brookings Institution.

Carter, Anne P., and Andrew Brody (eds.). 1970a. *Input-Output Techniques, Vol. 1, Contributions to Input-Output Analysis*. Proceedings of the Fourth International Conference on Input-Output Analysis, Geneva, January 1968. Amsterdam: North-Holland.

Carter, Anne P., and Andrew Brody (eds.). 1970b. *Input-Output Techniques, Vol. 2, Applications of Input-Output Analysis*. Proceedings of the Fourth International Conference on Input-Output Analysis, Geneva, January 1968. Amsterdam: North-Holland.

Carter, C. 1992, 1994. *The Sporting News Pro Football Guide*. St. Louis: The Sporting News Publishing Co.

Carter, Craig, and Mark Broussard (eds.). 1996. *The Official NBA Guide*. St. Louis: The Sporting News Publishing Co.

Carter, Craig, and Alex Sachare (eds.). 1996. *The Official NBA Guide*. St. Louis: The Sporting News Publishing Co.

Cassing, James, and Richard Douglas. 1980. "Implications of the Auction Mechanism in Baseball's Free Agent Draft." *Southern Economic Journal*, 110–121.

Center for Business Research, Arizona State University. 1996. *The Economic Impact of Super Bowl XXX*. Tempe, Arizona, May.

Center for Economic and Management Research, University of South Florida. 1991. *Economic Impact Analysis of Super Bowl XXV on the Tampa Bay Area*. Tampa, Florida, June.

Chapman, K. S., and L. Southwick, Jr. 1991. "Testing the Matching Hypothesis: The Case of Major-League Baseball." *American Economic Review*, 81, 1352–1360.

Chelius, J. R., and James Dworkin. 1980. "An Economic Analysis of Final Offer Arbitration as Conflict Resolution Device." *Journal of Conflict Resolution*, 293–310.

Chizmar, J. F., and T. A. Zak. 1984. "Canonical Estimation of Joint Education Production Functions." *Economics of Education Review*, 3, 37–43.

Chizmar, J. F., and T. A. Zak. 1983. "Modeling Multiple Outputs in Educational Production Functions." *American Economic Review*, 73, 17–22.

Coase, Ronald. 1960. "The Problem of Social Cost." *Journal of Law and Economics*, October, 3, 1–44.

Coffin, Donald A. 1996. "If You Build It, Will They Come? Attendance and New Stadium Construction." In John Fizel, Elizabeth Gustafson, and Lawrence Hadley (eds), *Baseball Economics: Current Research*. Westport, CT: Praeger.

Cohn, Jordan. 1993. *The Pro Basketball Bible 1993–1994 Edition*. Marina Del Rey: Basketball Books Ltd.

Coughlin, Cletus C., and O. Homer Erekson 1985. "Contributions to Intercollegiate Athletic Programs: Further Evidence." *Social Science Quarterly*, March, 65, 194–202.

Coughlin, Cletus C., and O. Homer Erekson 1984. "An Examination of Contributions to Support Intercollegiate Athletics." *Southern Economic Journal*, July, 50, 180–195.

Cymrot, Donald J. 1983. "Migration Trends and Earnings of Free Agents in Major League Baseball, 1976–1979." *Economic Inquiry*, 545–556.

Daly, George G. 1992. "The Baseball Player's Labor Market Revisited." In Paul M. Sommers (ed.), *Diamonds Are Forever: The Business of Baseball*. Washington, DC: The Brookings Institution.

Daly, George, and William J. Moore. 1981. "Externalities, Property Rights and the Allocation of Resources in Major League Baseball." *Economic Inquiry*, 19, 77–95.

DeBrock, Lawrence M., and Alvin E. Roth. 1981. "Strike Two: Labor-Management Negotiations in Major League Baseball." *The Bell Journal of Economics*, 12, 413–25.

Demmert, Henry G. 1973. *The Economics of Professional Team Sports*. Lexington, MA: Lexington Books.

Depken, Craig A., II. 1997. "Free-Agency and the Competitiveness of Major League Baseball." *The Review of Industrial Organization*, forthcoming.

Domazlicky, Bruce R., and Peter M. Kerr. 1990. "Baseball Attendance and the Designated Hitter." *American Economist*, Spring, 34, 62–68.

Drever, P., and J. McDonald. 1981. "Attendances at South Australian Football Games." *International Review of Sport Sociology*, 16, 2, 103–113.

Durbin, J. 1969. "Tests for Serial Correlation in Regression Analysis Based on the Periodogram of Least-Squares Residuals." *Biometrika*, 56, 1, 1–15.

Dworkin, James. 1981. *Owners versus Players: Baseball and Collective Bargaining*. Boston, Mass. Auburn House.

El-Hodiri, Mohamed, and James Quirk. 1971. "The Economic Theory of a Professional Sports League." *Journal of Political Economy*, 1302–1319.

Euchner, Charles. 1993. *Playing the Field: Why Sports Teams Move and Cities Fight to Keep Them*. Baltimore: Johns Hopkins University Press.

Farber, Henry S. 1980. "An Analysis of Final-Offer Arbitration." *Journal of Conflict Resolution*, December, 24, 683–705.

Farber, Henry S. 1981. "Splitting-the-Difference in Interest Arbitration." *Industrial and Labor Relations Review*, October, 35, 70–77.

Federal Reserve Bank of Cleveland. 1991. "Public Subsidies for Private Purposes." *Economic Commentary*, April 15.

Ferguson, Donald G., J.C.H. Jones and Kenneth G. Stewart. 1996. "Competition within a Cartel: League Conduct and Team Conduct in the Market for Baseball Player Services." Mimeo, University of Victoria.

Fizel, John, Elizabeth Gustafson, and Lawrence Hadley (eds.). 1996. *Baseball Economics: Current Research*. Westport, CT. Praeger.

Fleisher, Arthur A., III, Brian L. Goff, and Robert D. Tollison. 1992. *The National Collegiate Athletic Association*. Chicago: University of Chicago Press.

Fort, Rodney. 1970. "The Stadium Mess." In Daniel R. Marburger (ed.), *Stee-rike Four! What's Wrong with the Business of Baseball?* Westport, CT: Praeger.

Fort, Rodney. 1992. "Pay and Performance: Is the Field of Dreams Barren?" In Paul M. Sommers (ed). *Diamonds Are Forever: The Business of Baseball*. Washington, DC: The Brookings Institution.

Fort, Rodney, and James Quirk. 1996. "Overstated Exploitation: Monopsony versus Revenue Sharing in Sports Leagues." In John Fizel, Elizabeth Gustafson, and Lawrence Hadley (eds.) *Baseball Economics: Current Research*. Westport, CT: Praeger.

Fort, Rodney, and James Quirk. 1995. "Cross-subsidization, Incentives, and Outcomes in Professional Team Sports Leagues." *Journal of Economic Literature*, 33, 1265–1299.

Frank, Robert H. 1997. *Microeconomics and Behavior*, 3rd Edition. New York: McGraw-Hill.

Frank, R. H. and Cook, P. J. 1995. *The Winner-Take-All Society*. New York: The Free Press.

Frederick, David M., William H. Kaempfer, and Richard L. Wobbekind. 1992. "Salary Arbitration as a Market Substitute." In Paul M. Sommers (ed.), *Diamonds Are Forever: The Business of Baseball*. Washington, D.C.: The Brookings Institution.

Freund, J. E. 1971. *Mathematical Statistics*. Englewood Cliffs, NJ: Prentice-Hall.

Fulks, Daniel L. 1994. *Revenues and Expenses of Intercollegiate Athletics Programs*. Overland Park, Kan. The National Collegiate Athletic Association, August.

Gaski, John F., and Michael J. Etzel. 1984. "Collegiate Athletic Success and Alumni Generosity: Dispelling the Myth." *Social Behavior and Personality*, 12, 1, 29–38.

Goff, Brian L., William F. Shugart, III, and Robert D. Tollison. 1988. "Disqualification by Decree: Amateur Rules as Barriers to Entry." *Journal of Institutional and Theoretical Economics*, June, 144, 515–523.

Greene, W. H. 1990. *Econometric Analysis*. New York: Macmillan.

Grimes, Paul W., and George A. Chressanthis. 1994. "Alumni Contributions to Academics: The Role of Intercollegiate Sports and NCAA Sanctions." *American Journal of Economics and Sociology*, January, 53, 27–40.

Gyimah-Brempong, K., and A. O. Gyapong. 1991. "Characteristics of Education Production Functions: An Application of Canonical Regression Analysis." *Economics of Education Review*, 10, 7–17.

Hadley, Lawrence, and Elizabeth Gustafson. 1997. "Increased Revenue-Sharing for Major League Baseball?" In Daniel R. Marburger (ed.), *Stee-rike Four! What's Wrong with the Business of Baseball?* Westport, CT: Praeger.

Hadley, Lawrence, and Elizabeth Gustafson. 1991. "Major League Baseball Salaries: The Impacts of Arbitration and Free Agency." *Journal of Sport Management*, 5, 111–127.

Hart-Nibbrig, Nand, and Clement Cottingham. 1986. *The Political Economy of College Sports*. Lexington, MA: D. C. Heath.

Helyar, J. 1995. *Lords of the Realm*. New York: Del Rey Books.

Helyar, John. 1994. *Lords of the Realm: The Real History of Baseball*. New York: Villard Books.

Hilgert, Raymond, and Sterlung H. Schoen. 1993. *Cases in Collective Bargaining and Industrial Relations: A Decisional Approach*, 7, 38. Homewood, IL: Irwin.

Hill, James. 1985. "The Threat of Free Agency and Exploitation in Professional Baseball: 1976–1979." *Quarterly Review of Economics and Business*, 68–82.

Hill, James, and William Spellman. 1983. "Professional Baseball: The Reserve Clause and Salary Structure." *Industrial Relations*, 1–19.

Hill, J. R., H. Madura, and R. A. Zuber. 1982. "The Short Run Demand for Major League Baseball." *Atlantic Economic Journal*, 31, 2, 31–35.

Hirschberg, Joseph G., Gerald W. Scully, and Daniel J. Slottje. 1992. "Efficiency Aspects of the Major League Baseball Players Market." In Gerald W. Scully (ed.), *Advances in the Economics of Sport*, 1. Greenwich, CT: JAI Press.

Hofler, Richard A., and James E. Payne. 1997. "Measuring Efficiency in the National Basketball Association." *Economic Letters*, August, 55, 293–299.

Hollander, Zander (ed.). 1996. *The Complete Handbook of Pro Basketball "1996."* New York: Signet Books.

Hollander, Zander (ed.). 1995. *The Complete Handbook of Pro Basketball "1995."* New York: Signet Books.

Hollander, Zander (ed.). 1994. *The Complete Handbook of Pro Basketball "1994."* New York: Signet Books.

Hollander, Zander (ed.). 1993. *The Complete Handbook of Pro Basketball "1993."* New

York: Signet Books.

Hollander, Zander (ed.). 1992. *The Complete Handbook of Pro Basketball "1992."* New York: Signet Books.

Horowitz, Ira. 1994. "On the Manager as Principal Clerk." *Managerial and Decision Economics*, 15, 413–419.

Hotelling, Harold. 1929. "Stability in Competition." *Economic Journal*, March, 41–57

Irani, Daraius. 1996. "Estimating Customer Discrimination in Baseball Using Panel Data: 1972–1991." In John Fizel, Elizabeth Gustafson, and Lawrence Hadley (eds.) *Baseball Economics: Current Research.* Westport, CT: Praeger.

Jennett, Nicholas I. 1984. "Attendances, Uncertainty of Outcome and Policy in Scottish League Football." *Scottish Journal of Political Economy*, 31, 176–198.

Kahn, L. M. 1993a. "Free Agency, Long-Term Contracts and Compensation in Major League Baseball: Estimates from Panel Data." *Review of Economics and Statistics*, 75, 157–164.

Kahn, L. M. 1993b. "Managerial Quality, Team Success, and Individual Player Performance in Major League Baseball." *Industrial and Labor Relations Review*, 46, 531–547.

Kahn, L. M. 1992. "The Effects of Race on Professional Football Players' Compensation." *Industrial and Labor Relations Review*, 45, 295–310.

Kahn, L. M., and P. D. Sherer. 1988. "Racial Differences in Professional Basketball Players' Compensation." *Journal of Labor Economics*, 6, 40–61.

Knight Foundation Commission. 1991. "Keeping the Faith with the Student-Athlete: A New Model for Intercollegiate Athletics." *Report on Intercollegiate Athletics*, March.

Knowles, Glenn, Keith Sherony, and Mike Haupert. 1992. "The Demand for Major League Baseball: A Test of the Uncertainty of Outcome Hypothesis." *The American Economist*, Fall, 36, 72–80.

Koch, James V. 1983. "Intercollegiate Athletics: An Economic Explanation." *Social Science Quarterly*, 64, 2, 360–374.

Koch, James V. 1978. "The NCAA: A Socio-economic Analysis." *American Journal of Economics and Sociology*, July, 37, 225–239.

Koch, James V. 1973. "A Troubled Cartel: The NCAA." *Law & Contemporary Problems*, Winter/Spring, 38, 135–150.

Koch, James V. 1971. "The Economics of 'Big Time' Intercollegiate Athletics." *Social Science Quarterly*, September, 52, 248–260.

Lederman, Douglass. 1991. "College Athletes Graduate at Higher Rates than Other Students, but Men's Basketball Players Far Behind." *The Chronicle of Higher Education*, March 27, A1, A39–A44.

Leonard, John, and Prinzinger, Joseph. 1984. "An Investigation into the Monopsonistic Market Structure of Division One NCAA Football and Its Effect on College Football Players." *Eastern Economic Journal*, October–November, 10, 455–467.

Leonard, Wilbert M., II, and Jonathan E. Reyman. 1988. "The Odds of Attaining Professional Athlete Status: Refining the Computations." *Sociology of Sport Journal*, June, 5, 162–169.

Leontief, Wassily. 1936 "Quantitative Input-Output Relations in the Economic System of the United States." *Review of Economics and Statistics*, August, 18, 3, 105–125.

Lipton, Eric, and Mark Markey. 1995. "Va. Denied a Ball Club for 1998." *The Washington Post*, online March 9.

Long, James E., and Steven B. Caudill. 1991. "The Impact of Participation in Intercollegiate Athletics on Income and Graduation." *Review of Economics and Statistics*, August, 73, 525–530.

Major League Baseball. 1997. *Basic Agreement between the American League of Professional*

Baseball Clubs and the National League of Professional Baseball Clubs and Major League Baseball Players' Association, effective January 1.

Major League Baseball. 1990. *Basic Agreement between the American League of Professional Baseball Clubs and the National League of Professional Baseball Clubs and Major League Baseball Players' Association*, effective January 1.

Malkin, Michelle. 1997. "If They Build It, You Will Pay." *Wall Street Journal*. June 25.

Marburger, Daniel R. 1997a. "Gate Revenue Sharing and Luxury Taxes in Professional Sports." *Contemporary Economic Policy*, April, 15, 114–123.

Marburger, Daniel R. 1997b. "Whatever Happened to the 'Good Ol' Days'?," In Daniel R. Marburger (ed.), *Stee-rike Four! What's Wrong with the Business of Baseball?* Westport, CT: Praeger.

Marburger, Daniel R. 1997c. "Why Can't Baseball Resolve Its Differences in the Off-season"? In Daniel R. Marburger (ed.), *Stee-rike Four! What's Wrong with the Business of Baseball?* Westport, CT: Praeger.

Marburger, Daniel R. 1996. "A Comparison of Salary Determination in the Free Agent and Salary Arbitration Markets." In John Fizel, Elizabeth Gustafson, and Lawrence Hadley (eds). *Baseball Economics: Current Research*. Westport, CT: Praeger.

Marburger, Daniel R. 1993. "Exchangeable Arbitrator Behavior: A Closer Look." *Economics Letters*, 43, 219–220.

McCormick, Robert E., and Roger Meiners. 1987. "Bust the College Sports Cartel." *Fortune*, October 12, 235–236.

McCormick, Robert E., and Maurice Tinsley. 1990. "Athletics and Academics: A Model of University Contributions." In Brian Goff and Robert Tollison (eds.), *Sportometrics*. College Station, TX: Texas A&M University Press.

McCormick, Robert E., and Maurice Tinsley. 1987. "Athletics versus Academics? Evidence from SAT Scores." *Journal of Political Economy*, 95, 5, 1103–1116.

McGraw, Dan. 1996. "Playing the Stadium Game." *U.S. News and World Report*, June 3, 46–51

McKenzie, Richard B., and Thomas Sullivan. 1987. "Does the NCAA Exploit College Athletes? An Economics and Legal Interpretation." *Antitrust Bulletin*, Summer, 32, 373–399.

McLaughlin, K. J. 1994. "Rent Sharing in an Equilibrium Model of Matching and Turnover." *Journal of Labor Economics*, 12, 499–523.

Medoff, M. 1986. "Baseball Attendance and Fan Discrimination." *Journal of Behavioral Economics*, 15 Spring/Summer, 149–155.

Medoff, Marshall H. 1976. "On Monopsonistic Exploitation in Professional Baseball." *Quarterly Review of Economics and Business*, 16, 2, 113–121.

Mildner, Gerard C. S., and James G. Strathman. 1996. "Stadium Ownership and Franchise Incentives to Relocate." Paper presented at the Western Economics Association, San Francisco, June 30.

Miller, Marvin. 1991. *A Whole Different Ballgame: The Sport and Business of Baseball.* New York: Birch Lane Press.

Miller, Ronald E., and Peter D. Blair. 1985. *Input-Output Analysis: Foundations and Extensions*. Englewood Cliffs, NJ: Prentice-Hall.

Mills, Edwin S. 1993. "The Misuse of Regional Economic Models." *Cato Journal*, Spring/Summer, 13, 1, 29–39.

Murphy, Robert G., and Gregory A. Trandel. 1994. "The Relation Between a University's Football Record and the Size of Its Applicant Pool." *Economics of Education Review*, September, 13, 265–270.

Nakamura, David. 1994. "New Group Seeks Team in Virginia." *Washington Post,* September 15.

Neale, Walter. 1964. "The Peculiar Economics of Professional Sports." *Quarterly Journal of Economics,* 78, 1–14.

Neyer, Rob. 1996. "Who Are the "True" Shooters?" *STATS Pro Basketball Handbook, 1995–96.* New York: STATS Publishing.

NFLPA (National Football League Players' Association). 1993. *NFL Collective Bargaining Agreement 1993–2000* (NFLCBA), New York, NY.

Noll, Roger G. 1991. "The Economics of Intercollegiate Sports." In Judith Andre and David N. James (eds), *Rethinking College Athletics,* Philadelphia: Temple University Press.

Noll, Roger G. 1974. "Attendance and Price Setting." In Roger G. Noll (ed.), Government and the Sports Business. Washington, D.C.: The Brookings Institution.

Noll, Roger G. and Andrew Zimbalist (eds). 1997. *Sports, Jobs and Taxes: The Economic Impact of Sports Teams.* Washington, D.C.: The Brookings Institution.

Norton, Erle. 1995. "Football at Any Cost: One City's Mad Chase for an NFL Franchise." *Wall Street Journal,* October 13.

Ozanian, Michael K., Tushar Atre, Ronald Fink, Jennifer Reingold, John Kimelman, Andrew Osterland, and Jeff Sklar. 1995. "Suite Deals: Why New Stadiums are Shaking Up the Pecking Order of Sports Franchises." *Financial World,* 164, 11, 42–60.

Ozanian, Michael K., Ronald Fink, John Kimelman, Jennifer Reingold, Andrew Osterland, Jason Starr, and Brooke Grabarek. 1994. "The $11 Billion Pastime." *Financial World,* 163, 10, 50–63.

Ozanian, Michael K, Ronald Fink, John Kimelman, Jennifer Reingold, and Jason Starr. 1993. "Foul Ball." *Financial World,* 162, 11, 18–36.

Pacey, Patricia L. 1985. "The Courts and College Football: New Playing Rules off the Field?" *American Journal of Economics and Sociology,* April, 44, 145–154.

Pacey, Patricia L., and Elizabeth D. Wickham. 1985. "College Football Telecasts: Where Are They Going?" *Economic Inquiry,* January, 23, 93–113.

Padilla, Arthur, and David Baumer. 1994. "Big-Time College Sports: Management and Economic Issues." *Journal of Sport and Social Issues,* May, 18, 123–143.

Peel, David, and Dennis Thomas. 1988. "Outcome Uncertainty and the Demand for Football: An Analysis of Match Attendances in the Englich Football League." *Scottish Journal of Political Economy,* 35, 3, 242–249.

Places Rated Almanac. 1989. Englewood Cliffs, NJ: Prentice-Hall.

Porter, P. K., and G. Scully. 1982. "Measuring Managerial Efficiency: The Case of Baseball." *Southern Economic Journal,* 48, 642–650.

Quirk, James. 1997. "The Salary Cap and the Luxury Tax: Affirmative Action Programs for Weak-Drawing Franchises." In Daniel R. Marburger (ed.), *Stee-rike Four! What's Wrong with the Business of Baseball?* Westport, CT: Praeger.

Quirk, James and Rodney D. Fort. 1992. *Pay Dirt: The Business of Professional Team Sports.* Princeton: Princeton University Press.

Raimondo, Henry J. 1983. "Free Agent's Impact on the Labor Market for Baseball Players." *Journal of Labor Research,* 183–193.

Rascher, Daniel. 1998. "The NBA, Exit Discrimination, and Career Earnings." *Industrial Relations.* Forthcoming.

Rascher, Daniel. 1997. "A Model of a Professional Sports League." In Wallace Hendricks (ed), *Advances in the Economics of Sport,* 2. Greenwich, CT: JAI Press.

Riess, S. A. 1991. "A Social Profile of the Professional Football Player, 1920–1982." *The*

Business of Professional Sports. Urbana: University of Illinois Press.

Ringolsby, Tracy. 1997. "Base Issue: Does Washington D.C. Deserve a Team?" *Scripps Howard News Service,* online May 16.

Rottenberg, Simon. 1956. "The Baseball Players' Labor Market." *Journal of Political Economy,* 242–258.

Ruggiero, J. 1995. "Measuring Technical Inefficiency in the Public Sector: An Analysis of Educational Production." *Review of Economics and Statistics.* Forthcoming.

Ruggiero, John, Lawrence Hadley, and Elizabeth Gustafson. 1996. "Technical Efficiency in Major League Baseball." In John Fizel, Elizabeth Gustafson, and Lawrence Hadley (eds.). *Baseball Economics: Current Research.* Westport, CT: Praeger.

Rushin, Steve. 1993. "The Wooing Game." *Sports Illustrated,* November 29, 96.

Sack, Allen. 1991. "The Underground Economy of College Football." *Sociology of Sport Journal,* March, 8, 1–15.

Sack, Allen. 1987. "College Sport and the Student-Athlete." *Journal of Sport and Social Issues,* December, 11, 31–48.

Sack, Allen L., and Charles Watkins. 1985. "Winning and Giving." In Donald Chu, Jeffrey O. Seagrave, and Beverly J. Becker (eds.), *Sport and Higher Education.* Champaign, IL: Human Kinetics Publishers, Inc.

Schofield, J. 1983. "Performance and Attendance at Professional Team Sports." *Journal of Sport Behavior,* 6, 4, 196–206.

Scott, Frank Jr., James Long, and Ken Sompii. 1985. "Salary vs. Marginal Revenue Product under Monopsony and Competition: The Case of Professional Basketball." *Atlantic Economic Journal,* 13, 3, 50–59.

Scully, Gerald W. 1995. *The Market Structure of Sports.* Chicago: University of Chicago Press.

Scully, G. 1994. "Managerial Efficiency and Survivability in Professional Team Sports." *Managerial and Decision Economics,* 15, 403–411.

Scully, Gerald. 1989. *The Business of Major League Baseball.* Chicago: University of Chicago Press.

Scully, Gerald W. 1974a. "Discrimination: The Case of Baseball." In Roger G. Noll (ed.), *Government and the Sports Business.* Washington, DC: The Brookings Institution.

Scully, Gerald W. 1974b. "Pay and Performance in Major League Baseball." *American Economic Review,* December, 64, 6, 917–930.

Shropshire, Kenneth L. 1995. *The Sports Franchise Game: Cities in Pursuit of Sports Franchises, Events, Stadiums, and Arenas.* Philadelphia: University of Pennsylvania Press.

Shughart, William F., II. 1997. "Preserve Baseball's Antitrust Exemption, or, Why the Senators Are out of Their League." In Daniel R. Marburger (ed.), *Stee-rike Four! What's Wrong with the Business of Baseball?* Westport, CT: Praeger.

Shughart, William F., II, Robert D. Tollison, and Brian L. Goff. 1986. "Pigskins and Publications." *Atlantic Economic Journal,* July, 14, 46–50.

Siegfried, J., and J. Eisenberg. 1980. "The Demand for Minor League Baseball." *Atlantic Economic Journal,* July, 8, 59–69.

Sigelman, Lee, and Samual Bookheimer. 1983. "Is It Whether You Win or Lose? Monetary Contributions to Big-Time College Athletic Programs." *Social Science Quarterly,* June, 64, 347–359.

Sigelman, Lee, and Robert Carter. 1979. "Win One for the Giver? Alumni Giving and Big-Time College Sports." *Social Science Quarterly,* September, 60, 284–294.

Singell, Larry D., Jr. 1993. "Managers, Specific Human Capital, and Firm Productivity in Major League Baseball." *Atlantic Economic Journal,* September, 21, 3, 47–59.

Solomon, Mike. 1997. "Yes: Washington D.C. Deserves a Major League Team," *Scripts Howard News Service,* African News Online: Major League Baseball Features Page/The Baseball Server, May 16, 1–2.

Sommers, Paul, and Noel Quinton. 1982. "Pay and Performance in Major League Baseball: The Case of the First Family of Free Agents." *Journal of Human Resources,* 426–436.

Sport Management Research Institute, Barry University. 1995. *1995 Economic Impact Study: Super Bowl XXIX.* Miami.

Sperber, Murray. 1990. *College Sports, Inc.: The Athletic Department vs. the University.* New York: Henry Holt.

Staples, Brent. 1987. "Where Are the Black Fans?" *The New York Times Magazine,* May 17, 27.

Sullivan, Neil J. 1995. "Big League Welfare." *New York Times,* November 4.

Telander, Rick. 1989. *The Hundred Yard Lie: The Corruption of College Football and What We Can Do to Stop It.* New York: Simon and Schuster.

Thomas, S., and M. Jolson. 1979. "Components of Demand for Major League Baseball." University of Michigan Business Review, May, 31, 1–6.

Thorn, John, Pete Palmer, Michael Gershamn, and David Pietrusza (eds). 1997. *Total Baseball.* New York: Viking Press.

Thorn, John, and Pete Palmer (eds). 1993. *Total Baseball.* New York: HarperCollins.

Topel, Robert. 1991. "Specific Capital, Mobility, and Wages: Wages Rise with Job Seniority." *Journal of Political Economy,* 145–176.

Total Baseball. 1996. John Thorn and Pete Palmer (eds.). Portland: Curtis Publishing Company.

Tucker, Irvin B., III. 1992. "The Impact of Big Time Athletics on Graduation Rates." *Atlantic Economic Journal,* 20, 4, 65–72.

Tucker, Irvin B., III, and Louis Amato. 1994. "Does Big Time Success in Football and Basketball Affect SAT Scores?" *Economics of Education Review,* 12, 2, 177–181.

Tullock, Gordon. 1967. "Welfare Costs of Tariffs, Monopoly, and Theft." *Western Economic Journal,* June, 224–232.

USA Today. November 14, 1997, 14C.

USA Today. Friday, February 12, 1993 and Wednesday, January 18, 1995.

U.S. Bureau of the Census. 1997. "Metropolitan Area Population Estimates." Population Estimates Program, Population Division, Washington, DC.

Vader, J. E. 1995. "A Ballpark Would Be Great—Just Don't Ask to Pay." *The Oregonian,* October 16.

Vinod, T. 1976. "Canonical Ridge and Econometrics of Joint Production." *Journal of Econometrics,* 4, 147–166.

Vinod, T. 1968. "Econometrics of Joint Production." *Econometrica,* 36, 739–740.

Vinod, T. 1969. "Econometrics of Joint Production—A Reply." *Econometrica,* 37, 739–740.

Vrooman, John. 1997. "Franchise Free Agency in Professional Sports Leagues." *Southern Economic Journal,* July, 191–219.

Vrooman, John. 1996. "The Baseball Players' Labor Market Reconsidered." *Southern Economic Journal,* October, 339–360.

Vrooman, John. 1995. "A General Theory of Professional Sports Leagues." *Southern Economic Journal,* April, 971–990.

Welki, Andrew M, and Thomas J. Zlatoper. 1994. "US Professional Football: The Demand for Game-Day Attendance in 1991." *Managerial and Decision Economics,* September/October, 15, 489–495.

Wong, Glenn M. 1987. "Major League Baseball's Grievance Arbitration System: A Comparison with Nonsports Industry." *Employee Relations Law Journal*, 464–490.

Zak, Thomas A., Cliff J. Huang, and John J. Siegfried. 1979. "Production Efficiency: The Case of Professional Basketball." *Journal of Business*, 52, 3, 379–393.

Zech, Charles E. 1981. "An Empirical Estimation of a Production Function: The Case of Major League Baseball." *The American Economist*, Fall, 19–23.

Zimbalist, Andrew. 1997. "Baseball in the Twenty-First Century." In Daniel R. Marburger (ed), *Stee-rike Four! What's Wrong with the Business of Baseball?* Westport, CT: Praeger.

Zimbalist, Andrew. 1992a. *Baseball and Billions*. New York: Basic Books.

Zimbalist, Andrew. 1992b. "Salaries and Performance: Beyond the Scully Model." In Paul M. Sommers (ed). *Diamonds Are Forever: The Business of Baseball*. Washington, DC: The Brookings Institution.

Index

academic performance 6, 162, 163, 165,
  167, 169, 170
academics 163,167
American League (AL) 6, 36, 38, 97, 122,
  128, 129, 153–159
Anderson, Sparky 124
antitrust exemption 7, 99, 200
arbitration 101, 176, 179, 183, 184, 187,
  188, 191, 192, 194, 197, 198
attendance 13, 29–31, 35-38, 42–44, 50,
  57, 58, 76–78, 79–81, 84, 86, 88–91,
  95–107, 111, 119, 124–126, 128, 129,
  153, 156, 161, 179, 180

basketball 21, 22, 35, 44, 57, 75, 78–91,
  93, 133, 135–137, 139, 163, 165
Bulls 43

capacity 19, 24, 32, 35, 61, 62, 67, 69,
  71, 76, 78–80, 83, 87, 89, 90, 125,
  128–132
capacity constraints 4, 5, 61, 62, 72
career length 203, 204, 207, 208
cartel 4, 11, 12, 50, 109
CBA 214–216, 218–222, 224, 225
cheating 4, 12, 20–24
Cobb–Douglas 97
Cobb, Ty 5, 110, 112, 114, 115, 117
collective bargaining agreement 7,
  191–193, 214
college football 4, 11–13, 16, 19–22

collusion 7, 176, 177, 182, 185–189
competitive balance 3, 4, 11, 15, 16, 19
customer discrimination 36

demand 4, 27–30, 34–38, 43, 49, 58, 64,
  68–70, 81, 82, 125, 127
designated hitter (DH) 6, 154–159
Devil Rays 193
Diamondbacks 193
distribution of income 7
draft 27,

efficiency 123, 138
expansion 4, ,49, 50, 55, 56, 58, 59, 76,
  81
expansion teams 4, 55, 56
externalities 4, 12

Fan Cost Index 32, 34, 36, 38, 45
franchise 4, 5, 12, 50–52, 56–57, 59,
  75–77, 79–88, 90, 91
free agency 7, 27, 111, 177, 184, 187,
  199, 201, 213–215, 217, 219, 220,
  223–225

Gini coefficient 218, 219
Golden Glove 180, 181, 183, 187, 189
grade point average (GPA) 6, 162, 163,
  165–168, 170, 171
Grand Prix Racing 61

history 214
hitting 97, 111, 112–114
hockey 80, 83–86, 164, 169
Hotelling's location model 49

income distribution 219, 224
Industry Growth Fund 195, 197
input–output 62, 109

joint
    production 97–99, 102, 107
    venture 12

location 49, 50, 52, 58, 61, 75,
Lorenz curve 218, 219
luxury tax(es) 7, 27, 192–198

Major League Baseball (MLB) 4, 5, 7,
    29, 30, 50–55, 61, 75, 78, 96, 109, 119,
    176–180, 183, 185, 187–189, 191,
    192, 203, 213, 214, 218, 219
Major League Expansion Committee 49
managers 6, 95, 119, 120, 123, 124, 132,
    135
marginal revenue product 17, 19, 20,
    22–24, 135, 155, 176, 177, 180, 196
Mariners 30
market viability 49, 55–59
Marlins 50, 195
metropolitan 4, 50–54, 56, 76, 81–86,
    89, 90
metropolitan areas 4, 50–54, 56, 76,
    83–86, 89
Miller, Marvin 203
monopsony 3, 13, 18, 22, 23, 175, 178,
    213, 216
Most Valuable player (MVP) 181, 183
moves 50, 81, 89, 90, 206, 208, 210
MRP 135, 136, 178, 180, 195, 196
multipliers 61, 64

National Basketball Association 5, 6, 30,
    34, 75, 78, 135, 136, 193
National Collegiate Athletic Association
    (NCAA) 11–13, 15, 17–24, 62, 72,
    161, 171
National Football League (NFL) 12–15,
    18, 24, 65, 84, 85, 91, 192–194, 213,
    214, 216, 218, 221, 223, 224

National Hockey League (NHL) 80, 83,
    91
National League (NL) 6, 57, 59, 102, 121,
    122, 131, 153–156, 186, 187, 195
network 4, 26
Nomo, Hideo 33

Oakland A's 30
odds data 29, 33–35, 43
Olympics 61

Park, Chan Ho 33
payroll tax 197
PGA 61
pitching 110–112, 120
player
    mobility 24
    representatives 7, 203, 205, 208, 211
Pro Bowl 222
production 4, 5, 27, 61, 95–99, 101, 102,
    105–107, 136, 142, 143, 147, 151, 154,
    159
production function 95–98, 102, 105, 106
public
    ownership 5, 80, 86, 87, 89, 91
    subsidies 58, 63

quality 4, 6, 16, 19, 27–30, 32, 33, 35, 36,
    96, 111, 124, 156, 158

regional impact analysis 61
relocation 5, 59, 75–77, 81
rent 76, 84, 146, 147, 175, 200
rent-seeking 18, 24
reserve clause 214
revenue 4, 7, 11, 15–24, 27–30, 49, 51,
    58, 89, 95, 135, 137, 144, 155, 156,
    163, 165, 167, 177, 180, 189, 192,
    195–197, 200, 201, 220
revenue sharing 7, 23, 24, 28, 58, 80,
    192, 196, 200, 201
Rockies 50
rules 15, 17–22, 27, 109, 153, 155, 159,
    199
Ruth, Babe 5, 112, 114, 115, 117

salaries 7, 12, 23, 28, 76, 175–181,
    183–188, 193–195, 214, 215,
    217–219, 224

salary caps 27, 28, 192–194, 214, 217, 224
SAT scores 14, 15, 23, 24, 162, 165, 171
scholarships 17, 18, 20
service days 198
sports industry 3
sports revenue 167
stadium ownership 77, 80
stadiums 49, 50, 58, 75–80, 86–91, 128
strike 176, 191, 199, 200, 228
subsidies 58, 63, 75, 77, 80, 89, 196
Suns 43
Super Bowl 4, 5, 61, 62, 65–73, 222

team quality 28–30, 32, 102, 158
technological change 109
tempo 139, 142, 143, 150

ticket prices 34, 76
trades 6, 135–137, 146–149

viability 56–58
violations 21, 161

win
    percentage 12, 24, 34–37, 43, 84, 87, 97, 99, 100–102, 104, 107, 119, 180, 187
    streaks 6, 119, 120, 128, 133
World Series 95, 153, 191

Young, Cy 180, 181, 184

About the Contributors

David J. Berri is an Assistant Professor of Economics at Coe College in Cedar Rapids, IA. In addition to his interests in the economics of sports, he has also published in the field of international trade and is currently an associate scientist with the Cooperative Institute for Research in the Atmosphere in Fort Collins, CO.

Stacey L. Brook is Assistant Professor of Economics at the University of Sioux Falls, and previously was a faculty member at Clarkson University. His areas of interest include domestic and international competition policy and economics of professional team sports.

Thomas H. Bruggink began his academic career at Fordham University in 1976, and has continued that career since 1978 at Lafayette College in Easton, PA. He has published papers on the economics of natural resources, public utilities, and the economics of the baseball industry. He is currently researching structural differences in production between different eras in baseball history.

Donald A. Coffin is Dean of the School of Business at Indiana University Northwest. He has previously taught at Illinois State University, Western Kentucky University, West Virginia University, and Alderson-Broaddus College. He also worked as an economic analyst for the city of Indianapolis. His primary research interests include urban economic development and the economics of professional sports.

Craig A. Depken II is an Assistant Professor of Economics at the University of Texas at Arlington, which he joined in 1996. His research focuses on theoretical and empirical industrial organization, including market structure, demand analysis, and the economics of advertising. His recent research in baseball includes the effect of free agency on competitiveness, customer-based discrimination, and the estimation of fan loyalty.

John Fizel is Professor of Economics at Penn State University in Erie, PA. Dr. Fizel conducts research in applied microeconomic topics that have included nursing home efficiency, oil market pricing, mutual fund performance, and the economics of sports. He has published papers on momentum in football, relationships between football attendance, competitive balance and televised games, basketball coaching efficiency and retention, and baseball arbitration.

Rodney Fort is Professor of Economics at Washington State University. His numerous publications include *Pay Dirt: The Business of Professional Team Sports*, a paper on baseball performance and compensation in *Diamonds Are Forever: The Business of Baseball*, and a literature review on the economics of professional team sports in the *Journal of Economic Literature*. His theoretical analyses of professional sport leagues (with James Quirk) are among the most important contributions in this area.

Elizabeth Gustafson is Associate Professor and Chair of Economics at the University of Dayton. She previously held positions at Miami University and the University of Cincinnati. Her area of expertise is econometrics and her research interests focus on applied econometric models, most recently in the area of the economics of baseball.

Lawrence Hadley is Associate Professor of Economics at the University of Dayton. He was a member of the faculty at Hartwick College and at American University in Cairo before joining the University of Dayton faculty in 1977. For the past few years, his professional research has dealt with efficiency and labor market issues in Major League Baseball.

Timothy R. Hylan is a health economist at Eli Lilly and Company. He has also worked as an economist for CNA Corporation and was Assistant Professor of Economics at John Fisher College from 1993 to 1994. He has presented and published several papers dealing with the economics of baseball players' salaries and with the impact of free agency on the allocation of players between major league teams.

Sandra Kowalewski is a Doctoral Candidate in Economics at Temple University in Philadelphia, PA. In addition to the economics of sports her research interests include finance and industrial organization.

Maureen J. Lage is an Associate Professor of Economics and Affiliate of Women's Studies at Miami University where she has worked since 1990. She has presented and published several papers that focus on economic issues in Major League Baseball. Her professional areas of interest include applied econometrics, health economics, and gender economics.

Michael A. Leeds is Associate Professor of Economics at Temple University in Philadelphia, PA. His research interests include labor economics and applied microeconomics as well as the economics of sports.

Daniel R. Marburger is Associate Professor of Economics at Arkansas State University. He edited *Stee-rike Four! What's Wrong with the Business of Baseball?* and contributed chapters to *Diamonds Are Forever: The Business of Baseball* and *Baseball Economics: Current Research*. He was also retained as an expert in personal injury cases involving former Major League Baseball players. His research interests include the economics of sports, interest arbitration, and economic education.

Gerard C. S. Mildner is Assistant Professor of Urban Studies and Planning at Portland State University. His primary research interest is in the economics of local government and urban planning. He is co-author of *Scarcity by Design: The Legacy of New York City's Housing Policies*.

Philip K. Porter is Professor of Economics at the University of South Florida in Tampa, FL. His research interests include law and economics, labor, public choice, and, of course, sports.

James Quirk's academic career has included appointments at Purdue University, the University of Kansas (University Professor), and Cal Tech. He is currently retired from full-time teaching but continues his long and distinguished career in economic research. His published writings investigate general equilibrium theory, decision making under uncertainty, qualitative economics, and futures markets. He has published many papers in the area of sport economics, and his theoretical models of professional sports are among the most important contributions in this area. His published books include *Pay Dirt: The Business of Professional Team Sports* and *Minnesota Football, the Golden Years: 1932–1941*.

Daniel Rascher is a sports economist and antitrust economist at LECG. Previously, he was an Assistant Professor of Sport Management at the University of Massachusetts at Amherst. His research interests focus on understanding the effects of team and league decision making on the product market and labor market in sports.

Robert Rosenman is Professor of Economics at Washington State University. His research interests focus on applied microeconomics, with publications in the fields of health economics, natural resources, environmental economics, and financial economics.

John Ruggiero is an Associate Professor of Economics at the University of Dayton. His major research interests include the measurement of technical efficiency, public finance, and the economics of education. His recent publications focus on technical efficiency in the school districts.

Timothy Smaby is an Associate Professor of Finance at Penn State University in Erie, PA. His primary research interest is capital markets. He has published papers on the behavior of foreign exchange rates, stock market efficiency, and the profitability of short-selling.

James G. Strathman is Professor of Urban Studies and Planning and Assistant Director of the Center for Urban Studies at Portland State University. His primary research area is in transportation, regional science, and economic development. His publications include articles in the *Journal of Public Transportation, Land Economics, Transportation Research Record,* and *Journal of Urban Affairs.*

Michael Treglia is Senior Health Economist at Eli Lilly and Company. Besides the economics of sports, his research interests include health economics and topics in microeconomics. His previously published research on Major League Baseball focused on the impact of institutional changes in the industry.

Justin M. Zamparelli is a graduate of Lafayette College and is currently a law student at Cornell University.